America's Except.
Economic Problem

With an good
wister

Warwick

First published 2017 by Searching Finance Ltd, 8 Whitehall Road, London W7 2JE, UK

ISBN: 978-1-907720-65-9

Designed and typeset in the UK by Deirdré Gyenes

America's Exceptional Economic Problem

By Warwick Lightfoot

About the author

WARWICK LIGHTFOOT is Director of Research and Head of Economics and Social Policy at Policy Exchange. He is an economist with specialist interests in monetary policy, public expenditure, taxation and labour markets. Formerly the economics editor of *The European*, he was for many years a frequent contributor to *The Wall Street Journal* and has written for the *Financial Times*, *The Times*, the *Sunday Times*, the *Daily Telegraph*, the *Sunday Telegraph*, the *Guardian* and *The Spectator*. His articles on economics and public policy have also been published in specialist journals that range from *Financial World, International Economy*, and the *Investors Chronicle* to the *Times Literary Supplement* and the *Journal of Insolvency Practitioners*.

Warwick Lightfoot has worked in UK government departments as Special Adviser to the Chancellor of the Exchequer from 1989-92, initially appointed by Nigel Lawson and later reappointed by John Major and Norman Lamont. He was also Special Adviser to the Secretary of State for Employment, Norman Fowler between 1987 and 1989. From 1992 to 1997 he was Treasury Economist at the Royal Bank of Scotland. In the 1980s he was capital markets economist at Hill Samuel & Co and started his career at Merrill Lynch International.

About Searching Finance

Searching finance Ltd is a dynamic new voice in financial services, business and economics. Our mission is to provide expert, highly relevant and actionable comment, information and analysis. We bring you the latest industry insight and best practice guidance, provided by writers who are renowned experts in their field, to give you the knowledge that will gain an edge for you and your organisation.

To learn more, please visit www.searchingfinance.com

Contents

Figures

Tables

Acknowledgements

This book benefits from and draws on the research literature of the international economics community. I have benefited for many years from talking to Professor James Gwartney at Florida State University, to Professor Douglas Holtz-Eakin and to officials and economists at the Congressional Budget, Office Council of Economic Advisers, the Joint Economic Committee of Congress, and the United States Treasury Department and from the Federal Reserve System and its network of regional reserve banks. Over several years I have enjoyed seminar discussions led by Vito Tanzi hosted by Politeia. I appreciated help from Professor Price Fishback, at the University of Arizona on the economic history of the Great Depression and wider comments on the role of fiscal policy. I benefitted from talking to Professor Laurence Kotlikoff at the University of Boston and from his research on the effects of taxes and transfer payments. Dr David Steiner the former New York State Commissioner of Education and Director of the Johns Hopkins Institute for Education Policy offered valuable guidance on the policy challenges in American education. I am grateful to the late Professor Arnold Relman, who was for many years the professor of medicine and social medicine at Harvard Medical School and editor of *The New England Journal of Medicine Medical*, for his help and comments on the chapter on health care. I benefited from talking to Josh Barro about his work at the Manhattan Institute on public sector pay and employment. I had the benefit of talking to Professor Ira Katznelson at Columbia University and draw on his research on the role of the New Deal and post Second World War policies' impact on minority households. I would like to thank Professor Kevin Gaines at the University of Michigan for his comments on the economic welfare and position of minority communities. The project benefited from suggestions by Professor Ken Mayhew at Oxford University. I would like to thank Dr Louise Newman at the University of Florida, Rebecca Coulson, Christopher Chantrill, Jonathan Dupont,

David Goodhart, Therese Raphael, Clive Tucker and David Stanton for their comments and statisticians at the Congressional Budget Office, the Bureau of Economic Analysis, General Accountability Office, the IMF, the OECD, and the United States Census Bureau.

Dedication

This book is dedicated to my Mother and to the memory of my late Step-father, who for many years happily made their home in Upstate New York.

Statistical Note

General government expenditure provides the most comprehensive consolidation of public sector activity within national income. There are two sources of data for general government expenditure – the domestically produced national accounts from the US Bureau of Economic Analysis (BEA) and the internationally produced national account measures generated by the Organisation for Economic Co-operation and Development (OECD).

The OECD data is constructed for the purposes of consistent international comparison. The OECD international accounting conventions result in a ratio of general government expenditure to gross domestic product (GDP) that is slightly higher than the national accounting conventions used by the BEA. The OECD ratio is around 38 percent and the BEA ratio is around 36 percent. The OECD guidance shows that the difference is explained by the scoring of purchases of weapon systems by the US Defence Department and government owned non-transit utilities. The US National Income and Product Accounts (NIPA) employed by the BEA scores expenditure on weapons systems as part of gross capital formation. The OECD System of National Accounts (SNA) scores such purchases as current expenditure. The difference is estimated to be about 0.5 percent of GDP. Non-transit utilities owned and operated by government bodies that do not charge market prices are scored by the OECD as part of general government expenditure. This increases the level of government spending and its level as a ratio of GDP. The issues are explored in a BEA paper

The NIPAs and the System of National Accounts by Charles Ian Mead, Karin Moses and Brent Moulton in the *Survey of Current Business*, December 2004.

The international comparisons in this book are based on OECD data, which provides the best available consistent benchmark for international comparison. The main point of comparison is the size of the US public sector relative to that of other advanced economies. This book uses the OECD figure for general government expenditure, which yields a ratio of around 38 percent of national

Income in the US compares to an OECD average of 40.8 percent. Data expressed in relation to GDP drawn from American sources, such as the Office for Management and Budget Government, the Council for Economic Advisers, the Congressional Budget and the General Accounting Office will be given in terms of the BEA's national accounts using the NIPA accounting conventions. For example, data and projections taken from the *Budget of the US Government* or the Congressional Budget's Office *Long-Term Budget Outlook* that express spending, taxation and borrowing in relation to GDP use the BEA's national accounts' estimate of GDP. There is little difference between data on federal government activity from the two estimates of national income. The principal difference comes from where the full public sector, including state and local government activity, is consolidated with that of the federal government. The difference in scoring the data makes little difference to the broad picture of an extensive public sector accounting for around two-fifths of national income that is projected potentially to rise by around a further third over the next 25 years.

Chapter 1

Introduction

This book looks at the longer term challenges that the US economy faces. The title *America's Exceptional Economic Problem* is intended to denote the gravity and awkwardness of the challenges that the US economy faces. These are a historically large public sector, extensive unfunded public sector liabilities and an aging population. Many people still perceive the US economy as being significantly different from other advanced economies. Instead it is much more similar to an average OECD economy than many people think and shares many of their structural challenges. This book is principally about the need to strike an appropriate balance between the operation of private markets and public intervention to maximise economic welfare conventionally, albeit imperfectly, measured by GDP.

It is not about the immediate matters of the recent banking crisis and what economists have come to call the Great Recession. Although it deals with aspects of the policy response to it, such as the use of active fiscal stimulus measures, in so far as they touch on the longer term issues that are its main focus. It is not intended as a contribution to the currently fashionable literature exploring American decline. America's political and strategic place in the word will be shaped by many things far beyond the scope of this book. The international economy is not some form of zero sum mercantilist balance, where one economy's progress is another's regression. The oddity historically is not the current economic progress of China and India, but rather their relative eclipse in the world economy after 1820.

The principal matter that should concern American residents is not the progress of the Chinese economy, but how to maximise their own economic welfare and GDP per capita.

An economy cannot be understood outside its economic history and the institutions that have been created by its political history. The recognition of the importance of history and the evolution of institutional structures is necessary when studying any institution such as a central bank and it is significant for the study of political and economic communities. A failure to take account of, for example, the way that the US presidential election is decided through an electoral college rather than through a direct popular vote, could mislead a person about the chances of a candidate being elected or obtaining legitimacy through the process of the electoral college. In most years the results of the Electoral College and the popular vote coincide, but in 2016 they significantly diverged.

This book therefore gives careful attention to the economic history and legacy of the 1930s Great Depression. The depression was an event of huge social and political importance. It continues to be perceived in folk memory as a catastrophe and continues to shape the principal institutions of the federal government from the Federal Reserve Board to the Social Security. The intellectual study of the 1930s Great Depression, its causes, consequences and potential remedies is far from recondite. It was the seminal moment in the evolution of macro-economics and looking at the economy as a system. The recent Great Recession has returned to the centre of economics, the fundamental questions about the capacity and policy instruments that policy makers have to manage the economic cycle.

This book is principally concerned with the long-term structural challenges of the American economy. It is not focused on one period in the economic cycle compared to another or the performance of one administration compared with another. The Great Recession, however, is by any measure an immense event. It was a huge shock that exposed and amplified many of the longer-term challenges in the US labour market and in the cost bases of state and local governments in the US. But it did not create the structural challenges that are at the heart of this book and the discretionary measures taken to address it and to remedy the shortfalls in revenue, make little difference to them.

Much of the debate about American public policy focuses on the federal government in Washington DC and its programmes. One of the main purposes of this book is an attempt to marshal an intelligible account of the US public sector as a whole, including state and local government authorities, as well as the federal government. The federal government accounts for some 21 percent of GDP. To ignore the other components of general government expenditure in the US would be to underestimate significantly the role of the American public sector. Likewise to assess the impact of the public sector on the economy by only looking at ratio of public spending to GDP, that ignores over a trillion dollars of tax expenditures, would underestimate the impact of collective decision making in the US.

The book also attempts to place the US public sector in the context of the markets where public policy is normally used to correct market failures and supplement the under-provision of merit or beneficial goods and services that may be under produced in a market economy, such as health and higher education. It offers a perspective on US public policy that attempts to look across each of the levels of government: federal, state and local and at the range of markets that modern public sectors have evolved to supplement or improve. When they are not straightforwardly misleading, generalisations about the US are usually clumsy glosses on a rich and diverse set of political communities that work within a transcontinental economy. Constructing anything other than a superficial account of the American public sector, its institutions and the economy that it helps to shape is necessarily a daunting task, but a fascinating and rewarding one. One of the principal purposes of this book is to offer a coherent analysis of the role of the public sector as whole in the US economy.

The evolution of a country's living standards

In 1985 Martin Feldstein presented a paper to the American Economic Association entitled *Supply Side Economics: Old Truths and New Claims.* In it he elegantly summarised the key to a community's long-term living standards, writing that the 'evolution of a nation's real income depends on its accumulation of physical and intellectual capital and on the quality and efforts of its work force'. He explained that means ensuring government policy does not hinder the working of labour and product markets and that regulation and the burden that arises from public expenditure is not excessive. Advanced economies have faced these challenges for more than a generation and have made little progress in improving the long term working of their economies. At the heart of their problems is a historically high level of public expenditure.

Public Expenditure has a cost

A fundamental proposition informs the analysis in this book. It can be briefly summarised as, public spending has a real cost. That cost is higher than the simple cash cost of the spending involved, because of the economic distortion that arises from the taxes collected to finance it, the so called dead-weight or excess cost. This means that supporters of public expenditure programmes have to be mindful to ensure that a particular spending programme yields benefits that exceed the cost of the taxes needed for it. They also have to be mindful of the principle of diminishing returns at the margin. Simply increasing the inputs into a desirable activity will not yield results. What is required is realism about the costs and potential benefits of public sector activity.

Being realistic about both the cost and potential diminishing returns to public spending does not mean that a modern economy does not benefit from what historically is a large public sector. Striking an appropriate balance between an effective public service and the private market economy that finances it, is the central challenge. Pretending that public spending does not have a cost and always yields benefits is to resile from the central challenge of modern public policy. In the same way that seeking to dismantle much of the public intervention developed to improve social welfare in the first half of the 20th century is to step aside from the difficult judgements that have to be made. Deciding how that the balance should be struck and how costs will be controlled are the matters that cannot be evaded.

Modern market economies benefit from a public sector

The book rehearses the reasons why a public sector that is much larger than that in place in the first part of the 20th century yields improvements in the working of the modern market economy. Much of the benefit of public intervention comes from the fact that properly functioning market economies will have a wide dispersion of earnings and many households will need collectively financed assistance to raise their level of welfare. The US economy exhibits this dispersion of income to a greater extent than other economies. There are also genuine practical matters that public policy ought to address that arise from modest growth of average household income over a protracted period.

The US is unusual in that unlike most other major advanced economies it has a significant proportion of its residents who are relatively impoverished as the result of public policy. Black households have lower wealth and income than the average and participate less in the labour market. This is the result of a long and complex history of public policy that discriminated against them. Public policy has a legitimate role and interest in attempting to correct previous discrimination, through policies such as improved training, wider active labour market polices and re-examining the structure of benefits for low income households including Milton Friedman's original ideas for a negative income tax. Fully integrating black men and women into the labour market would not only raise their welfare, but would increase the level of GDP and reduce some public spending.

5

It offers a genuine opportunity to improve the performance of the US economy.

35 percent rule of thumb

As a rule of thumb, public spending should be kept on average over the economic cycle to 35 percent of GDP. The central challenge that mature advanced economies have is how to finance a historically large public sector which has extensive future liabilities that will raise the ratio of public expenditure within national income over the next twenty-five years. OECD countries already have large public sectors that result in structural economic challenges that impede the operation of product and labour markets and slow economic growth. The US economy is in a similar position to that of other advanced economies. The US has already broken the 35 percent rule. General Government Expenditure accounts for around two fifths of national income. On present policies, over the coming twenty-five years the ratio to public spending within GDP, using projections made at various times from the Congressional Budget Office and General Accountability Office, will easily exceed fifty percent of national income. Spending on such a scale would have a progressively damaging impact on the future trend rate of economic growth, which combined with higher spending would result in a ratio of total public spending to GDP closer to sixty percent. Long-term projections of this sort are highly sensitive to the assumptions made about demography, productivity, the trend rate of growth, prices and interest rates. The US federal government carries in common with most other OECD governments' huge unfunded intergenerational health and pension liabilities. The numbers and projections used in this book from US public authorities are illustrative of a direction of travel and the potential scale of the public expenditure challenges that policy makers will face in the coming thirty or forty years on unchanged policies.

US shares problems in common with other advanced economies

This book attempts to explore these challenges and to show that America is not different, but is in many respects similar to other advanced countries. The principal differences being the relative generosity of public policy towards older people and the great expense of the chosen methods of assisting them in relation to health care. Medicare and Social Security are both generous. Much of the focus of discussion is about the narrow construction of their rules relating to their narrow financial solvency. In terms of present policy both are unsustainable. Yet the real debate should be about the wider economics of the efficient provision of medical services and how households are assisted to save and make provision for a protracted retirement in old age and the appropriate role that collective provision should make in contributing to that.

The central issue is total public spending. How public spending is financed through borrowing and taxation is a secondary matter compared to the actual level of spending itself, provided borrowing is growing in line with national income and the tax base. Part of the public expenditure problem in the US arises out of the Federal Government's structural budget deficit that is accumulating debt faster than any realistic assessment of growth in either the present tax base or the underlying economy. This book tries to describe the range of American government institutions and explores their context. Public policy does not operate in a vacuum. Institutions and policies reflect the political choices that were made when they were established and have to be understood in their historical context.

The American public sector at both the state and federal level needs extensive change to reduce its cost and improve its economic efficiency. Much the same can be said for several important private and semi-private markets in health care and higher education. What is interesting is how it has reached the present position. Expensive and malfunctioning private markets particularly in health care both raise public spending and directly reduce private household welfare as well as damaging the economy's wider performance.

Although this book principally focuses on structural problems that arise out of public expenditure, there is no doubt that important matters of private sector corporate governance need to be addressed. The separation of ownership and control of joint stock firms have led to egregious issues of agency and rent seeking over the last twenty years. Executives who manage and effectively control corporations are able to divert profits from dividends to shareholders into various forms of executive compensation, often presented as aligning executive and shareholder interests.

A large public sector exceeding any careful assessment of what an optimal ratio of public spending within GDP should be is a common problem that the US now shares with most other advanced OECD economies. The US has a large, expensive and lumpy public sector that absorbs too many resources to accomplish the tasks given to it. Despite being only slightly smaller than the OECD average it offers only a limited and partial social safety net and does not offer general assistance with medicine and healthcare for people of working age.

Where it does provide health care for people of working age it is through Medicaid. A means tested system that withdraws access to care as incomes rise. This contributes to a complex system of federal, state and local taxes and social transfer payments with effective marginal tax rates that have significant malign implications for work incentives for households across most of the earnings distribution.

This complicated pattern of work incentives appears to be creating structural labour market difficulties that will not disappear as the economy stabilises and recovers from the Great Recession. The adverse shock of the loss of output during the great recession appears to have exposed a structural problem in the labour market.

Health costs

The principal driver of the Federal Government's unsustainable fiscal deficit is Medicare. The combination of an increasingly elderly population and rising health care costs aggravated by defective private markets in medicine and health insurance places the Federal budget on an unsustainable trajectory.

The challenges in American health policy extend beyond the debate surrounding the Affordable Care Act passed in 2010. The medical profession is not properly regulated to protect the public and to control costs. Medical costs are further aggravated by third party payments that mean that whoever foots the bill – government, insurance companies, private firms or private individuals – medicine in the US is very expensive. And it does not represent value for money. It is the key to understanding why the Federal Government's finances on present policies are not sustainable. It is also part of the explanation for weaker growth in real wages over the last thirty years. Health benefits provided by employers have absorbed a rising proportion of the Employment Cost Index. Given that households with insurance have to make sizeable co-payment, as do households benefiting from Medicare they are highly resistant to proposed increases in the effective tax burden

A large and financially expensive higher education sector also aggravates both the public expenditure pressures in the US and the structural challenge of the US economy. Higher college and university fees increase pressure for greater federal assistance with college education. It is also contributes to the heavy burden that households carry.

Ubiquity of American Economics

This book is written from the perspective of an economist who began his professional working life in an American investment bank Merrill Lynch. Most bank economists working in large trading rooms spend a significant part of their time commenting on the flow of American statistics, economic reports, the actions of the Federal Reserve and the ebb and flow of policy in

Washington DC. The monthly US Employment Report remains the most influential statistic shaping the sentiment of international financial markets. When New York is closed for a public holiday, such as Thanksgiving, financial centres like London have relatively quiet trading days where markets tend to be less liquid, thinner and more erratic in their prices. This is to explain that for an economist working in international financial markets the American economy is ubiquitous.

The intellectual influence of America's economic community cannot be exaggerated. This is a function of the quality and range of academic institutions and quasi-academic research institutes, think tanks and campaigning bodies. The range of research from official bodies, such as the regional banks that make up the Federal Reserve System, the Congressional Budget Office and the General Accountability Office is immense. If you want to look at a question, such as how effective constitutional fiscal rules may or may not be or the impact of different tax policy regimes, the US is as good a place to start, as any. The scope that different state governments have to experiment is considerable and there is likely to be an extensive research literature that has explored it. The intellectual imperialism of economics in America moreover recognises few boundaries or limitations. Economists led by the late Gary Becker have applied their intellectual tools to questions that range from gender and race discrimination to education and training, the law, arts and culture.

My own interest in the US was further stimulated, because for many years my parents made their home there. Visiting them gave me the opportunity through their friends and neighbours to explore the real life practicalities of things like paying both state and federal taxes, the tax-paying season itself, co-payments in Medicare, local property taxes, referenda on high school rebuilding proposals, the vitality of local church communities and voluntary action and the sheer fun of events, such as groundhog day. Behind every statistic and artefact of analysis in economics are people, individuals who are flesh and blood. They go shopping, they make plans and they often face difficult choices. And in a transcontinental economy when the weather is bad they change those plans and adjust their lives accordingly whether it is snow, floods or hurricanes.

Over many years I have benefitted from visiting economists and officials at the US Treasury Department, the Council of Economic Advisers, the Congressional Budget Office, the Joint Economic Committee of Congress and the Federal Reserve System. The American economy is too big and complex to be easily or simply described. Its political institutions are complex and the policies they yield often match that complexity. I have greatly appreciated the time and help that many people have given to me.

America's 20th century legacy: capability and generosity

As a child I grew up in a family that impressed upon me the fact that America in the darkest period of the Second World War saved Britain from going under. My grandmother regularly told me 'they fed us, they financed us and they armed us, I don't know where we would have been without them'. To a small child the significance of the US assistance to Britain in a war that had only ended twelve years before I was born was re-enforced by the place where I lived. It was a remote rural part of Devon, the South Hams. An area noted for the beauty of its landscape and coast. It was the area used by American armed services to practice ahead of the D-Day landings in 1944. Chosen, because the landscape is what geographers call a *bocage* landscape, and is similar to that in Normandy. Tragically many hundreds of them lost their lives on Slapton Sands, the beach where I first swam as a child. Their deaths are commemorated by the American War Memorial there. From the adults around me, I was therefore alert to America's role in the world and the help that it had given to Britain. I should add that it was not a straightforward or saccharine appreciation. Often when you help people they resent the much needed assistance, even when they appreciate it. As I grew up I was made aware of the financial and industrial assets that Britain had to transfer in return for that assistance; the abrupt cessation of Lend Lease at the end of the war in 1945 that Lord Keynes in a Treasury memorandum called a 'financial Dunkirk'; and the exclusion of Britain and Canada from information about atomic technology that they had helped to create as part of the Manhattan Project, under the 1946 McMahon Act. Yet despite these resentments, that my grandparents felt strongly, the overwhelming impression I had was one of American generosity and capability, exemplified by the Marshall Aid programme to Europe.

I went to school in Totnes, a small market town that benefited from American philanthropy on a magnificent scale. An American heiress, Dorothy Elmhirst the widow of Willard Straight, used her money to help her second husband, Leonard Elmhirst to found Dartington Hall. They rescued a ruined medieval manor house, created a wonderful garden and set up an arts and education foundation that continues to flourish. It is now best known for its international music school in the summer. As a teenager Dartington was my imagination. It was where I went to listen to concerts, see films and experience serious drama. The first 'proper' play I ever saw, *Sizwe Bama is Dead*, was there. Dartington as an institution had a significant influence on my school. Many of the people who worked for the Trust sent their children to it and for many years Leonard Elmhirst was the chair of the school's governors. We all knew that it was Mrs Elmhirst's money from America that had made it all possible.

Structural economic problems in advanced economies are tractable

All countries go through difficult periods. In the second half of the 1970s stagflation was widely perceived as an intractable problem in the US. Indeed many economic and social problems were regarded as intractable. A perception reinforced by what became known as President Carter's malaise speech. I first arrived in the US in January 1981, President Carter was in the White House. President Reagan had yet to take the oath of office and American diplomats were detained in Iran. When the hostages returned,

I stood and watched the ticker tape parade, near Wall Street alongside a friend from work, who was Iranian. Two months later President Reagan was shot. Inflation was running at around 13 percent and the economy was in a protracted double-dip recession. Paul Volker was the Chairman of the Federal Reserve, having been appointed by President Carter in 1979. Volker was using a regime of tough monetary and reserve targets to restore monetary discipline.

In the 1980s, inflation was reduced through a policy of deliberate disinflation. That was followed by an extended period of economic expansion. Huge deficits were created by what the *New Republic* magazine dubbed as President Reagan's war Keynesianism – increased spending on defence when tax revenue fell because taxes were cut and economic activity was weak. These deficits seemed pretty impossible when President Bush took the oath of office in 1989. Ross Perot ran for president on a third party, fix the deficit, ticket in 1992. Yet eight years later in President Clinton's second term the budget was not just balanced, but in surplus albeit in the context of strong revenues from an overheated economy.

Moreover, in the 1980s major changes were made in response to the Greenspan Report that stabilised the financial position of the Social Security Trust Fund. In 1986 a bipartisan revenue neutral tax reform act that simplified the income tax system and widened the tax base was passed by Congress.

I rehearse these episodes in contemporary history to emphasise that while the structural challenges that the US economy faces are very awkward they are tractable. What is required is realism. It is not the same challenge as recreating a functioning market economy after a protracted period of full socialist planning or developing an economy where people have very low levels of physical and human capital per capita. In principle it is manageable.

Three pieces of music serve as a metaphor to my ear for modern America. They are Aaron Copland's *Appalachian Spring* and *Fanfare for the Common Man,* and Leonard Bernstein's music for *Candide*. Copland's pieces convey to me both the space that America has and the can do practicality that distinguishes the ability of Americans to adjust. Bernstein's music expresses the vitality and optimism of American culture. The long-term structural economic challenges that the US economy needs to address are exceptional in their gravity. If any country is able to meet those challenges, on past performance, it should be the US.

Chapter 1

America's structural economic problem

There is a perception that the American economy is the epit-
ome of free enterprise, unsupported markets and unbridled
individualism.

This sense of an unimpeded, capitalist America is also part
of the broader self-perception that Americans have about their
country being exceptional. It is part of the tradition of the frontier, self-reliance and rugged individualism. Modern America
is regarded as home to capitalism, where its manifestation is
red in tooth and claw. This long-standing picture is shared by
much of the world. Werner Sombart's brilliant essay, *Why There
is No Socialism in America,* established a presumption about
American capitalist free enterprise. Yet even at the time of its
publication in 1903 it was anachronistic – Sombart concluded
that the particular circumstances that impeded the emergence
of a working class socialist party on the model of the German
Social Democrats may have been about to change.

One of the interesting features of the 2016 presidential
election campaign, given this history, was the impact that a self-
styled socialist Senator Bernie Sanders had in the Democrat
Party primary. His campaign drew effectively on the legacy
of the Occupy Wall Street Movement. It got traction against a
background, where there was a perceived revival of American
working class consciousness following the Great Recession and
the continuing changes in labour markets and manufacturing
communities arising from greater international competition. It
attempted to draw political support out of the alienation explored

by David Vance in his book, *Hillbilly Elegy: a memoir of a family and culture in crisis*, (Harper 2016). Mrs Clinton took account of the success of Senator Sanders's socialistic campaign and tried to win over his supporters by letting them write the Democratic Party platform. George Packer writing in the *New Yorker* on 31 October 2016, *Hillary Clinton and the Populist Revolt*, described that platform as 'the farthest left of any in recent memory'.

What is interesting is that the beneficiary of the alienation of a significant proportion of the working class electorate in these communities in 2016 was the Republican candidate Donald Trump. This was explored after the election result by Professor Joan Williams in, *What so many people, don't get about the US working class*, published in the *Harvard Business Review* (10 November 2016) shortly after the election. The perception of Mr Trump's business acumen – the billionaire who can cut a deal and get things done – was often more persuasive than the detailed policy agenda of Democrat politicians, such as Mrs Clinton and Senator Elizabeth Warren.

The reason why Sombart originally thought that American politics may change and become more similar to early German 20th century politics that were marked by the emergence of the Marxian social democrats, was the growing interest among American policy makers at the state level in collective action. When developed countries like Britain and Germany were taking their first significant steps to collectivism at the end of the 19th century, the US was also taking decisive steps in that direction. These were not steps towards a socialism of the late 19th century German Marxian sort. Instead they were the first attempts to use public policy to regulate and supplement deficient private markets. American public policy was in many respects in the vanguard. It was an intellectual policy agenda shaped by American economists, who themselves were often influenced by contemporary German ideas. Public education advanced further and faster in America than in any other advanced economy at the time. The antitrust legislation to promote competition and to break up concentrations of economic power is an early and important example of collective state action in the 1890s. During the Progressive Era, Republicans and Democrats in state and federal governments at the end of the 19th and in the early years of the 20th century passed collectivist legislation to regulate trade and employment and to improve social conditions.

Progressive tradition of regulation

State governments pioneered worker's compensation pensions, social insurance and the public control and regulation of utilities. Active governors such as Theodore Roosevelt in New York and Robert La Follette in Wisconsin, both Republicans, personified Progressive policymaking, involving economists and social scientists and creating the role of the expert or technocrat in public policy. At the federal level, it was during Woodrow Wilson's administration that the breakthrough came. The Federal Reserve System was created and a federal income tax was established by constitutional amendment. The creation of the Federal Reserve was the recognition, following the banking crisis in 1907 that financial markets could not be left to themselves. Federal income tax provided the federal government with a powerful instrument to extend its role and purpose – a buoyant source of tax revenue. By the time President Wilson was re-elected on a pledge of keeping the US out of World War I in 1916, the tools were in place at the federal level massively to expand the role of the government. The mobilisation of the American economy for World War I significantly expanded the role of the state and raised the level of federal expenditure.

The Great Depression, FDR and the expansion of federal government

The 1920s was the decade of the 'return to normalcy', as President Warren Hardy expressed it, where the 'business of America was business'.

The age of the *Great Gatsby* was a decade of rapid growth and huge optimism based on the expectations about the opportunities that new technology such as radio would bring. It was a boom period similar to the run-up to the dotcom boom and tech-wreck in 2000. A huge over-accumulation of capital and an asset price bubble resulted in a stock market collapse in 1929 and was followed by a protracted and very deep fall in output in the early 1930s. This economic contraction was aggravated by the Federal Reserve Board's actions in relation to monetary policy. The social and economic disaster that resulted stimulated a huge federal government response. First under President Herbert Hoover who, although described as 'do-nothing Hoover', was active in his response to the Great Depression, and then Franklin Roosevelt's massive extension of federal government activity through the New Deal. The combination of public works measures and the creation of federally chartered corporations, the Securities Exchange Commission, along with social security insurance to provide unemployment insurance and pensions in old age, enormously extended the role of the public sector – and the federal government in particular.

The folk memory of the Great Depression continues to shape contemporary public debate in America. Not least because of the literary and artistic legacy, from the novels of Steinbeck to cinema and popular music exemplified by the lyrics of *Buddy, Can You Spare A Dime?* A significant part of the intellectual energy of American economists since the 1940s has been devoted to trying to understand the Great Depression and identify where policy-makers made mistakes. The lessons for mainstream economic analysis have been not to aggravate a fall in demand by trying to cut a deficit generated through the automatic effects of higher spending and lower tax revenue, not to tighten monetary policy prematurely when there remains substantial unused capacity in the economy, and not to engage in trade protection that damages the international economy as a whole. Two of the principal economists involved in American policymaking during the recent recession, Ben Bernanke, the chair of the Federal Reserve Board and Christina Romer, President Obama's first chair of the Council of Economic Advisers, are both scholars that have devoted a great deal of effort to understanding the Great Depression.

The New Deal settlement

That extension of public sector activity through the federal government's New Deal during the Great Depression followed an expansion of public sector activity at the state and local government levels.

State and municipal authorities took an active role in developing public utilities and managing natural resources such as rivers for hydroelectric power generation. There was important further development of education and the development of institutions of higher education, but state governments were often involved in much more ambitious social expenditure. A good example would be Louisiana, where Governor Huey Long established state charity hospitals, over 30 years before Medicare and Medicaid were introduced in the 1960s. Roosevelt's New Deal saw the establishment of Social Security – giving people pensions and unemployment benefits in the 1930s – which, along with the mobilisation of the US economy in World War II, massively extended federal regulation of private economic activity in the labour, product and transport markets. Prices, incomes and production were all controlled in America during World War II. It left a permanent legacy in terms of an expanded military and intelligence sector that was maintained in peacetime because of the fear of the USSR.

Roosevelt's New Deal then became the benchmark for the progressive part of the American political spectrum. President Truman offered the American people the Fair Deal in 1948 and President Kennedy proposed the New Frontier in the 1960s. The Kennedy and Johnson administrations further expanded the role of the public sector at the federal level with the creation of Medicare for older people and Medicaid for low-income households.

The military-industrial complex that emerged during the 1950s as the Cold War entrenched concern about national security into a permanent condition represented a further step in the creation of an extensive public sector and what amounted to an industrial strategy. The scale of the business interests involved were so great that President Eisenhower spoke about it in his farewell broadcast to the American people in 1960. With hindsight, the military-industrial complex left a smaller footprint on the American economy than Social Security, Medicare and Medicaid. Neither President Reagan's conservative counter-revolution nor President George W. Bush's international interventions and compassionate conservative social spending appear to have altered the fundamental landscape. President Barack Obama was elected in 2008 on a platform that promised transformation, summarised in his campaign slogan 'yes we can.' It promised affordable healthcare, reform of schools and more affordable colleges, a green, cleaner and more sustainable energy policy, enhanced labour and employment legislation to promote trade union collective bargaining and a pledge to redistribute the tax burden from the middle class to the rich. In many respects, this was a backward-looking agenda. Its most sympathetic analysts often expressed themselves in the rhetoric of policy nostalgia. A good example is the title given to a book published by the Russell Sage Foundation examining the Obama administration's domestic policy – *Reaching a New Deal: Ambitious Governance, Economic Meltdown and Polarised Politics in Obama's First Two Years*. The title reflected the continuing historical importance of the New Deal policies and the impact of its legacy on contemporary policy discussion. The shadow of this legacy and its nostalgia was reflected in Mrs Hillary Clinton's decision to launch her presidential campaign for the 2016 election on Roosevelt Island in New York City in 2015. Mrs Clinton framed the opening of her speech around President Franklin Roosevelt's four freedoms.

The political process and crony capitalism

The legacy of President George W. Bush's administration was to make Medicare more expensive, increase spending on most other areas of domestic spending and to revive some of the worst examples of rent-seeking in the military-industrial complex as a result of its interventions in Afghanistan and Iraq. The American political process during the George W Bush administration further exhibited the marks of crony capitalism that distort political policy making and the efficient operation of markets and economic performance. The same complex process of corporate and other interest group lobbying resulted in the Obama administration's main policy initiatives being seriously distorted. Both the fiscal stimulus measure passed in 2009 and the Affordable Care Act passed in 2010 reflected the distorting influence of vested lobbying, even when the President's Democrat Party controlled Congress.

The fiscal stimulus that Obama administration passed in 2009 was captured by vested interest groups that persuaded Congress to use it to fund local projects and union concerns, which meant that it failed to be timely, targeted and temporary. Introduction of comprehensive healthcare insurance was a huge political achievement for the Obama administration and its political significance could not have been exaggerated. Yet it came at the price of not only avoiding the key issues in healthcare that must be addressed, such as the future financial incentives that shape doctors' clinical decisions and the costs that result. It has likely aggravated those costs and raised the structural rate of unemployment, while the business, insurance and union interests involved in healthcare provision have been protected and rewarded.

The US shares many of Europe's structural rigidities and may amplify some of them

Whatever America may be, it is not a straightforward capitalist society with a limited public sector, low levels of public expenditure, and few regulations that is uniquely well-placed to meet the challenges that confront other advanced economies.

It is much more of a mainstream OECD economy. It has a large, somewhat lumpy public sector that fails to offer comprehensive social protection while being expensive and inefficient. It has some public policy and structural economic challenges it shares in common with other advanced economies. These are a large and inefficient public sector and several additional distinct structural challenges that can be properly described as exceptional in that they are specific to public policy in the US. These uniquely American structural challenges are the way that the healthcare and further and higher education markets are organised, the methods of financing used to pay for public services and the development of commercial law, and tort law in particular, over the last 40 years.

The condition of federal public finances

These structural economic challenges are best exemplified in the condition of the US federal government's public finances. In 2010, following the Great Recession the federal government borrowed around 40 cents of every dollar it spent. Spending accounted for around 25 percent of GDP, and it had a budget deficit close to 10 percent of national income. As the economy recovered the deficit fell to 2.5 percent in 2015. In 2016 deficit rose to 3.2 percent of GDP, The Congressional Budget Office in its *Monthly Budget Review: Summary for Fiscal Year 2016* note that this was a significant increase in the deficit from the year before albeit partially explained by the timing of payments by the Federal Government. Spending on the Federal Government's three largest entitlement programs: Social Security, Medicare, and Medicaid. These rose by 3 percent, 5 percent, and 5 percent respectively. Spending on Medicaid grew largely because of new people enrolling as a result of the expansion of coverage authorized by the Affordable Care Act. With that growth, Medicaid spending increased by almost 40 percent in the three years to 2016. The combined outlays spent on the three programs were equal to 48 percent of federal spending and 10.0 percent of GDP in 2016. The gross stock of federal government debt to GDP in 2016 was 75 percent of GDP and is projected, by the Congressional Budget Office, to increase to over 140 percent of GDP in 2046. *The 2016 Long-Term Budget Outlook* expects the ratio to exceed its historical peak of 106 percent of GDP recorded just after the Second World War. This increase in public debt is driven by a permanent or structural federal budget deficit. Average annual deficits as a ratio of GDP are projected to rise from 3.8 percent in the coming decade to 8.1 percent. Over the period federal tax receipts hardly change as a ratio of GDP, averaging around 18.2 to 19.1 percent of national income. While spending is projected to rise from just over 21 percent of GDP to over 27.2 percent of GDP. Money spent on servicing federal government debt rises as a share of national income from 1.4 percent to 5.4 percent of GDP. The future evolution of interest rates will play a critical role in determining the future cost of the US federal government.

A significant proportion of that debt is currently held on the balance sheet of America's central bank, the Federal Reserve Board. Managing a large deficit is more difficult when the stock of debt is large in relation to national income, and it is further complicated when it is being partly financed by the central bank. A large public debt that is partly monetised presents acute challenges for the conduct of monetary policy. When adding in unfunded federal government liabilities that will rise as a result of an ageing population, the US appears to face fiscal challenges that are greater than any other G7 economy apart from those of Japan, and arguably the UK. The combination of direct public sector debt, unfunded public sector liabilities and private debt is also significantly worse than that in the Eurozone taken as a whole.

How well is America's labour market functioning?

One of the most significant structural challenges to emerge in recent years is the labour market. Over the last 30 years, a distinguishing feature of the US economy has been the efficiency and flexibility of its labour market. Part of the mantra of public policy commentators and economists describing the US economy has been the recognition of the capacity of it to adjust to changing economic circumstances. A flexible labour market was at the heart of that adjustment.

Structural problems tend to be exposed when economies suffer a shock. The credit crunch in 2007 and the Great Recession that started in 2008 have exposed a labour market that is not working as well as it once did. While the recovery in economic activity eventually significantly lowered unemployment the pace of the recovery in employment was slower than in previous cycles and the participation rate, the ratio of the labour force in work has been disappointing low. 59.7 percent in November 2016 it was 59.7 percent. The participation rate had recovered from 58.2 percent in July 2011, but remains lower than its peak of 63.4 percent in December 2006. There are a series of factors that emerged out of the house price bubble ahead of the credit crunch that may partly explain the poor performance of the US labour market, following the Great Recession. These include an over-expansion of construction, followed by a sharp and concentrated contraction in that sector. House prices fell and this locked some homeowners who would otherwise have rented into particular areas where there is no work, because they cannot move house. Yet even taking this into account, there now seems to be evidence that the US labour market is no longer as flexible and as efficient as it used to be. This means that as output recovers, employment will not automatically follow as it did in previous expansions. The result of this is that the US economy may well experience higher levels of structural unemployment that will remain entrenched regardless of the macroeconomic performance. In short, with unchanged policies, the US may be about to exhibit to some extent the kind of structural unemployment challenges that European economies have had over the past 25 years.

American exceptions: tort, health and university costs

These structural economic issues are located in the public expenditure, taxation, borrowing and regulation choices that American policymakers have made. Several others problems have emerged not so much out of deliberate policy choice, but from the interaction between the US common law tradition and its 18th century constitutional texts and their interaction with statute law. These complex legal processes have resulted in two specific outcomes that are significant contributors to America's structural rigidities.

The first relates to healthcare, where judicial decisions partly turning on late 19th and early 20th century anti-trust legislation have given priority in healthcare to conventional competition focused on profit maximisation rather than to the challenges of regulating a profession where asymmetries of information between the consumer and provider expose limitations in the efficient operation of the price system. More generally, the development of civil law and tort law has led to expensive and erratic costs for companies and every organisation engaged in employing people and offering services to the public. The effect of the costs that come from the American courts' approach to torts is similar to costs that arise from imposing extensive and expensive regulation of economic activity. Measures have been taken to contain the costs of litigation in American jurisdictions in recent years, but further progress needs to be made.

A further challenge in America is the cost of its best further and higher education system. The US has established since the 1630s the world's greatest and most successful universities, which have been very successful in attracting endowments and offering some of the finest environments for scholarship that the world has ever seen. Yet for undergraduates and graduate students who need to use them to complete their general education and prepare for their professional lives, the costs that universities demand the community bear are very high. Schools, such as Harvard had, for many years, effectively 'taxed' a significant portion of the potential earnings premium the beneficiary of a Harvard education might enjoy. Harvard is not unique in having done this. Harvard today along with a number of elite universities, such as Princeton use their huge endowments to offer applicants effectively free 'needs blind' places, but many liberal arts colleges and good state universities that represent the backbone of higher education for most families, charge high and rising fees. For many households, the cost of completing a higher and professional education is a huge burden on lifetime earnings. It appears that a large number of schools that are in a position to do so exploit what is an economic rent, and in the process add to the structural economic challenges American households face.

The cost of higher education is probably the least-recognised structural economic issue the US faces.

Struggling average American households

Some of the structural challenges the US economy faces have been around for some time. Among them is the recognition that the federal government has growing, unfunded healthcare liabilities and underfunded social security liabilities. But some of these problems have something to do with the longstanding sense that things are not as good for average and below-average income households as they were a generation or two ago.

The combination of constrained real income growth, higher healthcare costs even for families with insurance cover paid for by an employer and the costs of higher education have contributed to the perception that average-income American households now have fewer opportunities, carry greater financial burdens and are more economically insecure than they were. This perception has been compounded by a widening in the dispersion of earnings and wealth exhibited by the US economy over the past 30 years. The so-called 'winner takes all' aspect of contemporary American economic activity worsens this dispersion of earnings through failures in corporate governance and the opportunities that exist for rent-seeking by senior managers, both in private firms and in not for-profit bodies. Part of the explanation for a widening earnings distribution during a relatively constrained growth in incomes is the impact of increased international trade and the competitive emergence of countries such as China, Brazil and India. The result is that both home and international markets are more competitive and more contested than they were before. Manufacturing is in the traded goods sector, where the competition is fiercest. It has to face a competitive challenge compounded by domestic structural economic constraints that raise its costs and place it at a greater disadvantage than it would otherwise have. The social and political consequences of this featured in the presidential campaigns of the leading protagonists in both parties during the 2016 election cycle. Trade was an issue in the platforms of Mrs Hilary Clinton, Senator Bernie Sanders and Mr Donald Trump.

America's large public sector

America's economic welfare is diminished by significant structural economic challenges that do not go away as the economy recovers and expands. Structural rigidities tend to be exposed and aggravated by contractions in output.

In common with most advanced OECD economies is a level of public expenditure that is too high and a public sector that is expensive and not delivering. The American federal system makes it harder to score the full scope of the public sector. The combination of federal, state and local government is not as easy to consolidate as the public sectors in largely unitary states such as France, Japan and the UK.

Public sector organisations of one sort or another absorb about 45 percent of US national income, when account is taken of tax expenditures that are used to yield results comparable to public expenditure.

As the US does not provide publicly funded healthcare to most households of working age, and provides a less systematic and coherent framework of social assistance to households of working age, it is surprising this ratio is so high. It suggests that for what it does, the public sector is overly large and expensive. The US federal government spends more on defence than other OECD countries as a proportion of GDP, but that alone does not explain the high level of public sector spending, its recent growth and its future projected growth.

Absorbing over 40 percent of national income, including tax expenditures, American public spending has passed the point where the returns to spending at the margin meet or exceed its full cost. During the 20th century the role of the state massively expanded in providing education, healthcare, old-age pensions and unemployment assistance. The international evidence suggests a range of economic and social indicators improved significantly, but once spending reached around a third of national income there was less clear evidence of social improvement and increasing evidence of the economic cost of higher spending. It appears in rough terms that governments can accomplish all they can realistically achieve if they limit spending to about 35 percent. When spending increases above that level it starts to do economic damage for little clear social benefit. The US has gone beyond that level and will continue to raise the ratio of national income devoted to public sector spending on present policies. The heart of this rising ratio of spending to national income is the federal government's longstanding commitments to Medicare and a structural federal budget deficit that is accumulating future public expenditure liabilities at a faster rate than either the tax base or national income can be expected to match.

Raising revenue in a clumsy and expensive manner aggravates the economic cost of tax collection

In public finance, the key issue is total spending. How it is financed in terms of taxation and borrowing is a secondary matter, unless the government is borrowing so much it is compounding its future debt service costs at a faster rate than a realistic assessment of its future tax revenue and growth in the economy.

With a continuing permanent or structural federal budget deficit that is accumulating debt at a faster rate than the trend rate of GDP, the US is doing precisely that. Where the federal government levies taxes it does so principally through income, corporation and capital taxes, and a payroll social security levy. It makes little use of expenditure taxes. Income and capital taxes are more distorting and damaging to incentives to work, savings and investment than expenditure taxes.

The tax structure that has been constructed suffers from a further set of serious defects. It has many exemptions and allowances that create tax subsidies or expenditures that distort economic behaviour in a negative way and narrow the tax base, requiring higher marginal tax rates. In the first decade of the 21st century Congress passed laws cutting taxes for protracted periods that then, in law, were due to lapse, creating further uncertainty in what is already a complex and defective set of tax arrangements. Most tax systems are imperfect, but the US government has constructed a regime that aggravates economic cost and distortion.

America's structural economic rigidities require a systematic reform agenda

American policymakers have seven major challenges.

First, US policy makers have to finance their public sector with a realistic assessment of spending and borrowing. This means cutting borrowing and collecting taxes in a more effi-cient way that reduces distortion and deadweight cost to the economy. Part of this should include raising revenue from a neutral comprehensive tax on expenditure, designed to be as non-distorting of economic activity as possible. This is mainly a matter for the federal government, but is also an issue for state and local governments as well.

Second, they need to reduce the proportion of spending and tax expenditures within national income and increase the effi-ciency and productivity of their programmes, while making the tax system more efficient. Policy makers must regulate and supplement the private healthcare and higher education markets. In these sectors, costs must be lowered and opportunities for rent-seeking reduced. The financial exploitation of brands by many higher education institutions and the asymmetry of information in healthcare, along with the limitations of insurance markets, damage economic welfare.

Third, action must be taken to improve further the functioning of the US legal system at both state and federal level to ensure that the damages awarded as a result of tort litigation are more proportionate and consistent with the public interest. Civil law damages raise the cost of most economic activity in a way that is both erratic and expensive. This increases employment costs for employers and the cost of healthcare, as well as business costs in general.

Fourth, action must be taken to improve the functioning of product and labour markets. American policy makers need to examine at both federal and state level the regulations that hinder the working of competitive markets, prevent new entrants from challenging existing businesses. Part of this action should be an examination of the way the labour market operates, the effects of licences on professions and potential role that more active labour market policies could play in raising the rate of labour market participation. Systematic active labour market measures should be introduced to promote better links between schools, community colleges and higher education and employers to better help new entrants to the labour market. While labour market measures directed at older workers should help people who lose a job and suffer unemployment or spend periods out of the labour market for reasons ranging from family responsibilities, illness or a period of imprisonment. These measures should be partly designed expressly to raise the labour market participation rate of 'native' born minority communities in the US, as well as to improve the wider working of the labour market.

Fifth, the federal government and state governments need to look across their own policies and identify where high rates of tax, high net marginal rates of withdrawal of cash benefits or benefits in kind, such as access to the health care, damage employment and work incentives. This scrutiny of the tax system should include the operation of the federal tax credit system, the Manhattan skyline of the federal income tax system as credits phase in and out resulting in an effective marginal income tax structure that has little to with a person's place in the income tax distribution. It would involve an examination of the federal and state Medicaid rules and the withdrawal of subsidies for low income people within the Affordable Care Act policy regime. A part of it should include an examination of 'in work' assistance to very low income people at the bottom of the earnings distribution, who are on the cusp of participating in the labour market and the extent to which a more generous safety net is needed at the very bottom, not necessarily tied to the agenda of child poverty, to help to increase labor participation rates.

Sixth US policy makers in federal, state and local governments ought to examine ways of reforming taxation, benefits and the structure of taxes to create more efficient bases for taxation and spending. The objective should be a broadly based tax system with low marginal tax rates that is least distorting of economic activity and as neutral as possible. That suggests that extensive use should be made of expenditure taxes and they may work best when they are co-ordinated between federal, state and local government. Given the dispersion of economic activity among communities within the US and within individual states as part of that co-ordination some consideration should be given to revenue sharing to support effective education, health and social services in low income communities. More care should be given to developing shared finance to support basic necessary public services. Given the vulnerability of state and local government finances over the economic cycle and the differences in tax revenue available to finance public schools systems in neighbouring school districts, giving greater consideration to this is necessary.

Seventh, policy makers at every tier of US government from federal to local government need to invest in and maintain public infrastructure more carefully. Existing infrastructure needs to be better maintained and the benefits of repairing exist-ing infrastructure offer some of the highest rates of return on spending. Publically funded infrastructure investment needs to be rigorously costed in terms of its estimated returns and policy makers should be cautious about the wider economic and social benefits that are often asserted when infrastructure investment projects are prosed. The greatest returns are often to be found in more modest and local projects.

Ill-suited to reformation

American policymakers will find it difficult to tackle the kind of reform that is needed. The government in the US is divided between the executive, legislative and judicial branches. It is also divided between state and federal government.

This results in divisions both *between* and *within* tiers of government. These checks and balances make progress on a difficult agenda hard to achieve. The need to tackle these structural issues will become more pressing the longer reform is delayed. The US has one advantage over other countries faced with comparable challenges, in that it possesses a reserve currency the world still wants to own – which means the rest of the world is happy to continue to lend to its government. This is a huge advantage in the short term, but a long-term curse that allows the US federal government to avoid making necessary but difficult decisions.

In common with other advanced OECD countries, the US will face much greater international competition at the same time its population is ageing and its social security and healthcare commitments to older people will be increasing. It will need to nurture its private sector in order to maintain its public services. This will not be possible without an improvement in the supply performance of the US economy, which will be difficult without a systematic attempt to address connected structural economic challenges.

The combination of a federal system and the tradition of a divided government mean any one presidential administration or congress has little scope to do a great deal of damage. Presidents – and the rhetoric that surrounds them – are iconic players reflecting and shaping a mood rather than decision makers. Presidents can propose, but in many cases it is Congress and the states that decide. This applies even to presidents that appear, on election, to change the political weather such as Ronald Reagan and Barack Obama. President Trump for example benefited, on election, in principle from belonging to the Republican Party that controls both houses, yet has policies that are not necessarily fully coherent with the agenda of Republican senators or the Speaker of the House of Representative, Paul Ryan.

Much the same can be said of radical congresses. The Republican congresses first elected in 1994 on the *Contract with America*, left a public policy landscape mostly unchanged in its fundamentals, despite being accompanied by a Republican president for six years. Similarly, the Democratic congress elected in 2006 and the radical progressive mandate given to President Obama and the Democratic congress elected alongside him in 2008 did little to change the fundamentals of the American public policy landscape – despite the impressive amount of legislation, culminating in the extension of private health insurance and Medicaid assistance to American households, passed by President Obama, Speaker Nancy Pelosi and their Democrat colleagues in Congress. Yet the fundamentals of the policy landscape barely changed. President Obama's health care legislation represented a more limited change than the rhetoric that surrounded it and its impact was more limited than initially estimated by organisations such as the Congressional Budget Office. More broadly the policy agenda and its legislative expression pursued between 2008 and 2010 further compounded the structural challenges the American economy faces.

Chapter 2

The role of the public sector in advanced market economies

Modern societies and market economies need an efficient public sector providing goods and services that are best provided on a collective basis.

Public spending involves costs that go beyond the cash cost, because the taxes needed to pay for it impose a deadweight cost on the economy. So it is very important to ensure that public spending does not rise beyond the point where it generates clear benefits in excess of its costs. Diminishing marginal returns mean that at some stage, public spending costs on the economy exceed any benefits. Where the tipping point is precisely is difficult to identify. What is clear, however, is that spending over 35 percent of GDP or higher is approaching this tipping point. Any public spending ratio above 40 percent should be reduced.

Modern economies need large public sectors if they are to function efficiently. Markets also need a secure institutional framework of law, regulation and competition rules if they are to work well. This is the clear lesson from the experience of the transition economies in Central and Eastern Europe that have embarked on the process of establishing market economies following the collapse of Communism in 1989. Successful market economies also flourish when there is a clear appreciation of the need for substantial public intervention to balance the imperfections, defects and limitations that markets exhibit.

Public goods

Traditionally, the state was seen as necessary for providing certain public goods that markets could not easily provide. These included services such as street lighting, defence and criminal justice. Modern states rightly take on a much wider range of activities. Governments collectively organise and finance many services that could be done by private individuals or firms where there are either disproportionate costs to market provision or where low-income households would be unable to access the goods and services they need.

The wide dispersion of income and wealth that market economies exhibit requires collective action by governments to ensure all households have access to minimum standards of income and welfare. In modern societies, collective action by governments is an important part of ensuring both efficient markets and an optimal outcome in terms of individual living standards and welfare.

Going beyond public goods

Modern states intervene in a number of ways. As well as providing classic public goods they provide services such as education, health and pensions. These services could be organised and paid for privately, but the public interest in having them provided at an adequate level for all households results in government intervention.

Not all households value education, but because of the wider public interest in an educated society the state makes parents send their children to school. Given that many parents who do place a high value education are neither in the position to organise it nor pay for it for their children, the state organises it and pays for it. Insurance markets exhibit limitations that prevent some people from obtaining insurance for certain risks or only make it available at a disproportionate cost.

This is why governments intervene in the provision of healthcare, and also provide it for households that could potentially pay for it themselves, and also why they provide basic and earnings-related pensions to help low-income households and average-income households accumulate long-term savings and pension assets at a reasonable cost. Much of what the state does through collective provision is to assist people to smooth their incomes over their lifecycle. Households are given cash when they have children, when money is often scarce. Tax tends to be levied on individuals in middle age when earnings are highest and family responsibilities are lighter. And benefits are paid out in pensions, health and other services provided in old age when income is limited.

As these welfare services have been developed over the past century, there has been a huge improvement in a variety of economic and social indicators throughout the advanced OECD economies. Germany and Britain were in the vanguard of developing social insurance, which eventually led to the construction of comprehensive welfare states in Europe. In the 1950s and 1960s, welfare states were created throughout the advanced OECD economies, transforming the role of governments in the social and economic lives of their citizens. Levels of public expenditure and tax burden that once would only have been tolerated for brief periods of emergency became the peacetime norm.

Improving the functioning of market economies

Two economists have catalogued the international process through which efficient and extensive welfare states can improve the functioning of market economies. Vito Tanzi and Ludger Schuknecht have worked on fiscal policy at the International Monetary Fund (IMF). Their book, *Public Spending in the 20th Century: A Global Perspective*, sets out the secular rise in the ratio of state spending to national income.

In 1913, public spending accounted for about 13 percent of GDP in most industrial economies. In Germany it was 14 percent and in Britain and the US it was 12.7 percent and 7.5 percent respectively.

From 1918 to 1939, public expenditure rose sharply. Countries were starting to adopt embryonic social insurance schemes, but the main driver of higher spending was the fallout from the Great Depression. In Britain, there was a big expansion of state aid to industry and regions affected by the slump. In the US, New Deal programmes including the establishment of the Social Security pension system hugely expanded the role of the federal government. The French Popular Front government in 1936 expanded a wide range of social entitlements. Germany and Italy conducted experiments in self-sufficiency and state direction of the economy, along with rearmament spending that significantly increased state expenditure.

By 1937 the average ratio of public expenditure to GDP had risen from 19.6 percent after the end of World War I to 23.6 percent – in the US it was 19.6 percent, in France 29 percent, in the UK 30 percent and in Germany 34 percent.

In the following quarter of a century, the end of World War II and the establishment of comprehensive welfare states led to a further significant increase in the role of the state. In 1960, the average ratio of state spending to GDP was 28 percent, with the US at 27 percent, France at 32.4 percent, the UK at 32.8 percent and Germany at 34.6 percent.

Between 1960 and 1980 the average ratio rose more than a quarter by almost 13 percentage points to 41.9 percent. And between 1980 and 1996 it rose further to 45 percent. Tanzi and Schuknecht state:

'For the period up to 1960, a reasonable claim can be made that the increased public sector spending (on education, health, training, basic social security and so on) had led to measurable improvements in economic and social indicators'.

However, the further significant rise in public expenditure after 1960 has yielded little. They conclude that 'progress in improving the social and economic objectives slowed down considerably or even reversed in spite of a continuous large expansion in public spending in many countries'.

Market failure

The rationale for the increase in government spending in the 20th century and its expansion far beyond the provision of public goods is the need to correct imperfections and failures in markets.

In general, freely operating markets are the best way of using scarce resources. The conventional price mechanism does not consistently capture all the costs and benefits of providing goods and services. Costs at the margin do not always incorporate all benefits or damage generated by an activity. As well as negative costs, there may be positive benefits that are not reflected by the market. Some important areas such as insurance markets exhibit practical problems that make their private provision expensive as a result of adverse selection, asymmetries of information and moral hazard. Health insurance offers a good example of these constraints.

In market economies, incomes are widely dispersed. There will be many households that are not able to afford the range of goods and services the wider political community believes they should have access to. And because both expenditure on consumption and incomes are uneven over a lifetime, many households find it difficult to match their spending and income. This is partly because of imperfect knowledge of how long they will live and the imperfect savings and credit markets, and partly an element of myopia by households. This is why collective action is then taken to smooth household income over a lifetime.

State failure and the over expansion of the public sector

Identifying defects in markets is one thing, but remedying them efficiently is another.

As the public sector expanded in the 1950s and 1960s, economists began noticing examples of state failure that arise when resources are allocated through a political and bureaucratic process outside the price mechanism. American economists led this analysis. Economist James Buchanan made the point that while the neoclassical paradigm and the framework of Paretian welfare economics exposed market failures, the costs of rectifying them through state action should also be considered. His work led to the public choice school of economic analysis. The heart of this approach is to look at the consequences of vote-seeking politicians, supported by budget-maximising bureaucrats that create the conditions for state failure and an over-expansion of the public sector in modern democracies.

Diminishing returns to welfare spending

This significance of the research conclusions from, *Public Spending in The 20ᵗʰ Century: A Global Perspective*, is twofold.

First, is that a historically large public sector providing comprehensive welfare services in a generous manner helps a generally free economy to work better.

Second is that there must be a balance. Tanzi and Schuknecht believe governments should be able to accomplish much of what can be achieved through public spending within a rough range from 25-35 percent of GDP. Different countries will have different appetites for the collective provision of goods and services reflecting their unique traditions and cultural values.

The deadweight cost of public expenditure

Public expenditure imposes a cost on an economy, and that cost is greater than the cash of the spending involved, because public expenditure allocates resources outside the normal efficiency maximising framework of the price mechanism.

Both the spending itself and the taxes raised to finance it distort resource allocation in the economy. Expenditure has to be paid for in the long run by taxes, and taxation imposes a deadweight cost on the economy. This means that the cost in terms of economic output lost in the private sector is greater than the money or revenue raised through taxation to pay for it. Some forms of taxation are more distorting than others. Taxes on income, capital and trade appear to distort the economy more than taxes on expenditure. Government borrowing is effectively delayed taxation. The borrowing itself will also impose costs on an economy by competing for investors' funds in the bond markets and raising interest rates.

For many years, American policymakers have factored in the idea of deadweight to framing and costing US public expenditure programmes. In 1964, economist Arnold Harberger – who started this area of economic analysis – estimated that income taxes imposed welfare losses of 2.5 percent of tax revenue raised. More recent US studies have arrived at much larger estimates of deadweight losses. The Congressional Budget Office reports that 'typical estimates of the economic cost of a dollar of tax revenue range from 20 cents to 60 cents over and above the revenue raised'.

For several years, the Office of Management and Budget employed a 25 percent deadweight loss assumption when it carried out cost-benefit analysis on federal government spending programmes. The Office of Management and Budget's rules required that each additional dollar of tax revenue was scored as a cost of $1.25, because taxes 'create an excess burden that is a net loss to society'. This meant that a new spending proposal had to generate benefits that are at least 25 percent greater than the explicit financing costs involved.

Discussion of the deadweight consequences of taxation, or the 'excess burden' of taxation as it is sometimes referred to, has been at the heart of the American policy debate. For example, the President's Council of Economic Advisers in its *Economic Report to the President* in 2005, devoted a large part of their analysis to the effects of deadweight losses on economic behaviour. The report describes how taxation of savings and income distorts economic behaviour and results in inefficient use of resources, which leads to reductions in economic welfare that can exceed the amount of tax collected. These 'costs above and beyond the revenues collected are called the "excess burden" of the tax system. The level of distortion to economic decisions and the extent of the excess burden reflect the complexity of the tax system and the level of marginal tax rates.

Public spending and economic growth

There comes a point when public expenditure rises in relation to national income and the benefits are more than offset by the economic benefits, with the result that economic growth begins to slow down.

Many economists have looked at the connection between increased public spending and the long-term evolution of an economy's capacity to increase output and welfare. The economic literature establishes the proposition that relatively high public spending hampers economic growth.

Robert Barro, an economist at Harvard University, has taken a particular interest in economic growth and in the development of so-called new growth theory. He suggests that other things being equal, higher public spending will reduce economic growth.

Barro estimated that each additional one percentage point increase in the share of government spending in GDP was associated with a 0.14 percent retardation of GDP growth per head. Gerwin Bell and Norikazu Tawara, two IMF economists, looked at these issues in the 2009 paper, *The Size of Government and US-European Differences in Economic Performance*. They examine why European economies have, over the last 30 years, made little progress in closing the gap between their per capita GDP and that of the US. They examine the distorting effect of taxation on things like labour supply. They are careful to refute the blanket claim that differences in the size of government account for all of the differences in output and labour supply. They conclude, however, that 'the size of government does play a significant role in explaining lower European labour supply, while the size of European governments appears to imply large welfare costs'. They found there are large potential welfare gains to be made from 'cutting back government'.

Using data for 1992-2001, they found that in the UK a cut in marginal tax rates of five percentage points would have increased welfare gains equivalent to 4 percent of aggregate consumption, or 8 percent if the UK had adopted US tax levels accompanied by offsetting changes in government spending.

The 35 percent rule of thumb

As a rule of thumb, governments should aim to keep the ratio of public expenditure at around 35 percent of national income. By historical standards 35 percent of GDP would be considered a large public sector, although well beneath the current OECD average. It is slightly higher than the optimal ratio suggested by Tanzi and Schuknecht's research.

Bacon-Eltis thesis

In the mid-1970s, over-expanded public sectors were becoming a feature of European economies. No economy better exemplifies this than the UK in the 1970s.

Two academic Oxford economists, Robert Bacon and Walter Eltis, captured the challenges faced by the British economy in the 1970s in an arresting piece of contemporary economic analysis – *Britain's Economic Problem: Too Few Producers*.

Their thesis was straightforward. Britain had since 1961 shifted resources out of the production of marketable goods and services into non-marketable public services, and the extra public spending would need to be financed by higher taxation. That higher taxation would result in trade unions using their power in the work place to raise wages to offset the higher taxes. The resulting increased employment costs would cause private sector employers to shed labour and become reluctant to invest in future employment-creating capacity. If jobs were to be found for the displaced private sector workers, public spending must rise again so the state could take on the role of employer of last resort, which would raise taxes further and aggravate an already negative cycle.

They also looked at other OECD economies such as parts of the US and Canada, and suggested that that in the 1970s parts of the North American economy would begin to experience similar problems to Britain's as a result of expanding non-market sectors.

Bacon and Eltis originally set out their argument in a series of articles in *The Sunday Times* in 1975. Their analysis – although couched in terms of neo-Keynesian macroeconomic model – offered a frontal assault on the conventional economic policy in the post-war period that stated rising unemployment could be overcome if there was a sufficient increase in public spending.

A distinctive feature of the Bacon-Eltis thesis was the structural approach that it took, ad it is this approach that gives the book its continuing relevance to much of the OECD, including the US. This was highlighted by Robert Skidelsky in his foreword to the 20th anniversary edition of the book in 1996. Structural pathologies had, until then, been very the preserve of Marxist and neo-Marxist economists. It is possible to query the precise process in which government spending and borrowing crowds out private investment, whether it is possible to account for the one-for-one employment consequences that the their argument implies, and whether social security transfer payments played a bigger part in public spending for many years than direct purchases of goods and services – but their central point stands. Public spending has to be paid for through taxation or borrowing, which is delayed taxation. The Bacon-Eltis thesis is still relevant because it sets out what can go wrong when governments lose control of public spending.

Public spending crowds out the private sector

Many people find public expenditure attractive, but accept that beyond a certain point the cost in terms of taxation becomes prohibitive, even where someone else pays for it. This can be seen in the UK's regional economies since the 1960s and in the part of Germany that was once the German Democratic Republic.

American democracy has given the world some of the most vivid examples of the operation of the democratic political process. Much of the modern vocabulary of democratic discussion is of American origin – just think of terms such as gerrymander, lobbyist and pork barrel. These are all evocative political terms of American origin and have been the stuff of political history and literary fiction since the country's founding.

Lauren Cohen, Joshua Coval and Christopher Mallory in, *Do Powerful Politicians Cause Corporate Downsizing?* published in March 2011, assess changes in congressional chairs as sources of exogenous change in state-level federal expenditure. What they found is that fiscal spending shocks appear to significantly dampen corporate sector investment and employment. This negative response in private sector economic activity follows changes in Senate and House of Representatives committee chairs. They are most pronounced among large, geographically concentrated firms. The crowding out effects they identify are significant, and the mechanism that brings about public sector substitution for private sector activity is completely separate from the traditional causation of higher spending followed by higher taxation and interest rates.

The significance of Cohen et al's findings is that their paper offers a novel empirical approach that separates out changes in spending from other developments in the private sector and broader economy. When a congressional chair changes, the change has little to do with economic circumstances in the congressperson's state but leads to a positive reaction by the federal funds allocated to the new chair's state. Cohen et al found that through 232 changes in chair over 42 years, states receive an increase of spending. Earmarked federal spending increased between 40 to 50 percent, total state level government transfers increase by 9 to 10 percent and there is a 24 percent increase in government contracts. They found evidence of strong corporate retrenchment in response to increases in government spending.

In the year following an increase in government spending, capital spending by firms fell 15 percent. Firms also reduce employment and experience a fall in sales growth following an increase in government spending. These results are most pronounced when state-level employment and total US real GDP growth are at or above their long-term historical averages. They found that the increase in federal spending led to falls in state-level employment (-4.8 percent), GDP (-5.2 percent) and personal income (-5.8 percent). The parts of the private sector they identified as being most affected were manufacturing, construction and retail trade.

Shifting the same level of government spending between different states does not involve an overall increase in spending or taxation – only a different regional allocation. It therefore has no implications for taxation or borrowing costs. Cohen et al then identified distinct and separate channels through which public spending replaces private economic activity.

They conclude that 'crowding out occurs through factors of production, including the labour market and fixed industrial assets. These findings argue that the tax and interest rate channels, while obviously important, may not account for all or even most of the costs imposed by government spending. Even in a setting in which government spending is "free" – that is, it does not need to be financed with additional taxes or borrowing – its distortionary consequences may be nontrivial.'

This work on shifts in American federal government spending is similar to research into the effects of transfer payments in the European Union by economists at the European Central Bank. Cristina Checherita, Christiane Nickel and Phillipp Rother's paper, *The Role of Fiscal Transfers for Regional Economic Convergence in Europe* (ECB working paper number 1029, March 2009), finds that public expenditure transfer payments on average impede output growth.

There is a negative impact on the regions that receive fiscal transfer payments, and an even higher negative impact arising from net taxes on the growth of the regions that finance the transfers. The result is a 'process of "immiserising convergence" with output growth rates in the receiving poor regions declining by less than in paying rich regions in reaction to the tax-transfer scheme.

Conclusion

In advanced OECD economies there were many benefits from expanding the role of the public sector in the middle of the 20th century.

But much of the increase in public spending since the 1970s has been disappointing in terms of the results that it has yielded, and economies have performed less well in terms of growth of output and employment because of the opportunity cost arising from the higher spending.

There is a cost to public spending, in terms of distortions in activity and deadweight costs that is greater than the cash cost of the taxes needed to finance it. This means a balance must be struck between having public services that are best provided collectively, and recognition that there are both diminishing marginal returns and significant economic costs to such spending. It is therefore sensible to try to stabilise the ratio of general government expenditure at 35 percent of national income over the economic cycle.

The US has passed this threshold. It has a large, poorly focused public sector that fails to do many of the things that only the public sector can do, and provides many of the services it does carry out in an expensive and inefficient way. Without changes in policy and fundamental reform of healthcare, significant reforms to Social Security and measures to make state and local authorities more efficient in their employment practices, the ratio of US general government expenditure could on plausible projections exceed 50 percent of GDP in 25 years.

Chapter 3

The Great Depression

The Great Depression is an event of such magnitude and influence on American public policy that any discussion of the role and extent of the modern US public sector cannot ignore it.

Output fell between 1929 and 1933 by over a quarter in real terms, and by almost a half in nominal terms. Employment in nonfarm establishments fell by a quarter, and the average annual rate of unemployment rose from 3.2 percent to 24.9 percent. The rate of unemployment did not fall below 14.6 percent until 1941.

The 1930s in the US was a decade of mass unemployment. A full discussion of the Great Depression and its impact on American political policy is beyond the scope of this book, but a picture of one overriding factor accounting for the whole of the Depression is being replaced by a more nuanced analysis – one where a series of negative shocks interacted with the monetary policy of the Federal Reserve and caused the fall in output to deepen and to become more protracted. The Keynesian account focusing on a fall in confidence provoked by the Wall Street crash, a lack of demand, cash hoarding and a fall in consumption resulting in a new equilibrium of high unemployment has been supplemented with much greater focus on the role of monetary policy.

Role of monetary policy

Milton Friedman and Anna Schwartz in *A Monetary History of the US, 1867-1960*, published in 1963, challenged the Keynesian account and attributed the fall in output to a contraction in the money supply, deliberately engineered by the Federal Reserve to control inflation. The Federal Reserve was a relatively new and inexperienced central banking institution in 1929, only 16 years old. Much attention has focused on the weak and inexperienced leadership of its senior officials, a problem made greater by the premature death of Benjamin Strong, governor of the Federal Reserve Bank of New York, in 1928.

Domestic monetary policy in the US was made more complicated by international events, as the US remained on the gold standard until 1933. Barry Eichengreen and other economists have shown that this resulted in part from the Federal Reserve's focus. Even during banking crises this crisis meant that the reserve had to maintain domestic monetary conditions that were sufficiently tight to retain enough gold to ensure convertibility on demand. Despite falling output and a contracting money supply, at various times gold was moved to other financial centres such as London, and at critical moments the Federal Reserve was highly constrained in its policy actions.

In March 1933, the discount rate was actually raised. Christina Romer in a lecture, *Lessons from the Great Depression for Economic Recovery*, delivered at the Brookings Institute in 2009, argues this was one of the main reasons why the Federal Reserve did so little to counter the financial panics and banking crises. She also argued that when the US suspended the convertibility into gold temporarily, allowed the dollar to depreciate and then went back to gold at a new higher price, large quantities of gold flowed into the US. This then allowed the US Treasury Department to increase the money supply without operating through the Federal Reserve because it was able to issue gold certificates, which were interchangeable with Federal Reserve dollar notes. When gold flowed in, the Treasury issued more notes and the money supply, defined in terms of currency and reserves, grew by almost 17 percent between 1933 and 1936. As Romer put it: 'These gold reserves serendipitously continued to flow throughout the mid-1930s as political tensions mounted in Europe and investors sought the safety of US assets.'

Effectiveness of fiscal policy in 1930s

In folk memory of the 1930s, one of the principal problems was the personality and ideology of President Herbert Hoover. He is remembered as 'do nothing Hoover', in contrast to the ebullient personality of President Franklin D Roosevelt who transformed the federal government in an effort to put Americans back to work.

Price Fishback, in *US monetary and fiscal policy in the 1930s* in the Oxford Review of Economic Policy (2010; 26:3), surveys public policy in the Depression era. Fishback begins his examination of fiscal policy by commenting: 'Most observers do not realise how much the Hoover administration increased government spending. One reason is that Hoover remained a staunch advocate for balanced budgets throughout his presidency. Unlike Roosevelt, Hoover did not trumpet spending increases through new work relief programmes and public works programmes. Instead he expanded existing programmes.'

Federal spending rose under Hoover from $3.1bn in fiscal year 1929 to $4.6bn in fiscal year 1933. Fishback estimates that after adjusting for price changes – deflation – real federal government spending under Hoover peaked 88 percent above the level he started with in 1929. Federal spending on highways doubled, spending on river management and flood-control work carried out by the Army Corps of Engineers rose by 40 percent and the construction of the Hoover Dam, a project planned before the Depression, also contributed to increased spending on public works.

The Roosevelt administration almost doubled federal spending again between 1933 and 1936, taking spending to $8.4bn in 1936. Spending fell back in 1937 and 1938, before climbing to

$8.8bn in 1939. Despite this higher level of spending and the huge expansion of new public works programmes, the federal deficit during the Roosevelt administration was only significantly higher than the Hoover administration's in 1934, 1936 and 1939. Nor did Roosevelt's fiscal policy translate into a powerful stimulus of the sort advocated by Maynard Keynes. Professor Cary Brown, in *Fiscal Policy in the Thirties: A Reappraisal*, (American Economic Review 1956; 46) showed the scale of the deficits was insufficient to match the scale of loss of demand arising from the contraction of national income. It was not that spending did not rise, but that there was a succession of discretionary increases in taxation that raised revenue during the depths of the crisis. Brown said: 'The primary failure of fiscal policy to be expansive in this period is attributable to the sharp increases in tax structures enacted at all levels of government... the Federal Revenue Act of 1932 virtually doubled full employment tax yields.'

Hoover's Revenue Act 1932 was introduced because revenue was falling and spending was rising, creating a federal deficit for the first time since World War I. Although less than 10 percent of households earned enough to pay income tax in the 1930s, Fishback shows that those who did experienced sharp increases in taxation.

The income tax rate on individuals earning between $2,000 and $3,000 rose from 0.1 percent to 2 percent. The rate rose from 0.9 percent to 6 percent for incomes in the bracket between $10,000 and $15,000 and the top rate rose from 23.1 percent to 57 percent on incomes over $1m. The corporate income tax rate rose from 12 percent to 13.75 percent. The Revenue Act introduced new excise taxes on oil pipeline transfers, electricity, bank cheques, communications and manufacturers, which yielded $311m of revenue.

The Roosevelt administration initially left the tax regime inherited from Hoover intact, and tax revenue steadily increased as output recovered between 1933 and 1936. The Revenue Act 1934 made some modest adjustments to income tax, slightly lowering the rates in the lowest brackets and raising them for people earning between $20,000 and $1m. In the Revenue Act 1936, the Roosevelt administration raised income tax rates on individuals and families earning more than $100,000 from 31.4 percent to 33.4 percent, and on incomes over $1m the rate rose from 57.2 percent to 68 percent. This increase was also partly a response to a wider campaign, exemplified by Huey Long's 'Share our wealth' platform. The impact of fiscal policy in macro-economic terms was very modest. States faced with falling tax revenue also cut their spending to balance their budgets, as they were required to do by law. Fishback concludes that 'relative to a Keynesian deficit target designed to return to full employment, the deficits were miniscule'.

From 1937 the introduction of Social Security and the collection of the payroll tax to finance the social insurance pension resulted in a further tightening of fiscal policy, with around an additional $2bn of revenue collected.

In terms of monetary and fiscal multipliers, the research Fishback surveys is mixed. Even if fiscal deficits had been run on a large scale the multipliers suggest the effect on the economy would have been weak. His own work looking at government spending at the state, county and city level suggests the impact varied from programme to programme. On average, a $1 increase in net federal spending was associated with an increase of $1-1.50 in per capita personal incomes, but had little effect on unemployment.

Taxation and the supply-side performance

Fishback explains how the Roosevelt administration did little to reverse Hoover's 1932 Revenue Act and raised higher rates of tax in 1936. The combination of new excise duties on certain developing sectors and new rules and taxes on capital stock, dividends and excess profits – along with a surtax on undistributed profits in 1936 – distorted economic behaviour.

The revenue collected was small, but these taxes led to distortions in investment and company decisions about cash flow. The rules penalising undistributed profits particularly affected small firms undergoing rapid expansion in new sectors that tended to face difficulty in attracting external finance. The combination of much higher income tax rates at the top of the earnings distribution, new excise duties affecting the fastest growing sectors of the economy and investment distorting taxes on capital and dividends hampered economic activity and slowed the growth of new technology.

Microeconomic dimensions to the Great Depression

An interesting literature assessing microeconomic changes and the labour market has developed. Far from being some kind of apostle of free markets, Herbert Hoover had a strongly corporatist outlook. He was a supporter of free enterprise – provided it conformed to his understanding of efficiency, and his perception of efficiency was not always consistent with competitive markets. Indeed, Hoover was prepared to support high degrees of market concentration and monopoly power to avoid the 'inefficiency' of competition, so long as the monopoly profits were shared with workers in those industries through higher wages. He pursued this policy as Commerce Secretary in the Coolidge administration. The Justice Department was instructed not to enforce competition rules where market collusion was taking place, provided profits were being shared fairly with employees.

Wages were understood to be 'sticky' and the Hoover administration's approach to wage bargaining and competition aggravated this. Roosevelt's National Industrial Recovery Act (NIRA) actually raised cash wages, as well as limiting production and the number of hours worked. Harold Cole and Lee Ohanian have explored how total hours worked fell before 1933, but fell even further between 1933 and 1939. They argue that in 1933 the conditions were in place for a conventional vigorous recovery in output after a severe fall in activity. Productivity was growing rapidly, the price level was stable, interest rates were low and there was plenty of liquidity.

What prevented a conventional recovery were policies 'that violated the most basic economic principles'. These suppressed competition, the normal mechanisms for setting prices and wages and resulted in wages in many sectors being well above their normal levels. NIRA covered over 500 industries, and in each a code of fair competition was established to eliminate excess competition. These codes artificially raised wages and prices and restricted production. Cole and Ohanian calculate manufacturing wages were as much as 25 percent higher than they would have been without NIRA.

After the NIRA regime was dismantled in 1936 – having been declared unconstitutional by the Supreme Court in 1935 – the National Labour Relations Act 1935 gave unions substantial collective bargaining power. As a result, there were large wage increases that pushed wages above NIRA levels. Cole and Ohanian conclude that the New Deal's labour market measures extended the Great Depression by seven years.

This account of the Great Depression fits with work done by Lawrence Christiano, Roberto Motto and Massimo Rostagno in an ECB working paper *The Great Depression and the Friedman-Schwartz Hypothesis* published in 2004. They argue that while the Great Depression was principally a monetary event, 'a second shock plays an important role in our account of the Great Depression and helps resolve a puzzle that has constantly bothered scholars of this period. The puzzle is that hours worked recovered only slightly even in the face of the brisk upsurge in output growth in the second half of the 1930s... the answer to this is that there was a rise in the market power of workers. This feature of our story accords well with the widespread notion that the policies of the New Deal had the effect of sustaining wages and reducing employment by giving workers greater bargaining power.' In 1938, for example, President Roosevelt recognised in a speech that the American economy had become a 'concealed cartel system like Europe'.

Conclusion

There were clearly major mistakes made in public policy in the 1930s that turned an awkward contraction in output into the Great Depression that so colours modern thinking about the economic cycle.

The Federal Reserve's mistakes with monetary policy were probably the principal factor behind the scale and depth of the loss of output, and its concerns about inflation in 1937 resulted in a second leg to the Depression. Fiscal policy was wholly inadequate in scale given the fall in output and the discretionary tax increases destroyed most of any stimulus increased public spending could have offered. The tax policies pursued aggravated matters by increasing distortion and hampering innovative and technologically advanced sectors of the economy. Regulation of employment and product markets raised wages above their market rate and established the conditions for a protracted structural rise in unemployment. This meant that while more active monetary and fiscal policies could have raised output and income, their effect on employment would have been more muted.

In the post-war period, generations of economists found it easy to be critical of 1930s policymakers and to satirise their commitment to 'orthodoxy'. The fact that a recession was allowed to develop between 1937 and 1938 was greatly criticised, in much the same way that economic commentators have criticised Japan for its policy errors during its lost decade of deflation. Yet contemporary economic challenges seem increasingly difficult to navigate. The confusion and genuine dilemmas of modern policymakers mean that economists turn to the Great Depression to try to obtain some appreciation of what can go wrong.

The lesson least appreciated or understood is the need to be alert about policies that can inadvertently create structural rigidities that permanently raise the level of unemployment and reduce the trend rate of economic growth. The further lesson is that significant public policy developments such as the creation of Social Security in 1935 can have unexpected and highly disruptive consequences.

Chapter 4

Fiscal policy and demand management

There has been a contentious debate about the merits of the fiscal stimulus measure that was enacted by President Obama's administration in the American Recovery and Reinvestment Act 2009. It marked an extraordinary renaissance in the use of active fiscal policy to manage demand during contractions in economic activity. There is nothing inconsistent between having reservations about the extent of public spending and its long-term structural consequences, and recognising the role fiscal policy can have in short-term demand management. The active use of fiscal policy as part of demand management was generally accepted as the preferred method of ensuring resources were fully employed and demand was maintained over the economic cycle until the 1970s. The role of fiscal policy in active demand management was central to the Keynesian revolution of the 1940s.

The main structural economic challenges that the US faces are separate from the immediate issues of monetary policy and managing demand over the economic cycle. Given that active fiscal policy has made such a significant return, it is difficult to ignore its role in policy and the possible implications that it may have for the tractability of America's structural challenges.

Practical difficulty in making fiscal policy work

Fiscal policy was discredited as part of the broader collapse of the Keynesian system in the 1970s. It was considered at best ineffective, and at worst distorting and potentially destabilising. There were four reasons why policymakers had become sceptical about the use of fiscal policy as part of demand management. These were:

- the empirical record of effectiveness

- the practical difficulties of timing policy implementation

- the long-term consequences for the structure of micro-economic decisions

- the highly theoretical concerns over neo-Ricardian equivalence.

The discrediting of fiscal policy as a tool of economic management started in the US in the late 1960s. The combination of the cost of the Vietnam War and Lyndon Johnson's Great Society programmes aggravated inflation and pressures on the American balance of payments. American economic activity needed to slow down. The Johnson administration tried to do this by raising taxes, but these had little impact. American economic activity did not slow until the Federal Reserve tightened monetary conditions and raised interest rates. In 1975, the credibility of fiscal policy as a tool of demand management was further eroded by the Ford administration's attempt to use a tax cut to stimulate demand. Economists found that by the time tax cuts arrived in the hands of households, the recession in output was over. This illustrated the clumsy character of fiscal measures and the difficulty of executing them in a timely way.

In Britain the seminal event was the 1981 Budget. Sir Geoffrey Howe, the Chancellor of the Exchequer, tightened fiscal policy in order to reduce a structural budget deficit in the trough of a slump in output of 1981. Many economists said that this action was pro-cyclical rather than counter-cyclical and would ruin any recovery in output. As things turned out, GDP started to rise and the economy steadily expanded for nearly eight years. At the same time, the exchange rate fell, domestic interest rates were lowered and the economy was further stimulated by a real balances or Pigou effect arising from a greater than expected fall in inflation boosting the real value of money balances held by households and firms. This appeared to confirm the importance of monetary conditions compared with discretionary changes in taxation and spending that only directly affect a small ratio of total output – although the multiplier effects are always greater than the simple cash numbers may suggest.

Discretionary changes in taxation and spending as part of macroeconomic demand management were perceived as a source of instability. By the time changes took effect, the economy had moved on. Changes in taxes and spending amplified the economic cycle. Milton Friedman's charge against fiscal policy was that it was pro- rather than counter-cyclical. The level and composition of public expenditure, the tax burden and marginal tax rates were increasingly seen as important in shaping the evolution of an economy's supply performance in the medium term.

Not only did discretionary changes in taxation and spending amplify rather than smooth the cycle, they had negative effects on the economy. Increased government spending and new public sector programmes were politically difficult to cut once the immediate macroeconomic rationale for their introduction was over. Frequent changes in tax rates and the structure of income, corporation and capital taxes distorted economic decision making and undermined the supply performance of the economy in the long term.

Neo-Ricardian equivalence

If this catalogue of defects was not enough to finish off the appetite of policymakers for fiscal policy, theoretical work by Robert Barro in the 1970s did.

Barro, a Harvard economist, who has also done work on new growth theory and how economies experience and respond to adverse economic shocks, explored some concerns about the consequences of government debt that were first raised by British economist David Ricardo in the 19th century.

The essence of Barro's work is that people try to smooth their consumption to match some idea of their permanent income, and they have a long-term interest in the welfare of future generations. A government that tries to exit recession by spending money and running government deficits will find its efforts are ruined by the offsetting behaviour of private households. Household recognise that one way or another, government deficits will have to be paid for by future increases in taxation and will therefore cut spending and increase savings to pay for the future increased tax burden.

This idea of 'neo-Ricardian equivalence' may seem unknown and remote, but it has influenced the thinking of policymakers – particularly central bank and finance ministry officials.

Fiscal policy returns in 2008

Fiscal policy returned to fashion in a spectacular manner during the autumn of 2008, reflecting the scale of problems faced by central banks. It was not just governments that recognised fiscal policy had a role to play in policy at that time. Many of the world's central bankers accepted it as well, and in many respects the International Monetary Fund (IMF) led the world down this road.

The IMF changed in its attitude to fiscal policy. The speed of the change can be seen from its publications during the autumn of 2008. In November 2008 it published a supplement to its *World Economic Outlook*. The previous month, the core judgement in chapter 1, *Policy Challenges For The Global Economy*, its advice on the role of fiscal policy was cautious and hedged. The US fiscal stimulus in February 2008 was judged to be well-timed, but the 'potential costs' of these measures (the TARP and housing bailout measures) and the 'need for medium-term consolidation', however, meant 'adjustment measures will be required elsewhere'. In relation to the Eurozone, it stated 'fiscal policy is already providing support to the euro-area economy through automatic stabilisers and discretionary measures in some countries', and the 'limited scope for further fiscal easing available under the revised Stability and Growth Pact should be used to focus public resources on stabilising financial conditions, as needed'.

Within a month, in the November edition of the *World Economic Outlook: Update*, the tone had changed decisively. The IMF position was now that the 'room for further easing of [monetary] policy is limited as policy rates are already close to the zero bound. These are conditions where broad-based fiscal stimulus is likely to be warranted. Fiscal stimulus can be effective if it is well-targeted, supported by accommodative monetary policy, and implemented in counties that have fiscal space'.

The interesting thing is that before the extent of the financial crisis started to emerge in 2007, attitudes to fiscal policy among American economists were already changing, reflecting new evidence about the impact of the George W Bush tax cuts in 2001. Most economists, including those who supported cuts in marginal rates for supply-side reasons, assumed that the story would be much like the Ford administration's fiscal stimulus in 1975, when tax refunds were received by taxpayers after output had already started to recover. Empirical work on the impact of the 2001 tax cuts suggests they had a positive impact at an appropriate stage of the economic cycle. As a result, the balance of economic thinking about the efficacy of fiscal policy began to shift even before the financial crisis fully took hold.

The effectiveness of George W Bush's tax stimulus in 2001

A group of economists discussed the effects of the Bush tax cut in the *American Economic Review* in December 2006 (96;5) in the article *Household expenditure and income tax rebates of 2001*.

They found households spent much of their income tax rebate. Between 20 to 40 percent of the rebates were spent in the three months following receipt of the cheque from the Internal Revenue Service. Two-thirds of rebates were spent within three months. In national accounts terms, the tax rebates provided a substantial stimulus to the national economy. They added $38bn to personal consumption expenditure, about 2.2 percent, and 7.5 percent to nondurable expenditure in the third quarter of 2001. The behaviour of the savings ratio, which fell from 1.9 in the first quarter of 2001 to 1.2 in the second quarter, before recovering to 3.4 percent in the fourth quarter, was also consistent with evidence of the fiscal stimulus having 'anticipatory' effects. It appears that consumers ran down their savings and maintained or brought forward their consumption in the knowledge that the tax rebates would be coming.

This article was significant in modifying economists' views about the efficacy of fiscal policy in macroeconomic management. Dollar for dollar, it tracked consumer spending as a result of the tax cut and changes in consumer behaviour consistent with consumers being forward-looking. It may appear dull and technical, but it represents significant counter-factual evidence to most of what had been accumulated over the previous 40 or more years. There is no point in pretending that for policymakers and economists, who had come to accept Milton Friedman's judgment about the ineffectiveness of fiscal policy, this piece of work was a challenge they could not ignore. However accepted notions about the clumsiness and tardiness of fiscal policy have become, the arguments surrounding fiscal policy as a potential stimulus needed to be re-examined.

It would be a mistake to regard this renewed interest in active counter-cycle fiscal policy, after 2001 as either simply a political response or some kind of New Keynesian intellectual agenda. Among the economists looking again at these issues are Martin Feldstein and Michael Boskin – former chairs of the Council of Economic Advisers in the Reagan and Bush administrations and politically conservative mainstream economists. Feldstein has proposed that a fiscal stimulus should automatically kick in if certain criteria around output or employment are triggered.

In July 2008, the Federal Reserve Bank of San Francisco organised a seminar to look at research on the effect of fiscal stimulus as a policy tool. Boskin led the discussion and noted that there was now a consensus among American economists that counter-cyclical fiscal policy could mitigate the damage of economic slowdowns. He pointed to two changes of judgment about the efficacy of fiscal policy. The first change is the wide recognition that there is little evidence to suggest consumers actually modify their behaviour in response to government deficits, which disposes of the theoretical concern about neo-Ricardian equivalence. The second change is the recognition that in some circumstances, fiscal policy may work faster and more directly than changes in monetary conditions that normally act with a lag of between six and 18 months.

Timely, targeted and temporary

In 2008, a growing consensus emerged that said discretionary fiscal policies could usefully stimulate economic activity in certain circumstances. Ideally such policies should meet the criteria of the three Ts: timely, targeted and temporary.

The key idea is that they should give a temporary boost to demand, but not become entrenched in a way that permanently increases the stock of public debt crowding out private sector activity and capital investment in the medium-term. After the collapse of Lehman Brothers and the elimination of conventional monetary policy as an effective and independent instrument in September 2008, economists and governments turned to discretionary fiscal policy as the only practical tool available to stabilise the fall in output.

In the extraordinary circumstances in the autumn of 2008, similar to the circumstances that Keynes had written about so vividly in the *General Theory* in 1936, many economists who had previously been sceptical about fiscal policy began to support discretionary fiscal policies to stabilise output. It appeared that monetary policy only existed to the extent that fiscal policy backed the banking system – interest rates were at a level where changing them would no longer influence economic behaviour and output was collapsing.

Most major economies used fiscal policy to stabilize output in the Great Recession. As the US Council of Economic Advisers pointed out discretionary fiscal action was not the only form of fiscal stimulus that helped to stabilise output. The automatic stabilizers, such as unemployment benefits , welfare transfer payments, reduction in tax revenue collected arising from lower employment and economic activity - are triggered when an economy slows down. The size of automatic stabilizers present in an economy appears to be negatively correlated with the size of discretionary stimulus employed in different countries. Countries that had large automatic stabilizers in place already took less discretionary fiscal stimulus measures, although they were still providing significant fiscal support during the period of crisis.

Table 4.1: 2009 Fiscal Stimulus as Share of GDP, G-20 Members

Argentina	1.5%	Japan	2.9%
Australia	2.9%	Mexico	1.6%
Brazil	0.6%	Russia	4.1%
Canada	1.8%	Suadi Arabia	3.3%
China	3.1%	South Africa	3.0%
France	0.6%	South Korea	3.7%
Germany	1.6%	Turkey	2.0%
India	0.6%	United Kingdom	1.6%
Indonesia	1.4%	United States	2.0%
Italy	0.1%	**All G-20 Nations**	**2.0%**

Note: Values are average of International Monetary Fund and Organisation for Economic Co-operation and Development estimates for nations with expansionary fiscal policies.

Sources: Horton, Kumar and Mauro (2009); Organisation for Economic Co-operation and Development (2009)

Figure 4.1: Tax Share and Discretionary Stimulus

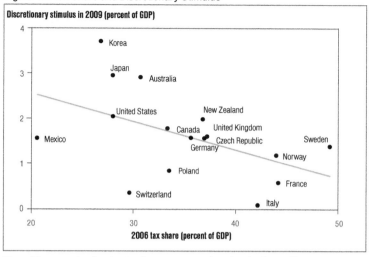

Notes: The regression line is stimulus = 3.8 – 0.06* (tax share). The coefficient on tax share is significant at the 90 percent confidence level. The R-square is 0.23.

Sources: Organisation for Economic Co-operation and Development, Tax Database Table O.1 (2009); Horton, Kumar and Mauro (2009); Council of Economic Advisers

From October 2008, fiscal policy staged a dramatic international comeback. Among the countries that announced – or in the case of the US extended – discretionary fiscal stimulus packages were Australia, the UK, China, France, India, Japan and New Zealand. The way was led by the IMF calling for countries to take measures equivalent to 2 percent of GDP. The European Commission, guardian of the European Union's Monetary and Stability Pact, called on member states to announce fiscal packages of 1.5 percent of GDP. The OECD endorsed fiscal stimulus measures, and on average OECD economies took discretionary fiscal measures that amounted to 2.5 percent of GDP. The only country initially determined in its opposition to fiscal measures was Germany, whose SPD finance minister dismissed such packages as 'crass Keynesianism' – and even Germany turned to fiscal tools in the end.

65

US fiscal policy in the Great Recession

The great recession following the credit crunch in 2007 resulted in real GDP falling slightly in the first quarter of 2008. The Council of Economic Advisers' *Economic Report of the President* 2010 catalogued the unprecedented policy response that the Great Recession provoked in the US.

The Bush administration and Congress passed a temporary tax cut in the form of a tax rebate. These rebates appear to have helped to stabilise output. During a period when household wealth was falling sharply, total household and non-profit wealth fell by 9.6 percent in the year to June 2008 – but consumption spending held up. Microeconomic studies of consumer behaviour suggest consumer spending was supported by the tax rebate, and real GDP rose in the second quarter of 2008.

An unprecedented policy response

The Emergency Economic Stabilisation Act was passed in October 2008. After the collapse of Lehman Brothers in September, the Bush administration proposed emergency assistance to stabilize the banking system. Congress eventually passed this in the Emergency Economic Stabilisation Act in October 2008, which provided $700 bn of assistance to the financial sector. Assistance that infuriated a lot of people, who felt that the financial industry brought this on themselves and should not have been bailed at the initiative of the Bush administration, after the collapse of Lehman Brothers.

It paid for the Troubled Asset Relief Program (TARP) that purchased distressed assets trading at a discount to their former perceived value and provided capital injections for banks. TARP money was divided into two tranches of $350bn. Under the terms of the legislation, the President had to seek Congressional approval for the use of each tranche.

The first tranche was used to buy preferred equity shares in banks to give them more capital at the height of the crisis. President George W Bush, at the request of Mr Obama, asked

Congress on 12 January 2009 to release the second tranche. The new administration used the money to try to address the related matters that worked to make financial markets unstable and continued to freeze the normal operation of credit flows.

The principal element of the Financial Stability Plan announced on 11 February 2009, was the Supervisory Capital Assessment Program, the 'stress test' to see if banks needed more capital. It was intended to ensure banks got additional capital if they needed it. The Consumer and Business Lending Initiative extended the Federal Reserve's Term Asset-Backed Securities Loan Facility intended to assist securitisation that had been announced in November 2008. This was extended and given a further $100bn to leverage $1trn of lending business. The purpose was to unlock consumer lending.

The Treasury Department combined with the Federal Deposit Insurance Corporation and the Federal Reserve to create the Public-Private Investment Program. Its purpose was to remove toxic assets of little value from bank balance sheets, thus increasing their ability to raise capital and lend. It leveraged limited public resources and used competitive markets to ensure that the federal government did not overpay for assets of limited value.

There was wide-ranging assistance given to the housing market to hold interest rates down and to help home owners stay in their homes. The failure of General Motors and Chrysler resulted in the George W Bush administration establishing an Auto Financing Program, using $17.4bn of funding from the first tranche of TARP in December 2008. In total, by September 2009 more than $80bn of assistance had been given to the auto industry, including help with consumer car warranties, balance sheet restructuring and assistance for pensioners and other creditors.

Monetary policy fuses with fiscal policy

In the great recession, the analytical and policy separation between fiscal and monetary policy was ended. The two, for all practical purposes, became one. Interest rates were close to zero and there was a textbook liquidity trap.

Without transfer payments from taxpayers to bank balance sheets, the financial system could not be stabilised. The balance sheet of the Federal Reserve expanded more than two and a half times, from just over $800bn in 2007 to over $2.2trn in 2009. Interest rates – the target rate for Federal Reserve funds – were cut from 5.25 percent at the start of 2007 to 0-0.25 percent in December 2008. In addition, the Federal Reserve introduced several unconventional monetary policy tools.

In March 2008, the Primary Dealer Credit Facility and the Term Securities Lending Facility were introduced and when the commercial paper market began to fail the Commercial Paper Funding Facility was brought in. In March 2009, the Federal Reserve announced it would buy $300bn of long-term Treasury debt to reduce long-term interest rates. It also said it would increase its purchases of debt issued by government-sponsored enterprises by a further $200m, taking its potential holding up to $1.25trn.

Figure 4.2: Assets on the Federal Reserve's Balance Sheet

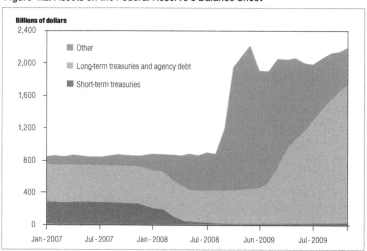

Sources: Federal Reserve Board, H.4.1, Table 1

Figure 4.3: Change in central bank assets

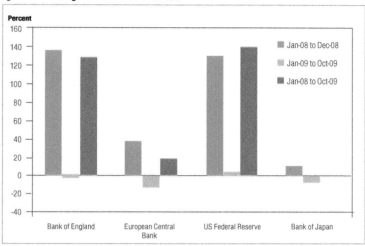

Sources: Country sources, CEA calculations

Figure 4.4: Policy Rates in Economies with Major Central Banks

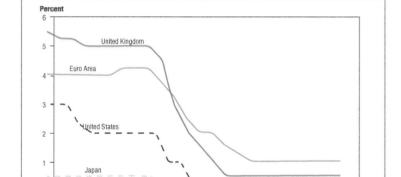

Sources: Country sources, CEA calculations

American Recovery and Reinvestment Act 2009

The American recovery and reinvestment act was passed in February 2009, to stimulate the economy and to expedite the recovery in output and employment.

Chair of the Council of Economic Advisers Christina Romer said the Act was to reduce unemployment by 2 percentage points by the middle of 2010 and create or save 3.65 million jobs by the fourth quarter of 2010. The stimulus plan was to raise GDP by 1-3 percentage points. The total cash deployed was $787bn, roughly equivalent to 2 percent of GDP in 2009 and 2.25 percent in 2010. It eventually cost $862bn, equivalent to 5.5 percent of GDP – albeit spread over a number of years. It was the largest fiscal stimulus ever attempted in American economic history; at its peak, the New Deal had a net impact of closer to 1.5 percent of GDP. It was designed to fill part of the shortfall in aggregate demand caused by the collapse of private demand.

Economists will have had plenty of opportunity to study its effects and to identify what worked and what did not. The first conclusions of the research into the efficacy of the American Recovery and Reinvestment Act are beginning to become available. The Congressional Budget Office looked at the effects on output of the 2008 tax rebates and the effect of the Act. It had expected 40 percent of President George W Bush's tax cut to be spent within six months, cumulatively raising consumption by 2.5 percent. Household surveys of direct consumer behaviour such as use of credit cards suggest that about a third of the tax rebate was spent. Other surveys of households, where people are asked questions about their spending, suggest only 20 percent of the rebate was spent. The Congressional Budget Office estimated the 2009 fiscal stimulus raised the level of GDP by between 1.7 and 4.2 percent and lowered unemployment by between 0.7 and 1.5 percentage points. Its research note estimated in 2009, increased federal government expenditure increased GDP cumulatively by 2.5 percent.

Several principles informed the design of the stimulus package. First, the measures were spread over two years because the Obama administration thought the economy would need substantial support for more than one year. It, however, wanted the stimulus to be explicitly temporary. Second, the stimulus should be diversified and should help the economy in different ways. And third, the emergency increases in government spending should address long-term needs, such as investment in infrastructure that would yield benefits in terms of productivity and economic growth.

The Congressional Budget Office estimated that $198bn of the stimulus directly helped individuals through extended unemployment insurance, help with Medicaid and so on. Some $281bn went on tax cuts – mainly the Making Work Pay credit of $800–and a temporary shielding of households from the Alternative Minimum Income Tax. And $308bn went on discretionary increases in public spending from roads to schools. The Congressional Budget Office estimated that by the end of the third quarter of 2009, 25 percent of the stimulus package would be spent, and an additional half would be spent over the following three quarters. A significant part of the package provided temporary assistance to help state and local governments balance their budgets without having to cut spending as sharply as they would otherwise have to, given the pro-cyclical character of state budgets.

Too small, too widely dispersed, too poorly targeted and too slow?

The stimulus package has been criticised by supporters of discretionary measures as being too small, the main criticism made by economist Paul Krugman. Martin Feldstein, president emeritus of the National Bureau of Economic Research, was concerned about its composition, arguing that more emphasis should have been placed on transfer benefits to raise consumption.

A general criticism of the stimulus package's structure was that it was too broad a brush, insufficiently focused and not timely enough. Part of this reflects the policy process, in that Congress had to agree the package and its members were well-placed to insist on their preferred schemes. President Obama was criticised for leaving too much of the shaping of the detail to the Democratic Congressional leadership. His administration's decision to conflate long-term infrastructure capital projects with a short-term stimulus to demand was mistaken. Much of this investment was part of an agenda that has nothing to do with the economic cycle and would take years to come through – up to a decade – and suggests there was insufficient attention to getting maximum immediate economic stimulus per dollar of tax loss or spending.

It contributed to the perception that the overall package was a hodgepodge of measures, which to a significant degree violated the 'temporary, timely, targeted' dictum of successful fiscal stimulus packages. Some of the measures that clearly yielded the greatest multiplier effect – such as extended unemployment insurance benefits – also have potential negative implications for microeconomic incentives in the labour market, operating to extend the duration of unemployment and as a result of this aggravating structural problems in the US jobs market.

In constructing the stimulus package Congress was subject to intense lobbying from interested parties, with the result that part of the funding available could only be spent on supporting public sector programmes that maintained union wage premiums and other rules, or through contracts that enhanced union collective bargaining. These reduced the microeconomic efficiency of some elements of the stimulus package, and aggravated other long-term problems such as efficiency in public spending and procurement, as well as local crowding-out effects.

Too little attention was given to 'shovel-ready projects'. Even where Congress used the American Recovery and Reinvestment Act to fund longstanding lists of projects, it is not clear that spending was actually swiftly delivered. The National Congress of American Indians in March 2010, for example published *Investing in Tribal Governments: Case Studies from the American*

Recovery and Reinvestment Act. It set out a significant list of spending projects in education, housing and healthcare, dating back over 10 years, to address the intergenerational disadvantages of Native people – but it did not explain how such projects immediately stimulated the economy. It was much more cogent in explaining how they are part of a much longer-term public expenditure agenda. Although its Congressional lobbyists would argue that they had a good record on having 'shovel-ready' projects waiting for federal money. The Obama administration also failed to offer a credible approach to reducing the federal government's unsustainable structural budget and debt position, although it did acknowledge it.

It is probably still too early to come to any definite conclusions about the effectiveness of the fiscal measures taken following the credit crunch and great recession in the US. Different research methodologies are yielding different results, and the data is still subject to revision. What is significant about this literature and debate is that it illustrates the vigour, range and rigour of the US public policy debate. Active fiscal policies that go above and beyond accommodating the operation of the normal automatic stabilisers should neither result in a permanent increase in public expenditure nor a permanent increase in the budget deficit. In political and practical policy terms, this is a genuine challenge. Even the operation of automatic stabilisers and 'recession'-related spending tend to permanently entrench and raise expenditure over the cycle. When the three Ts criteria – targeted, timely and temporary – for judging a fiscal stimulus package are used, it is obvious policymakers find it difficult to meet the 'temporary' criterion.

Alan Auerbach, William Gale and Benjamin Harris in *Active Fiscal Policy* looked at evidence around the effectiveness of fiscal policy, and argued President Obama's fiscal stimulus measures are best seen as part of a continuum, where policymakers have made much greater use of fiscal policy than previously. In the recessions in 1982 and 1990, fiscal policy was actually tightened. In 2001, President George W Bush cut taxes to boost the economy and it appeared to be effective. Auerbach et al argue that, in principle, there is a good case for the US to consider using discretionary fiscal policy, because automatic stabilisers play a less significant role in the American economy than they do in other OECD economies.

The tax cuts in 2001 were likely to have been effective given the interest that both the George W Bush administration and Congress had in reducing taxes permanently. Whereas in 2008, tax cuts were expressly temporary and the background to the public finances was one consistent with permanent future tax rises. The tax cut in 2001 went to all taxpayers, and in relative terms this should have resulted in a lower consumption effect than the 2008 tax cut targeted at low- and middle-income households. However, microeconomic research investigating household consumption suggests a similar behavioural response to both tax cuts.

The combined fiscal and 'fused' monetary measures taken between 2008 and 2009 were significant. Output was plummeting and the stimulus measures stabilised the economy. The US, the principal location of the cause of the credit crunch, lost less output than other advanced OECD economies. The extent to which the fiscal measures led to the economy recovering and using spare capacity to grow faster than its trend rate of growth before stabilising GDP growth at its trend rate is much less clear. The Federal Reserve Board's innovative monetary policy measures, the recapitalisation of the banking system, the Treasury Department's stress testing of bank balance sheets and the Federal Reserve's purchases of toxic bank assets played a critical role both in the stabilisation of output and the expansion that took place from 2009 to 2015. The role of the fiscal measures continues to be debate.

In years following the 2009 Obama administration's fiscal stimulus package there continues to be a contentious debate about its effectiveness. The Congressional Budget Office estimated that in 2012, the American Recovery and Reinvestment Act raised real GDP by between 0.1 percent and 0.8 percent and increased the number of people employed by between 0.2 million and 1.1 million.

The administration's economists confidently asserted that it saved jobs and raised output. The awkward challenge they face is reconciling what they expected to happen in their paper *The Job Impact of the American Recovery and Reinvestment Plan* and what actually happened. The administration's economists projected that with no stimulus, unemployment would continue rising during 2010, and would have peaked at around 9 percent and then stabilised at around that level for about a year. The stimulus, would have instead resulted in unemployment peaking in the third quarter of 2009, and would then start to fall, going below 6 percent. The Council of Economic Advisers illustrated economic forecast with a chart that that showed how the US economy would perform between 2009 and 2013 with and without fiscal stimulus. The chart showed that the projected unemployment rate would not reach 8 percent, if Congress passed the stimulus.

Figure 4.5a: Unemployment Rate with and without the Recovery Plan

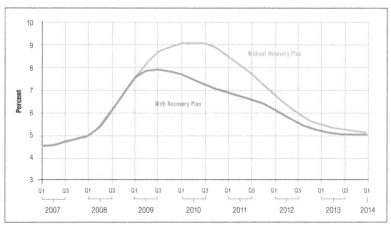

James Pethokoukis has produced a modified chart that shows what in the event happened after the passage of the stimulus.

Unemployment rose higher and faster than the administration's simulation of the performance of the economy without the stimulus. The unemployment rate peaked at over 10 percent and did start to fall until in early 2010, and did not fall as rapidly as projected in the administration's forecast.

Figure 4.5b: Unemployment Rate with and without the Recovery Plan

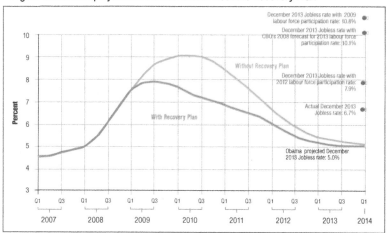

As well as the fiscal stimulus, James Pethokoukis points out that there were other factors in play. The head winds that the US economy faced were greater than the administration forecast; the weakness in economic activity in other advanced economies in Europe was aggravated by the crises in the Euro-zone; international oil and commodity prices rose sharply at the end of the Chinese boom; and recoveries following banking crises tend to be slow. The labour market itself changed, the extension of the duration of unemployment benefits reduced the supply of labour that contributed to a reduction in labour market participation. Demand in the US economy was also stimulated by a succession of unprecedented monetary interventions that expanded the balance sheet of the Federal Reserve from $800 billion to about $2.2 trillion between the end of 2008 and the end of 2009. Andrew Pethokoukis reasonably concluded that it is 'pretty tough to tease out the specific impact given everything else that was happening simultaneously from policy to macro forces that predated the downturn'.

He also makes the broader point that generally monetary policy has greater influence on demand than fiscal policy. Even when monetary policy would normally have been thought to be highly constrained by the zero rate boundary, the Federal Reserve's innovative policies ensured that monetary that point that maintained a powerful stimulus. A monetary stimulus that turned out to be sufficient offset the fiscal tightening that resulted from a higher payroll tax rate, and the rise in income taxes agreed following the end of the time limited tax cuts of the Bush administration in 2013. These measures tightened fiscal policy by around 2 percent growth, but did not prevent the rate of GDP growth from accelerating from 1.95 percent in 2012 to 2.7 percent in 2013. Pethokoukis pointed out that at the start of President Obama's second term in 2013, fiscal austerity in the U.S. was slightly greater than in the Eurozone at that time, yet the US economy 'did far better, solely due to the greater willingness of the Fed to do monetary offset'.

In terms of using active fiscal policy to stabilise the economy over the cycle part of the practical challenge policy makers confront is the wide range of estimates of the multipliers that determine its efficiency. The Congressional Budget Office, for example has estimated the multiplier for government purchases to be somewhere between 0.5 and 2.5 percent. A broad survey of estimates by University of California San Diego economist Valerie Ramey found that the range was usually between 0.8 and 1.5, although the data could support anywhere from 0.5 to 2.0 percent. Some of those multiplier ranges fall below the 1.0 percent. What that means is that the economic activity created by a stimulus is less than the original money spent, potentially as low as 50 cents on the dollar. Moreover, the precise timing and circumstances of the economy, and where it is in relation to the economic cycle, modifies these estimated multipliers.

Fiscal stimulus and a reserve currency

The fiscal measures are negligible in the context of the US government's medium- and long-term fiscal challenges. With the dollar as a reserve currency, the US can afford to trade some future growth for immediate economic activity, because international investors are prepared to lend to its Treasury and still turn to the dollar and US Treasury bonds as a safe haven. The use of fiscal stimulus is about sacrificing a measure of future activity level in order to increase output in the near term. This is easier if interest rates are low and markets are prepared to tolerate temporary deficits. As the ratio of debt to GDP rises and realistic estimates of trend growth are lowered, it becomes more difficult for governments to use fiscal policy.

For the time being, the US appears to have this scope. The OECD *Economic Outlook* in November 2016 took the view that lower short debt service costs gives the US 'fiscal space' to engage in infrastructure investment and active labor market measures. The difficult questions are the quality of the investment projects and the economic returns they may yield. The longer term outlook for debt and the federal deficit is more problematic. Whether a further fiscal stimulus is necessary, a proper examination of the multipliers involved and an analysis of the full costs and benefits of discretionary fiscal policy is beyond the scope of this book. There is nothing inconsistent in recognising the American economy's long-term structural challenge in an over-expanded public sector and the country's desirability to address this, while at the same time recognising the role of fiscal policy as an instrument for demand management over the shorter term in specific circumstances.

The dollar's status as a reserve currency means US policy-makers have greater scope to use discretionary fiscal policies compared with policymakers in other economies, especially smaller, more open economies. Such stimulus polices are also more likely to be effective if they are executed in the context of a smaller, rather than a greater, stock of public debt in relation to national income.

Chapter 5

Size and scope of the US public sector

The US has traditionally had a smaller public sector than other advanced countries in the OECD. Although Roosevelt's New Deal hugely extended the range of federal government activity in the economy in the 1930s, its permanent effect on the economy was more limited. Its most important legacy was unemployment insurance and old-age pensions for American workers. Large-scale federal healthcare programmes were not developed until the 1960s, when President Johnson established Medicare and Medicaid.

Social Security, Medicare and Medicaid have progressively become more expensive as larger numbers of people qualify for them and medical costs in the US increase.

Since 1945, the US has maintained a significantly larger military establishment than other developed countries, including its main allies. While military spending fell after 1990 following the end of the Cold War, it still remained much higher than in other comparable countries. After 2001, defence spending rose as a result of the interventions in Afghanistan and Iraq. This increased the proportion of federal government spending devoted to defence from slightly more than 16 percent to around 20 percent of total federal spending. Since 2010 the share of federal spending on defence has fallen from 20.1 percent to an estimated 15.3 percent in 2016. Over the past 30 years, defence spending has fallen both as a share of national income and as a proportion of the total federal budget.

A large public sector

At a glance, the US federal government spending of 21 percent of GDP looks low compared with that of other developed OECD countries. This is because it does not include the other components of general government expenditure carried out by state and local government in the US.

State and local governments spend around 15 percent of US GDP. States are sovereign authorities – they have their own taxation powers used to levy property, sales, income and capital gains tax, as well as imposing other licences and natural resource royalties. Some spending results from state administration of federal government programmes, such as Medicaid, where the state administers federal government money and often partly match it with their own funds. Many programmes are a combination of payments from the federal government supplemented by additional money collected by state authorities. In 2016, the OECD estimated that general government expenditure in the US was 38.1 percent.

Given that the public sector in US does not offer comprehensive healthcare financed by the taxpayer to individuals of all ages and does not spend as much on social protection and transfer payments for households as public sectors in other developed OECD economies do, a public sector spending ratio of over 35 percent of GDP is high.

The US has a large, expensive and inefficient public sector that is lumpy and porous in its coverage. Some things are done in a generous and expensive manner, and other things are not done at all or are carried out in a much less generous and systematic way.

General government expenditure in the US is 2.6 percentage points lower than the OECD average ratio of 40.7 percent of GDP. Its ratio of national income devoted to public expenditure is close to the OECD average, especially when the limited coverage of public sector healthcare is taken into account. When the use of tax expenditures is accounted for, it is clear that the overall influence of the public sector on the economy is close to the OECD average. The US makes much greater use of tax expenditures than other OECD economies and are roughly comparable to some 6 percent of GDP.

This shows that he US is not a dramatic outlier, but instead has a large public sector in common with the rest of the OECD. The outliers at the low end in the OECD are Australia, with a ratio of general government expenditure to GDP of 36.4 percent, and Switzerland, with a ratio of 34.3 percent in 2016. Moreover the US makes much greater use of expenditure taxes than other OECD economies.

Comparative composition of US public spending by function

While the US is not very different from other developed OECD economies in terms of the total scale, influence and size of its public sector, is does differ in the composition and organisation of its spending.

Public authorities in the US spend more on healthcare than most other OECD economies – in 2006 before the distortion of the Great Recession, public spending on health was 7.7 percent of GDP compared with 6.2 percent for its main OECD comparator countries.

Defence spending is roughly three times greater than that of the OECD average, with 4.3 percent spent on defence in 2006 compared with a 1.4 percent average across OECD countries. Other countries that spent a comparatively large proportion of their GDP on defence are still significantly below the level spent in the US, with the following countries spending strongly in the defence sector:

- Korea (2.8 percent)
- UK (2.5 percent)
- Greece (2.3 percent)
- France (1.8 percent)
- Germany (1.1 percent)
- Japan (0.9 percent).

However, in terms of social protection the US spends *less than half* of what an average OECD economy spends – 7 percent of GDP compared to an OECD average of 15.2 percent. It spends nearly a third more on public order, 2.1 percent of GDP compared to an OECD average of 1.6 percent. Over the past fifteen years, the US has devoted a growing proportion of national income to education and now spends almost 11 percent more through the public sector than the OECD average, devoting 6.2 percent of GDP to education compared to an OECD average of 5.6 percent.

The relative efficiency of the US public sector

Given the overall level of public expenditure in the US and the limited spending on health and social protection, there are serious questions about the efficiency of public services in the country.

The overall picture from international comparisons is that the US has a large public sector that is not much smaller than the OECD average. Given the scale of its spending and taking into account the services it does not provide, it would appear that significant parts of the public sector in the US exhibit efficiency, productivity and cost issues.

The effects of the economic cycle: the Great Recession

Public expenditure was elevated as a share of national income as a result of the effects of the great contraction in output that lowered GDP by over 5 percent between 2008 and 2009. This resulted in higher spending and lower tax revenue through the operation of automatic stabilisers, and from discretionary fiscal stimulus measures that both reduced taxes and increased spending.

The combination of higher spending and lower national income raised the ratio of public expenditure to GDP. The *OECD Economic Outlook* showed that general government expenditure increased from 37.2 percent of GDP in 2007 to 43.2 percent in

2010. The public sector's financial deficit rose from 2.9 percent of GDP in 2007 to 10.6 percent GDP in 2010. Some of these effects were reversed as economic activity recovered and the economy returned to a level of output consistent with its long-term trend of growth, which historically has been around 2.3 percent. In 2016 OECD estimated that ratio of public sector spending within GDP had fallen back towards 38 percent.

But long-term commitments and an ageing population mean public spending will progressively rise as a proportion of GDP unless policy is changed. *Analytical Perspectives Budget of US Government* document published as part of the Treasury's 2017 budget papers projected a real GDP growth rate of 2.3 percent in the long run. This is below the Office of Management and Budget's estimate of the average growth rate in the post-war period of 3.2 percent. *Analytical Perspectives* explains that the projected slower growth results from a decline in the growth rate of the working-age population and a decrease in the labor force participation rate caused by the retirement of the baby boom generation. The first cohort of the baby boom, born in 1946, reached the early-retirement age for Social Security benefits (62 years old) in 2008. Since then, the number of individuals in cohorts entering their retirement years has increased, and retirements are projected to continue increasing for the next eight years. Council of Economic Advisers in the *Economic Report of the President* and the Office of Management and Budget in 2016 estimated that the US trend rate of growth was 2.3 percent. While the Congressional Budget Office estimate that the US trend rate of growth is now 2.1 percent.

This means the US has a structural public expenditure problem.

This problem mainly arises from health spending commitments and a tax regime that cannot finance federal government spending commitments over the economic cycle, creating a structural budget deficit that increases future public spending. The federal government has a long-term structural budget deficit, and there are additional long-term spending pressures on state governments.

America's structural public expenditure problem

The Congressional Budget Office, in the 2011 *Long-Term Budget Outlook* published in June 2011, projected a rise in federal government expenditure (that accounts for about half of US total public spending) would increase the ratio of spending from 25 percent of GDP in 2010 to close to 34 percent by 2035.

State governments and local authorities will also exhibit further structural increases in spending as a result of their healthcare commitments and the specific healthcare and pension commitments made to public sector employees. The General Accountability Office's *State and Local Government's Fiscal Outlook* April 2011 estimated that without a change in policy, these commitments would raise spending by a further 6 percent of GDP over the next 50 years. Around half of this will take place in the next 20 years. Long-term estimates of this sort are very sensitive to assumptions and projections of the trend rate of growth, future interest rates, relative prices, health costs and demography and changes in policy. Since 2011 the Congressional Budget Office has revised these projections and lowered its estimate of federal spending and borrowing over the next twenty–five years, but it still refers to this document as an exemplification of the long-term challenges in federal spending. Over the last five years at both the federal level and in state and local authorities there have been changes in discretionary policies that have responded to these challenges. Hence the fiscal tightening recorded at the start of President Obama's second administration. Yet the broad challenges arising from structural budget deficits, health costs, an aging population, weaker productivity growth, college and university costs, unfunded intergenerational liabilities, a poor alignment between the tax bases and spending in federal, state and local government remain. Moreover the pressure for greater spending to support households with health, retirement incomes and college education remain. Both Mr Trump and Mrs Clinton offered improved federal support for families in the 2016 election campaign. Mr Trump pledged to protect Medicare and to provide something better than the Affordable Health Care Act. Mrs Clinton pledged to make college tuition free for students from families with incomes up to $125,000. There would in normal circumstances (leaving aside arguments about secular stagnation and reviving productivity and the trend rate of growth) be pressure to spend more on maintaining and improving US infrastructure.

The overall direction of travel projected is therefore worth looking at, the ratio of public expenditure to national income in the US was projected to rise by around 12 percentage points on the basis of unchanged policies. These projections of higher future spending were based on estimates that take account of future demography and make a realistic assessment of the evolution of things such as healthcare costs. This suggested that the ratio of total general government expenditure would increase to around 52 percent of GDP.

This implies that more than half of national income would be absorbed by the state. The Congressional Budget Office's projections did not take account of the complex economic implications that arise from such a significant increase in the ratio of federal government spending and the implication of such a higher expenditure ratio for the supply performance of the US economy and its future rate of growth. The Congressional Budget Office separately estimated that the cost of financing that level of expenditure could reduce the level of GDP by between 2 and 10 percentage points by 2035. This suggested that on unchanged policies, taking account of the crowding out and other effects of public expenditure, the US could have a ratio of public expenditure to national income close to 60 percent, roughly 20 percent higher than today. The introduction to this book emphasised how difficult it is to make long-term forecasts and projections. They are very sensitive to assumptions about population growth, productivity growth, the trend rate of GDP, interest rates and prices. The illustrative projections reported here show a direction of travel. They point to a destination where complex and difficult political, social and economic choices will have to be made about taxes, health spending and old age pensions for retired people.

Real resource cost of public expenditure

Much of the debate in the US focuses on the sustainability of public expenditure in terms of public debt and the levels of the federal government's deficit. There is also an extensive debate about the financial viability of specific federal programmes in relation to their legal obligation to pay benefits and the specific tax revenues assigned to finance them. Both debates are understandable.

Pension and healthcare programmes are crucial to many older people. Likewise, the federal government's deficit is on an unsustainable path. It is projected to accumulate on average at a faster rate than the trend growth rate of the economy. The cost of debt service is projected to increase faster than national income. Accumulating a public debt at a faster rate than national income and its tax base aggravates the future cost of public expenditure.

In narrow arithmetic terms, it is unsustainable when projected over the next 25 or 50 years. In many respects, however, the concentration of public debate on the federal deficit and the specific financial rules regulating certain programmes distracts attention from the central matter – the *real resource cost* of public expenditure.

The US has a historically large public sector that is expensive to finance, at the margin yields benefits that are lower than the full economic cost of financing it and is already creating structural problems that hinder the economy. An expensive, poorly focused public sector interacts with poorly functioning private markets for services such as healthcare and higher education. This further raises both overall spending and the structural impediments hindering the working of the economy. The level of public spending and test of whether it is yielding benefits that exceed its full economic costs is the critical issue. How it is financed and the arrangements governing specific programmes are, essentially, secondary questions.

The key challenge facing the US is finding a level of public expenditure that is consistent with optimally functioning markets where future national income and economic welfare are maximised. An overall level of public expenditure that is too high imposes further aggravated costs on the economy because of defective public policy. These additional costs come from the failure to regulate markets properly and the failure to collect sufficient revenue to finance government operations efficiently. Where tax revenue is collected, it is often raised in a manner that worsens the distortion and deadweight costs arising from nearly all taxes.

In short, the US has an expensive, poorly focused public sector financed in an unnecessarily expensive manner through debt and a badly constructed tax system.

Federal government and state and local government spending

Federal public expenditure accounts for over a fifth of the national income.

Spending by state and local authorities accounted for about a further 16 percent or more of national income on the OECD measure, of general government expenditure, giving a ratio of about 38 percent of GDP for total US public spending.

Some state and local expenditure is financed by transfer payments from the federal government. Data from the Board of Economic Advisers and the US Census indicate state and local authorities, including spending at the state level financed by federal transfer payments, accounted for 20 percent of local US GDP in 2008. In 2013 the proportion of states' expenditure financed by federal transfers had risen to 30 percent. It is important not to double count total federal spending and state and local spending when obtaining numbers for total general government expenditure, which is the best measure of spending on the public sector as a whole.

In 2008, before the impact of the Great Recession, total state and local government spending ranged as a ratio of state GDP from 15.46 percent in Delaware to 26.23 percent in Alaska. Some large states spent over 20 percent of their GDP. California and New York spent 21.70 percent and 23.75 percent respectively. Ratios were 22.51 percent in Alabama, 23.18 percent in West Virginia, 24.91 percent in South Carolina and 26.02 percent in Mississippi.

In 2008, before the full impact of the Great Recession federal government spending accounted for 20.2 percent of US GDP. In 2009 at the trough of the recession the ratio rose to 24.4 percent. Following the recovery in output the ratio is estimated to have fallen to 21.4 percent in 2016.

State and local authority expenditure

State governments are sovereign authorities. Under the constitution, all powers that are not explicitly vested in federal authority are left in the hands of the states.

In the 1890s, it was the state legislatures and executives that developed the collective regulations that influenced much of the practical detail of the Progressive political agenda. States like New York and Wisconsin – under the leadership of politicians like Theodore Roosevelt and Robert La Follette, who were both Republican governors – took the initiative in regulating sweated labour, workers compensation for accidents, housing rents and other economic and social conditions.

Individual states – beginning with Alaska in 1913, Colorado in 1927, Kentucky in 1926 and Maryland in 1927 – that developed old age pensions and social insurance years before the establishment of Social Security in 1937. Pensions for mothers were introduced even earlier, starting with Colorado in 1912, so that by 1920 most states had social security benefits arrangements, if not full pensions.

As Price Fishback shows in his paper *Social Welfare Expenditures in the US and Nordic Countries 1900-2003* (NBER Working Paper 15982, 2010) before the 1930s nearly all public welfare policy was the responsibility of local governments, with some activity at the state level. In 2011, around two-fifths of all public expenditure was at the state and local government level. It is not surprising that state spending remains significant even though the balance between federal government and state spending was transformed in the 1930s. States are involved in the delivery of several of the main federal social spending programmes such as Medicaid, where they are using federal funds and often supplementing them with locally collected tax revenue.

As sovereign political bodies, states have full tax-raising powers and they make extensive use of them. State governments also devolve these powers of taxation to local governments. There are state sales, income, capital gains and estate taxes. The main local government source of revenue is from property taxes, but there are also examples of local sales and income taxes levied by municipal authorities. State and local government authorities remain important public sector bodies in terms of both spending and taxation. In 2011, around 45 percent of all tax revenue raised in the US was levied by state and local authorities and half of all public expenditure went through state and local governments after federal government transfer payments are taken into account.

Figure 5.1: Federal Government Expenditure, Annual Amounts by Major Object Category: Fiscal Years 1983–2010

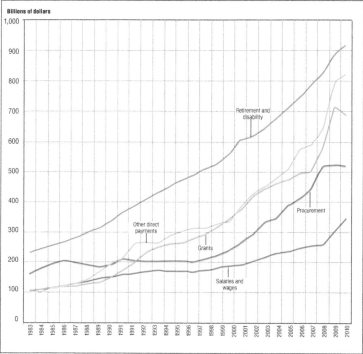

Source: US Census Bureau, Consolidated Federal Funds Report for Fiscal Year 2010

Figure 5.2: Federal Government Expenditure, Amounts and Percentages by Major Object Category: Fiscal Year 2010

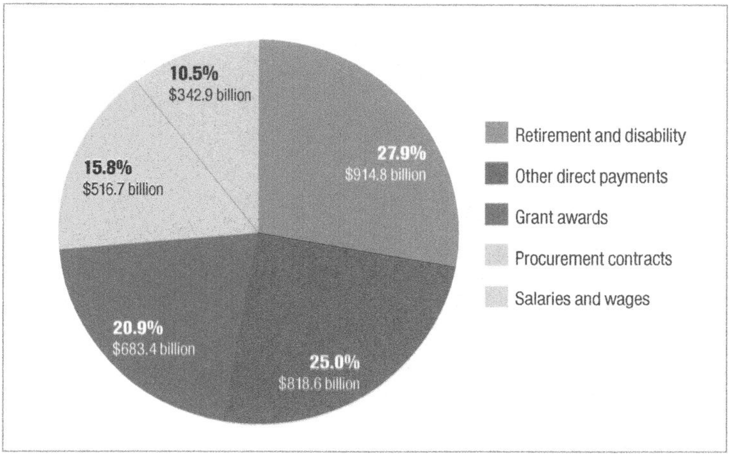

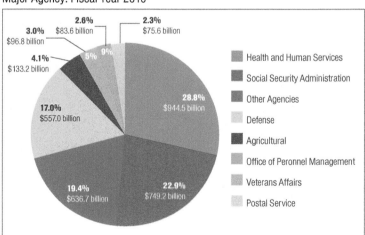

Source: US Census Bureau, Consolidated Federal Funds Report for Fiscal Year 2010

Figure 5.3: Federal Government Expenditure, Amounts and Percentages by Major Agency: Fiscal Year 2010

Source: US Census Bureau, Consolidated Federal Funds Report for Fiscal Year 2010

Figure 5.4: State and Local Government Expenditures: 2009

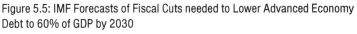

Source: US Census Bureau, 2009 Annual Survey of State and Local Government Finances

Figure 5.5: IMF Forecasts of Fiscal Cuts needed to Lower Advanced Economy Debt to 60% of GDP by 2030

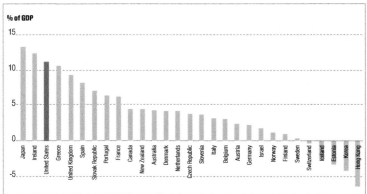

Source: "Shifting Gears: Tackling Challenges on the Road to Fiscal Adjustment," IMF Fiscal Monitor, April, 2011

Fiscal years

The federal government's financial year finishes in September. Forty-six states have budgets that run to June. The exceptions are New York, where the year runs to March, Texas to August, and Michigan and Alabama where it runs to September. Many local government budgets run to June or run on a calendar basis.

The American unsustainable fiscal arithmetic

Not only does the US have a large public sector, but a public sector that faces a series of long-term structural problems that arise from the manner they are financed. The federal government had a budget deficit of almost 10 percent of GDP in 2009 in the depth of the Great Recession. Since then the deficit has fallen from 9.8 percent of GDP to 2.5 per in 2015. The federal government's deficit has fallen sharply as a result in the recovery in output and the economic expansion since 2009, as the chart in the *Budget of the US Government 2017* shows.

Figure 5.6: Fastest Period of Sustained Deficit Reduction Since WWII, 2009–15

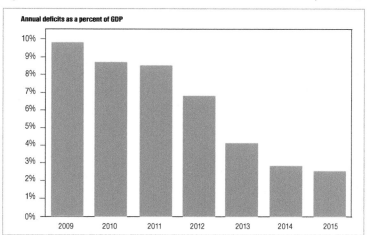

Source: Budget of the US Government 2017

93

Borrowing on the scale that took place during the Great Recession was unprecedented in peacetime and led to rapid the accumulation of a public debt. The fall in output caused by the credit crunch and the Great Recession, however, did not create the structural problem in the US federal government's finances. Rather it aggravated and exposed longstanding mismatches between spending and revenue. A significant proportion of the federal budget deficit melted away as output recovered and the economy expanded, but a significant proportion of the federal budget deficit is *structural* or *permanent*.

Without radical adjustment of either spending or taxation, the structural deficit will continue to increase. This is mainly because spending on healthcare has been steadily rising for over 20 years. The US Social Security system will exhibit challenges after around 2023, according to the latest estimates in the annual report of its Board of Trustees published in 2016. At that point contributions paid in through payroll Social Security tax and invested funds in its trust fund will no longer match its liabilities dollar for dollar. The Medicare and Social Security budgets are constructed in such a manner that by law, benefits have to be paid. The cost of those benefits are rising because the population is ageing, and the estimated tax revenues in place to finance them will not be sufficient to pay the projected costs. The more worrying issue is that of the economic cost in terms of the performance of the US economy that results from a public sector absorbing such a large proportion of national income. A fiscal crisis will arise from the mismatch between spending and tax receipts established by present law.

State and local governments had immediate budget pressures that come out from the economic cycle and were very awkward, but they do not amount to either a fiscal crisis or a full structural budget challenge on the scale that federal government faces. State and local expenditure does, however contribute to the overall structural public expenditure challenge that the US has. It exhibits problems of productivity, efficiency and a high cost base that are common to the federal government and other public sector authorities throughout the advanced OECD economies. Moreover state and local authorities are having more difficulty in balancing their budgets and face expensive inadequately funded employee health and pension liabilities.

The principal structural financial challenge that the states and local governments have is in the medium and long term. This is significantly unfunded pension liabilities for their public sector employees that cannot be managed without either higher employer contributions through higher taxation or a significant reduction in the retirement benefits that employees receive. Unlike most private sector occupational arrangements, in the US, public sector employers, such as states and cities have less flexibility in terms of being able to vary the generosity of pension benefits on grounds of affordability.

Balanced budget rules and the economic cycle

In practice, state and local authorities have a narrower tax base that is more dependent on property tax revenues than the federal government.

In an adverse economic shock, their tax revenue tends to fall more sharply than federal tax revenue. Given that most states have balanced budget rules written into their constitutions, a fall in tax revenue requires them to take decisive and often pro-cyclical measures to increase taxes and cut spending during recessions and in response to adverse economic developments. This means that the states have fewer unfunded, long-term liabilities than the federal government, although they more frequently face acute financial squeezes requiring severe discretionary action. Action at the trough of a recession that is pro rather than counter cyclical. The Center on Budget and Policy Priorities, for example in July 2010 estimated that in 2010 and 2011, state budget shortfalls totalled £375bn and that 30 states had raised taxes and 45 states had cut spending to cope with their budget problems. The General Accountability Office estimated that state governments would have budget deficits of 1 percent of GDP in 2010 and that their deficits would rise on unchanged policy to 2 percent of GDP in 2020, 2.5 percent in 2030 and to 3.35 percent in 2040. The credit crunch and the collapse of the financial market asset price bubble exposed and brought forward the main unfunded liability that state and local authorities have, which is their pensions. These were estimated to be around $1trn by the Pew Centre for the Study of States.

The federal government's structural fiscal problem

The main challenge that state and local government face in the US is controlling their cost base in terms of pay and pension liabilities and raising the efficiency and productivity of services.

The problem is in obtaining better value for money in schools and state systems of higher education. The federal government faces a fiscal crisis of a different magnitude. It has three dimensions.

The first is two expensive programmes – Medicare and Social Security – are demand-led and under their specific funding rules will run out of cash.

The second is unaffordable growth, in the economic sense of high spending imposing a huge opportunity cost on the economy, arising out of future increases in healthcare costs.

And third is a structural federal budget deficit that is unsustainable. It is the federal government's spending and borrowing that will present a serious structural problem, which has the potential to create a fiscal crisis on the basis of unchanged policies.

Chapter 6
The federal government's budget

America has a structural public expenditure problem. At is heart is the cost of nondiscretionary spending programmes that are principally demand led programmes providing health services and old age pensions. These mandatory spending programmes account for 68 percent of federal government spending. The most challenging will be the long-term course of spending on Medicare, along with spending on Medicaid and Social Security. They threaten the future financial solvency of the federal government. A number of factors combine to create an awkward cocktail in terms of future public spending. These include the sheer expense of medical care in the U.S. and the ageing of the population, which means both that medical services will be in more demand and that there will be fewer workers supporting many more retired beneficiaries. GDP would have to have exhibit much faster rates of growth than any realistic assessment of the trend rate of GDP growth to finance these programmes with in their current legal framework of benefits and at present tax and contribution rates. These problems are further aggravated by a long-term structural federal budget deficit that will result in debt service charges being accumulated at a faster rate than the economy will be able to finance without an increase in taxes or a reduction in spending. Normally the financing of public expenditure between taxation and borrowing is a second order matter. But when structural or permanent deficits incur higher debt services charges at a faster rate than the capacity of the tax system to finance them it becomes source of the public expenditure challenge in its own right. These federal programmes present a financial challenge. They also present an economic challenge. While in principle it would be possible to raise taxes to finance them, a rising ratio of public expenditure and a heavier tax burden would have malign implications for the supply performance of the US economy. Moreover, the federal government provides an expensive poorly focused social safety net that combines clumsy and expensive generosity with significant lacuna that public sectors in other advanced economies employing similar proportions of national income, provide.

The *Budget of the US government, Year fiscal 2017* reported that in 2016 the Office for Management and Budget estimated the federal government would spend $3,951.bn in outlays. This accounted for 21.4 percent of GDP. The spending was financed by total tax and other receipts estimated to be $3,335.bn, or 18.1 percent of GDP. The federal budget deficit was $546 bn, absorbing 3.3 percent of GDP.

In a recession spending is normally higher and tax revenues are usually lower as a proportion of national income and the budget deficit increases. The effects of the Great Recession have now largely melted away. Spending that rose from 19.1 percent of GDP in 2007 to 24.4 percent in 2009 has fallen back as a share of national income. Tax receipts that fell from 17.9 percent of GDP to 14.6 percent in 2010 have risen to 18.3 percent in 2015. And the deficit that peaked close to 10 percent fell back to 2.5 percent of GDP in 2015. Future projections of federal government expenditure and revenue, however, made by the Obama Administration, the Congressional Budget Office and the General Accounting Office were consistent in estimating that unchanged US federal government policy was financially unsustainable. It is clearly common ground that there is a structural problem in the US public finances.

Economists at the Federal Reserve Bank of St Louis in *The Federal Debt: Too Little Revenue or Too Much Spending?* published in July 2011 showed that between 1975 and 2007, federal government spending averaged 20.8 percent of GDP. Revenues from taxes and other sources have averaged 18.2 percent of GDP. On average, federal government spending increased by 2.5 percent of GDP between 1975 and 2007 compared with the period between 1960 and 1974, from 18.2 percent of GDP to 20.8 percent. In contrast, revenue only increased by 0.6 percent of GDP.

This has created a structural budget deficit. Spending mainly on increased transfer payments to individuals has been increased without corresponding reductions in other budgets or increases in tax revenue. As a consequence of this structural budget deficit, the gross public debt of the federal government has roughly doubled, from 32 percent of GDP in 1981 to 64 percent in 2007. Since then the impact of the Great Recession and the fiscal stimulus measures taken by the George W Bush and Obama administrations, gross debt has risen to 93 percent of GDP by 2010. Federal debt held by the public – a more accurate measure of the financial burden to the federal government – increased from 26 percent of GDP in 1981 to 35.2 percent in 2007, and by 2015 stood at 74.4. percent of GDP.

Federal spending: discretionary and mandatory outlays

The federal budget is divided into two distinct categories of expenditure: discretionary and mandatory.

The Budget of the US Government showed that under the Budget Enforcement legislation, mandatory expenditure in 2015 was scored at $2,524bn, 68 percent of the total federal budget and 14 percent of GDP. $ 1,165 bn, or 32 percent of the budget was scored as discretionary spending accounting for 6.5 percent of GDP.

Discretionary expenditure stood at $1,415bn, accounting for 37.1 percent of total spending and 9.4 percent of GDP.

Figure 6.1: Actual and Projected Primary Federal Spending as a % of GDP
1970–2035

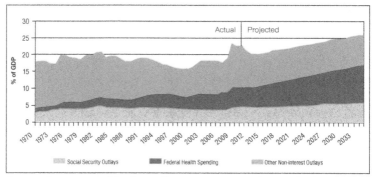

Source: Congressional Budget Office, Long-Term Budget Outlook, June 2010

Figure 6.2: Historical and Projected Federal Debt as a Share of GDP

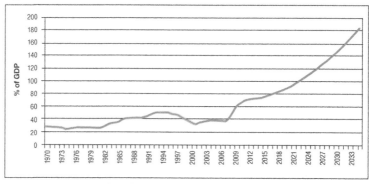

Source: Congressional Budget Office, Long-Term Budget Outlook, June 2010

Figure 6.3: Primary Fiscal Gap (in percent of GDP)

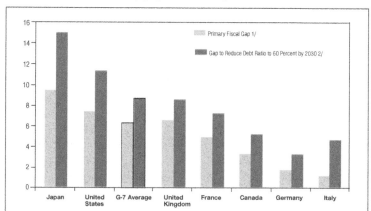

Sources: IMF Fiscal Monitor May 2010, IMF World Economic Outlook July 2010 and IMF staff calculations and estimates

Figure 6.4: Federal outlays, Fiscal Year 2010

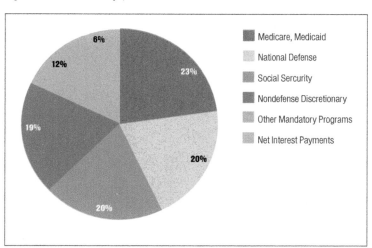

Source: Congressional Budget Office

Congress and the President have discretion over what is spent in areas of federal activity such as defence, homeland security, agriculture and the environment.

Every year, money is appropriated and spending on these areas is discretionary in the sense that it can be changed from one year to the next, whereas spending on Medicare, Medicaid and Social Security is mandatory. On these programmes, the payments are based on entitlements that do not change from year to year, such as the entitlement of a pension from Social Security or healthcare provided from the Medicare insurance programme. Spending is based on the number of people who are eligible and is demand-led. These entitlement programmes are funded by permanent appropriations that do not change from year to year and are considered mandatory under the Budget Enforcement Act 1997 as amended by additional legislation. People who meet the relevant eligibility requirements are legally entitled to them. There are some additional entitlement programmes, such as the Food Stamps programme, that are appropriated annually rather than permanently.

Figure 6.5: "Mandatory" programmes continue to gobble up a larger share of Government spending

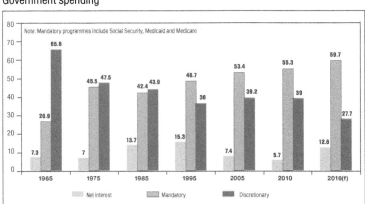

Source: US Office of Management and Budget

Money to pay interest on federal debt has been automatically appropriated since 1847. Over the last 50 years, mandatory spending has grown significantly. In 1962, 67.5 percent of federal spending was scored as discretionary and 32.5 percent was mandatory. Half a century later, the position is roughly reversed. Between 1966 and 2006, mandatory spending on Medicare and Social Security alone increased from 16 percent of the total federal budget to 40 percent.

Figure 6.6: Total Expenditures, FY1974 to FY2014

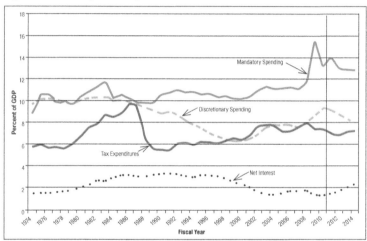

Sources: OMB, JCT and CBO

Not only has spending on mandatory federal programmes grown significantly and increased as a proportion of the total federal budget, but mandatory spending is expected to increase further.

The Congressional Budget Office's projected growth in mandatory spending on Medicare, Medicaid, Children's Health Insurance Programme and insurance subsidies provided through the Affordable Care Act 2010 would raise total federal health spending as a proportion of GDP from 5.6 percent in 2010 to between 9 and 10 percent in 2035. Spending on Social Security will rise by a further one percentage point of GDP. This means that nearly all available federal revenue receipts over the next 25 years will be absorbed by mandatory spending programmes, given that federal tax and other receipts usually average slightly more than 18 percent of GDP. Spending on such a scale would present a difficult challenge. Social Security and Medicare are driven by a shared dimension of fiscal arithmetic – in an aging society, the number of workers falls in relation to the number of people receiving the benefits. number of people receiving the benefits.

Figure 6.7: Composition of Total Expenditures, Selected Years

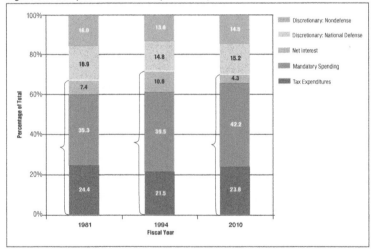

Sources: OMB, JCT and CBO

In 1960, the ratio of workers to retired people was 5:1. By 2016, this ratio had fallen to 2.8:1 and is projected by the Social Security Administration to fall to 2.1:1 by 2040. This means revenue from receipts falls and spending rises. In addition, the costs per person of Medicare will rise. Since the Great Recession the rate of growth in health care costs has moderated. Healthcare costs, however. apart from a brief pause in the 1990s, have been on a steadily rising trend for over 30 years. In 2009 the Medicare and Social Security Trustees reported: 'The financial condition of the Social Security and Medicare programmes remains challenging. Projected long-run programme costs are not sustainable under current programme parameters.'

Medicaid and Medicare

Medicaid is a means-tested programme jointly funded by federal and state governments directed at low-income groups. It was introduced in 1966 and is administered by the states, with the federal government matching state payments on a sliding scale. Federal funding is adjusted to take account of per capita income in states, with lower-income states receiving higher levels of matched funding. On average, the federal government pays about 57 percent of Medicaid costs. It is a healthcare programme directed at low income individuals, children and elderly people and provides access to healthcare and long-term care for older people, not an insurance programme. It is a means tested programme. Low income is not the only requirement for receiving benefits from the program. Eligibility is categorical and only available to people who fall into a category defined by statute; some of these categories include children below a certain age, pregnant women, parents of Medicaid-eligible children who meet certain income requirements, and low-income seniors. The details of how each category is defined vary from state to state. Access to care is provided in different ways in different states. In some states it is directly purchased by the state, while in others the state assists an individual to obtain medical insurance. The fastest growing area of spending in the Medicaid programme is nursing home care for people of retirement age.

The Patient Protection and Affordable Care Act (ACA) 2010 significantly expanded both eligibility for and federal funding of Medicaid. Under the law, all U.S. citizens and legal residents with income up to 133 percent of the poverty line, including adults without dependent children, would qualify for coverage in any state that participated in the Medicaid program. However, the

US Supreme Court decided in *National Federation of Business v. Sebelius* in 2012 that states do not have to expand Medicaid in order to continue to receive previously established levels of Medicaid funding. Many states have decided to continue with pre-ACA funding levels and eligibility standards.

Medicare is a social insurance programme fully funded by the federal government through a payroll social security tax, and offers health insurance to people over 65 and under 65 with certain disabilities and assists all people with renal disease. It also has a means-tested element.

Medicaid provides a wider range of healthcare services than Medicare. Among the categories of people eligible for assistance under Medicaid are low-income people, children, pregnant women, parents of eligible children and people with disabilities. Some people are eligible for services under both Medicare and Medicaid and are known as 'Medicare dual'. One-third of all American children and about 60 percent of low-income children are assisted by Medicaid. Almost 60 percent of all nursing home residents are covered by Medicaid and 37 percent of childbirths in the US receive assistance from Medicaid. An interesting feature of the Medicaid rules on assets is that the value of a person's home is excluded in calculating eligibility for nursing home care. Attorneys doing 'Medicaid planning' advise retired people to pursue homeownership in order to protect their assets.

Medicare provided healthcare insurance for 55.3 million people in 2015. Some 46.3 million of these were people aged over 65, and 9 million were disabled. It provides healthcare in four separate parts – A, B, C and D – each with specific funding. *The Annual Report of the Medical Insurance Trust Fund* published in May 2016 showed that $647bn was spent between these four parts in 2015.

Part A is hospital insurance (HI). This covers inpatient hospital services, skilled nursing care and home and hospice care. It is principally funded by a hypothecated payroll tax of 2.9 percent of earnings, divided equally between employers and employees.

Part B, supplementary medical insurance (SMI), covers GP services, outpatient services and home care and preventive services. The SMI trust fund is funded through beneficiary premiums set at 25 percent of the estimated programme cost and general revenues that fund the remaining 75 percent.

Part C, Medicare Advantage (MA), is a private option for beneficiaries that covers all HI and SMI services, apart from hospice care. Individuals who enrol in MA must also enrol in SMI. Part C is funded through the HI and SMI trust funds. Around 25 percent of Medicare beneficiaries enrol in these MA private healthcare plans that contract to provide HI and SMI health services.

Part D covers prescription drug benefits. Funding is included in the SMI trust fund and is financed through beneficiary premiums of around 25 percent and general revenues that cover 75 percent of its costs.

Medicare is an expensive public healthcare insurance programme, and its cost is projected to rise. The number of people enrolled in Medicare is expected to increase and the cost per person is expected to go up as well. Medicare exhibits the demographic dimension of a significantly ageing cohort similar to that of the Social Security programme. In addition, Medicare has experienced rapidly rising costs because of increasing healthcare prices.

Spending on Medicare and Medicaid is projected by the Congressional Budget Office to rise, and growth of these programmes will be the most important influence on future trends in federal spending. The Congressional Budget Office projects outlays will rise from 4 percent of GDP in 2007 to 12 percent in 2050, and 19 percent in 2082. Before the Great Recession the General Accounting Office's *Fiscal Brief* estimated that in 2007, the value of unfunded obligations under all parts of Medicare was approximately $34.1trn – that is the amount that would have to be set aside in 2007 to cover the principal and interest payments needed to cover the shortfall over the following 75 years. This is over six times the size of the unfunded liabilities of the Social Security programme, estimated to be $5.3trn.

Social Security

The Old-Age, Survivors and Disability Insurance (OASDI) is the official name of what is generally referred to as Social Security. It is essentially a social insurance programme with three components, funded through a hypothecated payroll tax.

Social Security's board of trustees, in their 2015 annual report, showed that in 2014, some 166 million people paid into the programme through payroll social security taxes, the fund had a total income of $884bn. This consisted of $786 billion in non-interest income and $98bn in interest earnings. 60 million people were paid $712.5bn in benefits. Total expenditures in 2014 were $859bn. Total asset reserves held in special issue U.S. Treasury securities grew from $2,764bn at the beginning of the year to $2,789 bn at the end of the year.

The Social Security fund's costs exceeded its tax income in 2014, and also exceeded its non-interest income, as it has since 2010. This relationship is projected by the Trustees to continue throughout the short-range period between 2015 and 2024. The 2014 deficit of tax income relative to cost was $74 billion and the deficit of non-interest income relative to cost was $73 billion. In recent years, the fund's tax income and non-interest income have differed as a result of a temporary reduction in the Social Security payroll tax for 2011 and 2012, made in response to the Great Recession, offset by reimbursements from the General Fund of the Treasury to the Social Security trust funds

Most of the beneficiaries were the 38 million retired workers who receive a pension from Social Security. In 2014 there were 2.8 workers per beneficiary. The Trustees' report shows how this ratio which had been extremely stable, remaining between 3.2 and 3.4 from 1974 through 2008, has declined since then due to the economic recession and the beginning of the demographic change of an aging population that will drive this ratio down over the next 20 years. The Trustees project that the ratio of workers to beneficiaries will continue to decline, even as the economy recovers, due to this demographic shift—as workers of lower-birth-rate generations replace workers of the baby-boom generation. The ratio of workers to beneficiaries reaches 2.1 by 2035 when the baby-boom generation will have largely retired, with a further gradual decline thereafter due to increasing longevity

The normal retirement age for pension benefit is 65, and for people born after 1938 the retirement age progressively rises until for people born in 1960 it is 67 years of age. In 2015 the average pension paid was per month was $1,287. The maximum monthly payment for a person retiring in 2015 aged 66 with a full 35 year record of contributions at the maximum rate was $2,663. A person who delays retirement until the age of 70, is entitled to delayed retirement credits that increase the pension by up to $3,515 a month or $42,182 a year. Less than two percent of Social Security beneficiaries delay receiving the benefits until they are 70 years old. Each year, benefits are up-rated by a cost of living adjustment to protect benefits from inflation. Offering maximum benefits of over $31,956 a year (at standard retirement age) and fully protected against inflation, Social Security offers one of the world's most generous basic social insurance pension schemes.

In its initial years, Social Security paid limited benefits to a few households that were eligible for benefits. In the 1950s and 1960s, the system enjoyed short-term surpluses that enabled Congress to pass legislation extending the benefits of Social Security and making the benefits themselves more generous. During this phase of policy evolution, Social Security legislation was normally passed in even-numbered years – the years when elections took place. This process of expanding benefits and increasing their generosity reached its height in 1972, when legislation was passed that increased benefits by 20 percent. This included the introduction of a cost of living adjustment (COLA), the raising of medium monthly benefits for low-income employees and the establishment of a supplemental security income

(SSI). Strictly, SSI is not a Social Security benefit – it is a welfare programme that gives benefits to elderly, disabled and poor people regardless of work history and record of contributions. It is not an entitlement and is scored separately as part of discretionary spending.

There was a technical mistake in the formula for the calculation of COLA, which resulted in double indexing that over-compensated for inflation. The result was that COLA actually increased benefits at twice the rate of inflation. This error was aggravated by the coincidence that the new regime of indexation took effect in 1975, when prices started to rise sharply and the economy suffered double-digit inflation. The result was that the Social Security fund moved from being in a position of comfortable surplus to one where its immediate solvency was in question. A combination of increased benefits, additional beneficiaries, high inflation, double indexation and lower than expected wages growth made the fund financially unsustainable. In 1977, legislation was passed to correct the error in the indexation formula and to change the tax formulas to raise more revenue.

Despite these changes, the Social Security fund remained financially unstable because forecasts for revenue were too optimistic. The combination of lower real wage growth and higher unemployment meant that in the early 1980s the Social Security fund had falling reserves and there was concern that it would not be able to pay out planned benefits after 1983. This resulted in the establishment of the National Commission on Social Security Reform being appointed by President Reagan, chaired by Alan Greenspan. Under Greenspan, the Commission recommended further tightening of the scheme's indexation formula, the application of income tax to Social Security benefits paid to higher income households – principally to generate short-term revenue – higher payroll tax rates, bringing additional employees into the scope of the tax, that the age to receive full benefits should be gradually increased on an incremental basis and up to half of all the value of benefits should be made potentially taxable income. The Commission's recommendations were broadly accepted.

These changes generated a large surplus in the Social Security trust fund. Their purpose was to ensure that there would be sufficient money invested 'to pay for the future retirement benefits of the baby boomers'. The surpluses were invested in special non-marketable US Treasury securities. Under the unified budget accounting rules adopted by the Johnson administration, this surplus on Social Security has been set against the on-budget federal deficit and has made it appear smaller as a proportion of GDP. There is contentious debate about the extent to which the Social Security trust fund has been saved or used as an excuse to finance other government spending or tax cuts.

The number of beneficiaries is expected to rise from 44 million in 2010 to 73 million in 2030. Spending on Social Security is projected to rise from 4.8 percent of GDP in 2010 to 5.9 percent in 2030. The Congressional Budget Office projects that payroll taxes would have to increase by 1.8 percent of GDP to balance Social Security spending and revenue over the next 75 years. Either the Social Security payroll tax would have to rise from 12.4 percent to 14.4 percent of wages, or benefits would need to be cut by 13.3 percent. Projections about the solvency of the Social Security fund are highly sensitive to assumptions about demographic change and economic growth, but a significant long-term problem is clear. In addition, the longer action is delayed, the greater that necessary action will be in terms of higher tax revenue or cuts in spending.

The problems of funding Social Security have been understood for many years. In the early 1980s, the Greenspan Commission's recommendations were adopted by Congress and the payroll tax was increased, with the result that by 2008 Social Security had received $180bn more in payroll taxes than it had paid out in benefits. This annual surplus has been accumulated in the Social Security trust fund and invested in special non-marketable Treasury securities. The surplus reduces the amount of debt that the US Treasury has to issue. At some point, Social Security payments would have exceeded both payroll taxes and the funds accumulated assets. At some point a gradual reduction in the fund's balance and will exhaust its non-marketable Treasury securities and there will be insufficient cash to pay full social security benefits.

Under current US law, the benefits will then be cut by 24 percent, given that only payroll social security taxes are permitted by federal law to be used to pay for social security benefits. Before the level of GDP was reduced by the Great Recession in 2007, Social Security spending equated to about 4.2 percent of GDP. From then the ratio of GDP spent on Social Security was projected to rise to 6 percent of GDP by 2050. The Social Security Trustees project in 2015 project that Social Security's cost as a percent of GDP will grow from 4.4 percent in 2008 to about 6.0 percent by 2035, then decline to 5.9 percent by 2050, and gradually increase to 6.2 percent by 2089. As the economy recovers, Social Security's non-interest income, which reflects scheduled payroll tax rates, increases from its current level of about 4.5 percent of GDP to about 4.8 percent of GDP for 2025. Thereafter, non-interest income as a percent of GDP declines gradually, to about 4.6 percent by 2089, because the Trustees expect the share of employee compensation provided as non-covered fringe benefits to increase gradually. Looking over a 75 year horizon the unfunded obligation, or shortfall, is equivalent to 3.9 percent of future taxable payroll or 1.3 percent of future GDP. In principle, the financial problems of the Social Security fund are tractable through changes in the retirement age, benefits and the employee and employer contribution rate. The question that US policymakers must address is how generous the basic social insurance pension should be. There would appear to be scope to reduce the maximum benefit available under the scheme.

Defence spending

There has been a fall in defence spending since the end of the World War II. After rising by 9 percentage points of GDP to reach 15 percent during the Korean War, spending on defence fell to around 3 percent of GDP in 2000. This fall in spending was interrupted by the Vietnam War in the mid-1960s and President Reagan's early 1980s military build-up, or what the *New Republic* called President Reagan's 'war Keynesianism'. As a result of the interventions in Afghanistan and Iraq, defence spending ran at around 4 percent of GDP after 2001. In 2010 it accounted for 4.7 percent of GDP. That higher ratio reflected the fall in output since 2008 and higher spending arising from operations in Afghanistan. By 2016 defence spending had fallen to 3 pct and in the medium-term, there should be scope to reduce defence spending to slightly under 3 percent of GDP, not least because of the inefficiency of the US defence procurement programme. The Trump administration may decide, given the uncertain and evolving geo-political position in relation to China and the Middle East, to make discretionary increases in defence spending in a manner that is analogous to the Reagan administration's defence policies that were directed at the USSR in the 1980s

Federal tax expenditures

There is a further category of federal expenditure that comes from the use of the tax system to achieve public policy objectives that would normally be obtained through direct government expenditure and would usually be achieved with more efficiently and less economic distortion through conventional direct public expenditure.

Tax expenditures are created through special deductions, exclusions, exemptions and credits within the tax regime. They are similar to direct spending and are used in place of mandatory and discretionary spending to achieve economic, social and political objectives. In many respects, they operate like mandatory entitlement spending commitments, given that anyone who qualifies for them is given them and the net cost to the federal budget depends on the rules of the programme involved, economic conditions and the behavioural response of economic agents. In addition, they remain entrenched within the tax code until Congress legislates changing them. Tax expenditures make the operation and cost of public policy more opaque. This and the defects of using tax expenditures have been recognised by policymakers for over 50 years. Walter J Blum wrote in *The Effects of Special Provisions in the Income Tax on Taxpayer in the Joint Economic Committee of Congress report Federal Tax policy for Economic Growth and Stability* that they are 'hidden in technicalities of the tax law; they do not show up in the budget; their cost frequently is difficult to calculate and their accomplishments are even more difficult to assess'.

The Joint Committee on Taxation of Congress recognised that tax expenditures should be reconsidered, and issued *A Reconsideration of Tax Expenditure Analysis* in May 2008 (JCX-37-08). It acknowledged the defects of the use of tax expenditures and offered an analytical framework to examine them. The starting point is a taxonomy that separated tax expenditures into two broad categories: tax subsidies and tax-induced structural distortions.

A tax subsidy is a provision that is deliberately inconsistent with the identifiable general rule of the law it modifies. Tax subsidies can be divided into tax transfers and social spending. A tax transfer gives cash to taxpayers regardless of their tax liability and includes the refundable parts of various tax credits, such as the Earned Income Tax credit. Social spending arises where a tax relief is created to influence changes in behaviour unconnected to the generation of income, such as deductions for charitable donations and for saving through individual retirement accounts and the non-refundable parts of tax credits.

The Joint Committee on Taxation identifies a further category of tax subsidy – synthetic business spending, which includes subsidies to influence behaviours directly related to the production of business income, such as energy tax subsidies. It concluded that tax-induced structural distortions materially affect economic decisions and impose substantial costs in economic efficiency. The differential taxation of debt and equity financing – where interest payments are subsidised, for example – distorts American corporate balance sheets by encouraging firms to raise capital in the form of debt instead of equity.

Christopher Howard, a political scientist at William and Mary College, coined the expression 'hidden welfare state' in his book *The Hidden Welfare State: Tax Expenditures and Social Policy in the US* published in 1997. Howard shows how tax expenditures have been used to encourage retirement saving, home purchases through mortgages and higher education. In 2010, tax expenditures scored in *Budget of the US Government* amounted to around $1trn and accounted for about a quarter of total federal spending. In *How Large are Tax Expenditures*, published in 2011, Donald B Marron estimated that in Fiscal year 2011 they may amount to almost $1.3bn – roughly equivalent to total revenue projected for individual and corporate income tax receipts.

When added to mandatory spending and debt interest payments, tax expenditures mean that overall more than two-thirds of federal spending is on 'automatic pilot' as part of permanent, demand-led spending rather than discretionary parts of the budget. Many of the tax expenditures – such as tax credits for education – would be better as direct government expenditure. This theme – extensive use of tax subsidies to accomplish objectives that would be better done through public expenditure – has broken the connection between taxation and revenue.

The US makes greater use of tax expenditures than other developed economies, a point made by the OECD in its *OECD Economic Surveys: US, September 2010* where it says 'tax exemptions [in the US] are more generous than in many other OECD countries'. The OECD uses the US Treasury's estimate and does not take account of state government tax expenditures. Overall, the combination of a ratio of general government expenditure that was about 2.2 percentage points lower than the OECD average in 2010 and above average use of tax expenditures means the impact of the public sector in the US is roughly comparable to that of an average OECD economy.

The Centre on Budget and Policy Priorities summarised US federal tax expenditures in a Policy Brief in 2016 as 'In fiscal year 2015, tax expenditures reduced federal income tax revenue by over $1.2 trillion, and they reduced payroll taxes and other revenues by an additional $128 billion. For comparison, just the federal income tax expenditures together cost more than Social Security, or the combined cost of Medicare and Medicaid, or defence or non-defence discretionary spending'. The General Accountability Office argues that tax expenditures require more scrutiny and points out that they now approach the size of the federal government's discretionary spending.

Figure 6.8: Tax expenditures are comparable in size to discretionary spending levels

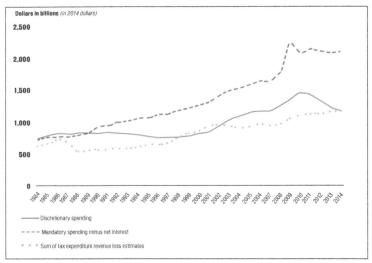

Source: GAO analysis of Treasury estimates and OMB historical data

Figure 6.9: Largest income tax expenditures in fiscal year 2014

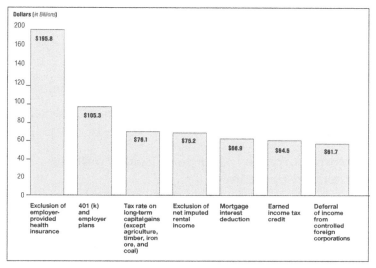

Source: GAO analysis of Treasury estimates

Federal budget deficit

The federal deficit is the difference between cash outlays and cash receipts.

Since 1970, the US federal government has had a budget deficit in every year except for the four-year period between 1998 and 2001. The brief interlude of modest surpluses was the result of tight control over discretionary spending during a period when the economy experienced a period of unsustainable economic growth fuelled by loose monetary conditions and an asset price bubble associated with the dotcom bubble that burst in 2000. From 2001 to 2009, spending increased by 6.5 percent of GDP from 18.2 percent to 24 7 percent. The principal drivers of the higher expenditure were:

- the costs of Medicare and Medicaid rose by 1.7 percent of GDP

- defence spending rose by 1.6 percent of GDP
- spending on unemployment insurance and food stamps rose
- 1.6 percent
- Social Security costs rose 0.6 percent
- all other categories of spending rose by 1.2 percent.

In short, there was a general increase across the board in federal government expenditure.

Clinton's surpluses, George W Bush's deficits aggravated by Obama

Between 2001 and 2009, federal tax revenue fell as a proportion of GDP from 19.5 percent to 14.8 percent. As a share of GDP, individual income taxes fell by 3.3 percent, payroll taxes fell 0.5 percent and corporate income taxes fell 0.5 percent. Part of the change reflects the impact of the economic cycle – the comparison between 2001 and 2009 is one between the peak revenues of one asset price bubble and the depressed revenue and increased spending during the trough of a recession. Yet even taking this into account, the picture is one where taxes have been cut while all areas of spending are rising and there is an entrenched structural budget deficit.

In 2001, the US Treasury was projecting budget surpluses for 'as far as the eye could see'. At the same time the Congressional Budget Office was forecasting average annual surpluses of around $800bn from 2009 to 2012 – the deficit forecast 10 years later for those years was $1.2trn. David Leonhardt's article 'America's sea of red ink was years in the making' in *The New York Times* (10 July 2009) described this as a swing from surplus to deficit of $2trn and attempted to identify the main drivers behind it. Its conclusion was:

- 37 percent of the change was due to the recession and economic cycle
- 33 percent was due to polices enacted by President George W Bush

- 20 percent was due to policies enacted by President George W. Bush that were supported or extended by President Obama
- 10 percent was due to new policies created by President Obama.

At least two-fifths of that deficit will be a permanent or structural feature of federal public finances. The federal budget is unsustainable in terms of its present level of healthcare and Social Security spending commitments and the taxes being collected to fund those commitments. As a result, federal government debt is being accumulated at a faster rate than tax revenue or GDP growth.

In 2008, the General Accountability Office estimated that double-digit GDP growth would be necessary for 75 years to match the projected increases in deficits and debt. Spending growth on mandatory healthcare and Social Security programmes will significantly exceed any projected growth in either the tax base or GDP. Future economic growth does not offer a reasonable resolution to the federal government's borrowing problem. No credible forecast suggests that future rates of growth of the US economy will be sufficient to eliminate the federal government's unsustainable structural or permanent borrowing requirement, without significant discretionary changes to present tax and spending policies.

The *Historic Budget Tables* report from the Office for Management and Budget shows that budget deficits of close to 10 percent of GDP during the Great Recession were higher than in any year since the end of the World War II. Periodic large budget deficits during slumps in economic activity or modest deficits that are lower than the economy's trend rate of economic growth are not a problem, but persistent deficits that accumulate debt at a faster rate than the economy can expand in the long-term represent a structural economic problem.

In fiscal year 2010, net interest payments on US debt were $197bn, equivalent to about 1.4 percent of GDP. Very low rates of interest held net interest payments below their historical average despite increases in borrowing to finance the deficit. The cost of net interest payments, however, could rise sharply once the economy recovers and interest rates rise. Net interest spending was projected by the Congressional Budget Office to rise to 4.4 percent of GDP in fiscal year 2021 and 8.9 percent in 2035.

The Congressional Budget Office projected that on unchanged policies, federal government spending will significantly exceed tax revenue and other receipts. Its 2011 Long-Term Budget Outlook published in June 2011 projects spending in 2035 of 33.9 percent of GDP and tax revenues of 18.4 percent of GDP with a primary (spending less debt interest) budget deficit of 6.6 percent of GDP and an overall deficit including interest rate spending of 15.5 percent of GDP. Debt held by the public has risen from 53 percent of GDP in 2009 to 69 percent in 2011, and is projected by the Congressional Budget Office to rise from 69 percent of GDP to 187 percent in 2035.

There was broad agreement between the Obama administration, the Congressional Budget Office and the General Accountability Office that the present structure of the federal budget is unsustainable. To return the US federal budget to a position where debt is stabilised at roughly the level it was in relation to national income before the Great Recession would require discretionary reductions in spending and increase in taxation equivalent to around 12 percent of GDP.

On-budget and off-budget federal deficit

Social security payroll taxes and benefit payments, along with net the balance of the US Post Office, are scored as off-budget. The costs of administering Social Security are scored as on-budget. The total federal deficit is the sum of the on-budget deficit and the off-budget surplus. Because the Social Security fund is in surplus, the total federal budget deficit is smaller than the on-budget deficit. That surplus is held by the Social Security trust fund in non-marketable US Treasury securities – these and other trust funds form part of the intergovernmental debt.

The total federal debt is divided into intergovernmental debt and debt held by the public. In fiscal year 2015, the on-budget federal deficit was $623.8bn. The off-budget surplus was $8bn. The resulting total federal government deficit was $615.8bn.

Public credit, the federal debt ceiling and the US credit rating

One of the first actions of Congress after the ratification of the Constitution in 1789 was to commission a report from Alexander Hamilton, the first Treasury Secretary, on public credit.

The original 13 colonies had taken on significant debts to finance the Revolutionary War and had found it difficult to manage them. Some colonies such as Virginia had paid them off, while others such as Massachusetts had incurred further debts, worsening the problem. Sorting out the legacy debt from the Revolutionary War was the first public finance challenge of the newly established federal political institutions. Hamilton in his *First Report on Public Credit* suggested that nations which faithfully pay their debts prosper in the same way that people who honourably pay their bills prosper. Hamilton argued the federal government should assume responsibility for these debts and should honour them. After a difficult and controversial debate, Hamilton's plan was accepted and the credit of the US was swiftly established. A succession of budget surpluses in the early decades of the new republic almost completely eliminated the debt by the 1830s.

The modern debt ceiling

The federal government periodically borrowed, usually for specific purposes, and required authorisation from Congress in order to do so. Each issue of debt was separately authorised, as were the types of financial instrument employed. In periods of war, such as during the Civil War in the 1860s, Congress provided the Treasury with greater discretion within a broad limit to choose the preferred debt instrument. The modern origins of an aggregate ceiling on debt can be traced back to World War I in 1917, when the Liberty Bond Act dropped certain limits on the maturity and redemption of bonds – although separate limits for previous debt issues remained in place. In the 1930s, Congress moved towards aggregate constraints on federal borrowing that gave the Treasury greater flexibility in debt management. In 1939, the first aggregate debt limit of $45bn was established, eliminating all other separate limits .

A powerful political tool for Congress

Over the last 30 years, arguments about increasing the debt ceiling have become an important feature of the institutional struggle between Congress and the executive branch of government when one or both houses of Congress is controlled by a party with a different affiliation to the President in the White House. President Reagan had difficulties with a Democrat-controlled House of Representatives and President Clinton had difficulty with a Republican-controlled Congress, that famously led the federal government to be shut down in 1995. That episode demonstrated how Congress could use the debt ceiling as a weapon against the executive branch, but it also showed that it was a double-edged weapon that could turn out to injure the political capital people wielding it. When the public cannot use day-to-day federal facilities such as a national park or a national museum, because of deadlock between two branches of the federal government, it has the potential to damage Congress as much as the President.

The Congressional Research Service note *The Debt Limit: History and Recent Increases* published 2011 points out that the debt limit 'provides Congress with the strings to control the federal purse, allowing Congress to assert its constitutional prerogatives to control spending'.

Marshall Robinson, in *The National Debt Ceiling: An Experiment in Fiscal Policy* published by the Brookings Institution in 1959, argued it 'expresses a national devotion to the idea of thrift and to economical management of the fiscal affairs of the government'. It certainly provides a powerful instrument for institutional conflict when the executive and legislative branches of federal government are divided.

Its overall economic significance is less clear. The debt ceiling has not prevented accumulating deficits over several economic cycles since 1979, and some public finance commentators such as Bruce Bartlett argue it should be eliminated. He says the modern budget-making process established in 1974 is a more appropriate framework for examining the prudence and sustainability of federal finances and that the debt limit has had little impact on the evolution of spending and the revenue policies that ultimately determine the level of the federal debt. The General Accountability Office concluded in its paper *Debt Limit Delays Debt Management Challenges and Increases* published in February 2011 that 'the debt limit does not control or limit the ability of the federal government to run deficits or incur obligations. Rather, it is a limit on the ability to pay obligations already made'.

The dispute over the debt ceiling that delayed raising it during the summer of 2011 resulted in the matter only being settled in August 2011, shortly before the US Treasury would have found it difficult to conduct normal business. The Republican House of Representatives delayed until there was a genuine risk of a default on the US' debt service obligations.

Some members of the Congressional Republican Tea Party caucus publicly explained, as part of the hard negotiations on the debt ceiling, that they were prepared to accept a federal government default. The episode provoked Standard & Poor's to reduce the AAA credit rating the US has had since the 1930s. The US had enjoyed an AAA credit rating since Moody's first gave such a rating in 1917, in the early years when credit scoring began. The decision by Standard & Poor's was hugely significant. The credit rating agency argued the impasse between Congress and the President over raising the debt ceiling implied that there was insufficient political agreement in the US to guarantee that its treasury could meet its debts in a manner that warranted an AAA credit rating.

Historically, the supply of public credit has depended on two things: financial and economic resources and the political will to mobilise those resources to meet public debt obligations. In the 17th century, the willingness of Dutch people to pay taxes to finance debt enabled the Netherlands to mobilise huge financial resources at a lower cost of borrowing against the Kings of Spain and France. In the 18th century, the British government was able to mobilise more resources through borrowing secured through taxes agreed by Parliament to fund the debt than the King of France was able to leverage. France was a larger country and arguably more prosperous, but people would not lend to it because the *ancien régime* could not be relied on to pay the money back – largely because it did not have popular representative political institutions that would consent to the necessary taxation needed to service the debt. Alexander Hamilton understood the importance of these lessons, and the implication of the Standard & Poor's downgrading of America's credit rating is that they are less well understood by contemporary politicians.

The possibility of the US Treasury defaulting on its debt is remote. The decision by Standard & Poor's to reduce the US credit rating to AA+ attracted a great deal of criticism. There was a complaint from the US Treasury Department drawing attention to an arithmetical error in the rating agencies initial announcement explaining the reasoning behind the decision to lower the AAA credit rating. This annoyance was shared by economists such as Paul Krugman and major investors such as Warren Buffet. The market reaction throughout the episode was to continue to use Treasury bonds during a period of international concerns about sovereign debt and banks in Europe, and weakening economic activity. Yields of Treasury instruments fell.

Cost of federal government debt

The impressive thing about the US federal government is the ease and low cost at which it continues to be able to borrow. Debt service costs the US Treasury Department about 1.5 percent of GDP a year. Although it is projected to rise in US Budget from 1.6 percent in 2016 to 2.8 percent of GDP in 2021. The question policymakers need to consider is the extent to which the US government is vulnerable to a change in the willingness of domestic and international investors to hold US government bonds paying relatively low levels of interest. The maturity duration of US Treasury debt is noticeably shorter than in other advanced economies. The maturity profile of US Treasury debt has been extended. Ten years ago about 30 percent of the debt matured in less than a year. The proportion of the debt that matures each year and has to be refinanced has fallen to just under 24 percent, but each year the Treasury will have to refinance over a fifth of its outstanding debt. Indexation constrains the benefits governments can obtain from allowing price inflation to erode the real value of their debt.

The OECD has pointed out that the share of inflation-indexed bonds in government debt is not negligible. Seven percent of US debt is index-linked, and among other major economies only France and the UK have higher ratios of outstanding debt in the form of debt index-linked to inflation. The *OECD Economic Outlook 2011* concluded that given the short-term maturity of much international government debt and indexation, the risks of using inflation to erode the real cost of debt would run the risk of requiring substantially higher rates of inflation, which would likely be associated with more adverse effects on the economy. The impact that higher inflation can have on the cost of debt service illustrated by the Congressional Budget Office's budget note in November 2016 that drew attention to the increase in federal spending that arose from higher outlays for net interest on public debt that increased by $23 bn, an increase of some 9 percent in 2016, largely because of higher inflation. As a result of having issued index linked bonds each month, to account for the effects of inflation, the US Treasury Department adjusts the principal of Treasury inflation-protected securities, using the change in the consumer price index for all urban consumers that was recorded two months earlier.

US debt will be a real burden on future economic welfare. It will not be easily avoided through a device such as deliberate or accidentally induced inflation. The headline gross stock of public debt is approaching the level that Carmen Reinhart and Kenneth Rogoff in *This Time is Different*, consider to be likely to hamper GDP growth, although it is important to note that the debt held by the public remains significantly below that level.

Chapter 7

Taxation in the US

The US federal government and individual state governments are sovereign political authorities with the full power to tax. State governments normally devolve some taxation powers to local authorities, such as city and county authorities. The distinguishing feature of American taxation is the variety of tax regimes in place in the individual states and the complexity that arises when they overlap with the tax-raising powers of the federal government. This mainly arises in relation to taxation income and capital gains. Not all states have income or capital taxes, but where they do state legislatures usually take great care to integrate them with existing federal tax structures, codes and marginal rates to avoid unnecessary duplication and complexity. In other cases, state governments have taken less care and have created interactions between state and federal taxation that can be complicated and expensive for certain bands of taxpayer.

In general, government authorities in the US levy taxes to fund their activities in a manner that is likely to aggravate the costs and economic distortions that inevitably arise from taxation.

The federal government makes extensive use of income and capital gains taxes that are much more distorting than expenditure taxes. The federal income tax system is complex and distinguished by extensive use of tax expenditures and subsidies, which narrow the tax base and require higher marginal taxes to yield a given level of revenue. The states make much greater use of expenditures taxes such as sales and excise duties, but have not consistently adopted non-distorting expenditure taxes model similar to the value added tax used by the European Union since the 1970s or the goods and services tax introduced by Canada in 1991 and by Australia in 2000. Some local authorities also have income and capital gains taxing powers that can introduce further complexity into the system. The principal taxes used to fund local authorities in the US, however, are property taxes.

The state governments have immense scope to experiment and innovate in public policy in general and taxation in particular. This provides interesting opportunities to benchmark and assess the effectiveness, costs and consequences from different policy choices. It offers benefits in terms of political choice and the opportunity to see what works and what does not. With taxation, it is difficult to avoid the conclusion that the way policymakers across the US use their powers comes at a price. The price is complexity and incoherence in the way that taxes are levied, which raises the costs and economic distortion that taxation inevitably causes. There, perhaps, should be more of a debate among governors and between the states and the US Treasury about working to develop a more coherent approach. Of course, the federal government would not be in any position to impose or direct such a debate. It does not have the power to impose different tax rules on the states, and perhaps more importantly its own tax system is far from being a paradigm of good practice.

Federal taxation in the US

In 2015, The federal government had total tax and other receipts of $3.2trn, accounting for 18.3 percent of GDP. The lion's share of this revenue came from individual income taxes and the payroll Social Security tax levied to finance pensions. Taxes on income raised 47.4 percent of revenue and Social Security taxes brought in 32.8 percent of total receipts. Corporation income taxes raised 10.6 percent of tax collected and excise duties brought in 3 percent. The striking feature of the federal government's tax system is how little use is made of expenditure taxes – total revenue from excise duties is 0.6 percent of GDP.

Figure 7.1: Social Security Spending and Revenues as a % of GDP 1985–2035

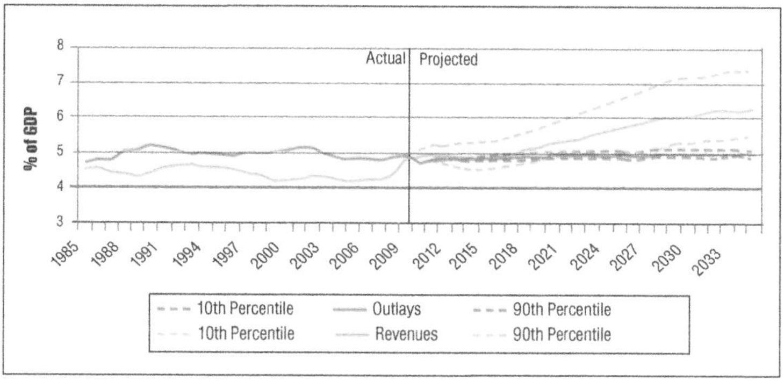

Source: *Congressional Budget Office, Long-Term Projections for Social Security Additional Information, October 2010*

This is a transformation of the historical position in the first three decades of the 20th century. In 1934, after the federal income tax had been in place for 20 years, the US collected 14.2 percent of its revenue from it and 45.8 percent of its revenues from excise duties. In the 1930s, income tax steadily rose as a share of revenue peaking at 20.3 percent of revenues in 1937 and then rising steadily in during World War II, peaking at 45 percent of revenue in 1944. Since the 1940s, income tax has accounted for between 40 and 49.9 percent of federal receipts.

Figure 7.2: Worker to Recipient Ratio for Social Security, 1980–2085

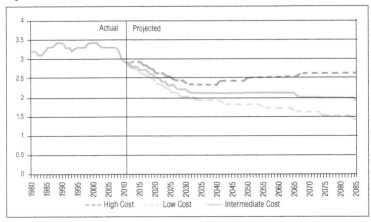

Sources: Trustees of OASDI, Annual Report, 2010

Social insurance receipts have increased steadily. In 1934, 1 percent of revenue was scored as coming from this source. The introduction of Social Security in 1937 increased it to 10.8 percent. Since then, apart from the war and post-war years there has been a steady trend where payroll Social Security tax receipts became a greater proportion of total tax collected. In the 1950s it was 11 percent, in 1960 15.9 percent, in 1970, 23 percent, in 1980 30.5 percent and in 1990 36.8 percent. In normal years, it stabilised at about 36 percent of total revenue. Since 2010 it has fallen from 40 percent to 33.8 percent of revenues in 2015 and is projected in President Obama's Budget Fiscal 2017 to fall to under 30 percent of total federal receipts. Corporation tax receipts have fallen steadily as a share of revenue from a peak of 39.8 percent of total receipts in 1943 to 10.6 percent in 2010.

Tax expenditures

The US income tax regime is too complicated. There are too many tax subsidies to collect revenue in an efficient and non-distorting manner. These tax expenditures narrow the tax base and result in higher rates of taxation than would otherwise be necessary.

Many of these expenditures result in significant distortion of market prices that change the behaviour of economic agents in ways that damage economic welfare. The housing market is clearly distorted by the tax subsidies assisting house purchase, and agricultural markets have been distorted by the tax and other subsidies offered to encourage the development of biofuels.

Figure 7.3: Ratio of the population aged 65 and over to the labour force

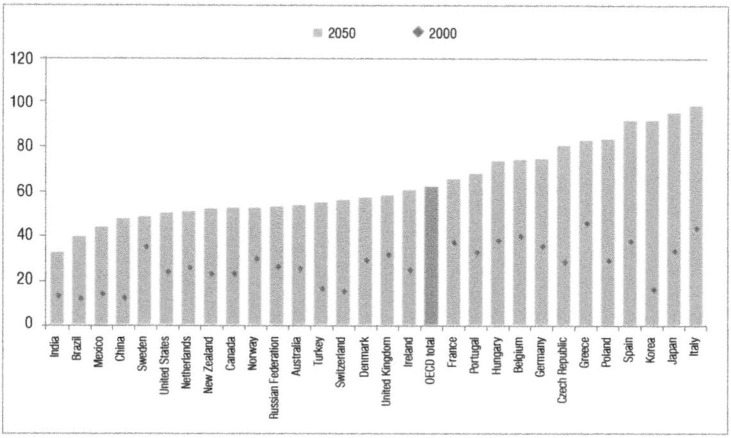

Source: OECD

In most instances, many of the public policy objectives of such subsidies are better and more systematically achieved through direct public expenditure rather than indirectly by the construction of a tax system with subsidies to change behaviour.

Tax reform and expenditure taxation

In 1986, the Reagan administration made a serious attempt to simplify the tax system, removing subsidies, widening the tax base and reducing marginal tax rates within a broadly revenue-neutral set of reforms. There is now increasing recognition that a similar reform is currently needed. Donald Trump's economic team have identified a tax reform programme based on widening the tax base and lowering marginal tax rates.

The Reagan reforms were not sufficiently comprehensive in their scope – for example, subsidies for home ownership were retained. They have now largely been undone as a result of continuous tinkering by Congress and also as a result of the Clinton administration's interest in the new growth theory, which assigned a special role to manufacturing capital investment and research and development. Various tax measures and credits were introduced as part of this agenda. In addition, the Clinton administration used the personal income tax system to try to accomplish policies that were constrained by the special set of rules imposed in the 1990s to limit growth in discretionary spending programmes in order to reduce the budget deficit.

Figure 7.4: Federal spending as a percentage of GDP by categories: 1950–2010

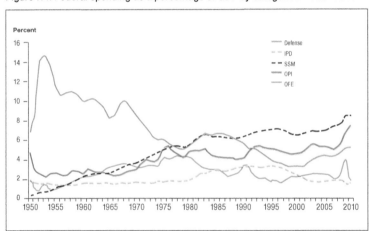

Source: Office of Management and Budget

Figure 7.5: Causes of rising spending on Medicare, Medicaid and Social Security

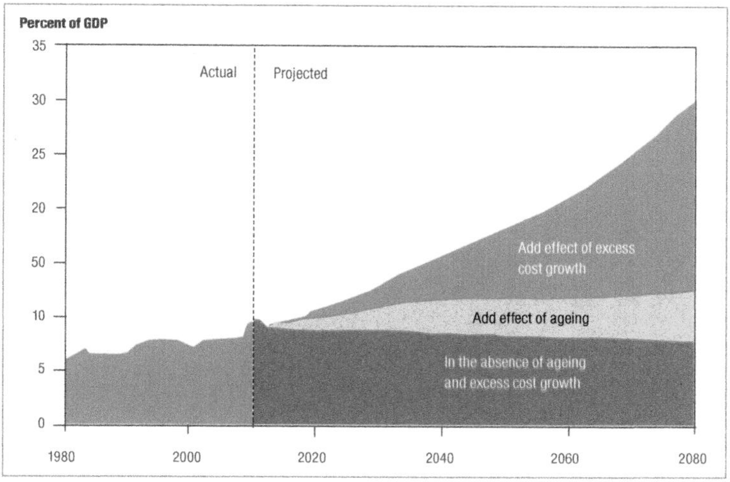

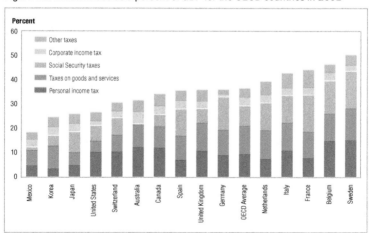

Source: *Office of Management and Budget (2010)*

Figure 7.6: Tax revenues as a percent of GDP for the OECD countries in 2002

Source: *OECD*

Figure 7.7: Top marginal personal and corporate tax rates for the OECD countries in 2004

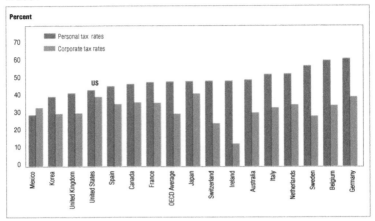

Source: OECD

Figure 7.8: The US tax-GDP ratio is low by OECD standards

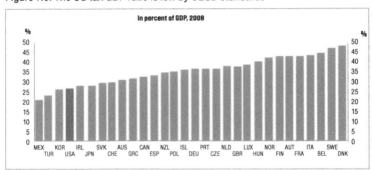

Source: Revenue Statistics database

Table 7.1: Tax expenditures in personal income tax: international comparisons

	Canada (2004)	Germany (2006)	Korea (2006)	Netherlands (2006)	Spain (2008)	United Kingdom (2006)	United States (2008)
Total	32.97	2.91	10.09	2.74	3.86	13.47	29.36
of which							
Retirement	10.72	0.05	0.10	0.16	0.46	6.38	5.77
Health	1.70	0.00	1.67	0.00	0.00	0.00	5.38
Housing	1.29	2.01	0.29	0.12	1.12	3.30	5.90
Intergovernmental	9.94	0.30	0.00	0.00	0.00	0.00	3.54
Other	9.32	0.55	8.03	2.46	2.28	3.79	8.77

Source: OECD

What is needed now is a major overhaul of the way the federal government collects revenue. That review needs to be realistic about the future spending that the tax system will be expected to fund and needs to consider in a basic way the most efficient method to collect tax so as not to damage the economy, in terms of distortion, work incentives and incentives to save and accumulate capital.

Part of the debate should be the consideration of a comprehensive value-added tax. A narrower debate around income, corporation and capital taxes would avoid the most obvious tax issue that the US needs to consider. This is the need to develop greater use of non-distorting expenditure taxes.

Clarity and certainty

One issue that specifically needs to be addressed is the bizarre manner in which the George W. Bush Administration and Congress cut taxes. US policy makers need to avoid cutting taxes and identifying the consequences for future revenue and deficits, as if taxes were cut on a temporary basis, enabling the fiction to be maintained that in future revenue would return as tax rates automatically returned to where they were before with the result that future revenue was scored higher.

This never made sense. People only respond to a tax cut if they believe it permanently raises their income. A 'temporary' tax cut would not, therefore, raise a household's permanent income. In addition, a tax cut that creates future budget deficits that will have to be financed by bond issues that taxpayers will then have to service also means taxpayers will not respond to the change.

In terms of accurate budget arithmetic, introducing clarity and certainty in the tax system and creating a rational tax policy, the US should establish a framework where people have some certainly about the tax system they will work under. This does not mean that the federal government should never engage in any active fiscal policy, but that in the main, tax policy should aim at clarity, simplicity and stability.

State and local taxation

State governments and local authorities raise around two-thirds of all the taxes collected in the US. They have balanced budget rules and have to adjust taxation and spending to changing financial circumstances. They can borrow for capital projects, but cannot operate unbalanced budgets. States as sovereign authorities are free to establish whatever tax policy regime they choose, and to delegate tax-raising powers to city and other local authorities within the states. They tend to make much greater use of expenditure taxes such as sales taxes and excise duties than the federal government. They also make use of income, capital gains and estate and inheritance taxes. The principal sources of tax revenue for city and local governments are property taxes. Some municipal authorities, particularly large cities, also operate full income tax regimes.

There can be extensive scope for tax levied by a state or local government authority to interact with federal taxation and to raise both the highest marginal tax rate that a person faces and to worsen the complexity of the tax system by applying tax rates to different tax bases. Some states have carefully tailored their income and capital tax regimes so that they interact with the federal regime in a way that mitigates the potential complexity.

The state and local taxation system – because it relies less on income taxes and more on sales and property taxes – can be less economically distorting than the federal tax system. There are states, such as New York and California, where the tax systems – when combined with federal tax – result in an effective tax burden as heavy as taxation in mainstream European economies, and arguably more burdensome in terms of complexity and tax compliance.

The US Census Bureau's *State Government Tax Collections Summary Report: 2014* shows that state governments collected $865.8 billion in tax revenue in fiscal year 2014. The principal source of revenue was from state income taxes that yielded 35 percent of taxes collected, followed by general sales and gross receipts taxes that raised 31 percent of revenue and selected sales taxes raised 16 percent of revenue and corporate income taxes raised 5 percent.

Figure 7.9: Total State Government tax collections by category

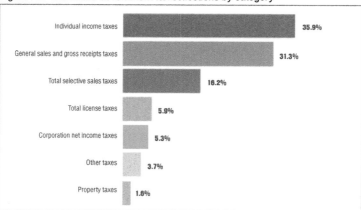

Note: Detail does not sum to total due to rounding.

Source: US Census Bureau, Annual Survey of State Government Tax Collections. <www.census.gov/govs/statetax>

Revenue from license taxes has risen sharply over the last twenty years. This includes motor vehicle licences, that made up $23.8 bn of the $51.1bn collected in licences, licenses paid as a condition for doing or operating a business and amusement licences for one-time casino start-up fees and annual licence obligations that raised $472.3 million.

The Economic Report of the President in 2016 drew attention to research illustrating the potentially malign effects of greater licencing for businesses and professions. The proportion of the U.S. workforce covered by state licensing laws grew five-fold in the second half of the 20th century, from less than 5 percent in the early 1950s to 25 percent by 2008. State licenses account for the bulk of licensing, when locally and federally licensed occupations are taken into account the share of the workforce that is licensed is 29 percent. The report recognises that while licensing can play a role in protecting consumer health and safety, there is evidence that some licensing requirements create economic rents for licensed practitioners at the expense of excluded workers and consumers. This increases inefficiency and potentially also increasing inequality. Employment barriers created by licensing raise wages for those who gaining entry to a licensed occupation by restricting employment in the licensed profession and lowering wages for excluded workers. Estimates find that unlicensed workers earn 10 percent to 15 percent less than licensed workers with similar levels of education, training, and experience. More restrictive licensing laws lead to higher prices for goods and services, in many cases for lower-income households, while purported benefits for consumers do not materialise. Some state-specific licensing requirements create unnecessary barriers to entry for out-of-state licensed practitioners, reducing mobility across state lines.

Figure 7.10: Total license taxes: 1994-2014

Figure 7.11: Share of workers with a State occupational license 1950-2008

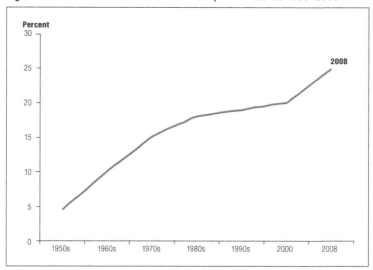

Source: Council of State Governments (1952); Greene (1969); Kleiner (1990); Kleiner (2006); and Kleiner and Krueger (2013), Westat data; CEA calculations

139

Chapter 8

States and local authorities

States and local governments are responsible for around 40 percent of all public expenditure in the US. In 2015, State and local government purchases were about 60 percent larger than Federal purchases and four times larger than Federal nondefense purchases. Government spending in state and local authorities rose by 68 percent between 1999 and 2008. The US Census Bureau's *State Government Finances Summary: 2013* published in 2015 showed that states spent $1,683 billion in 2013. *State Expenditure Report* published by the National Association of State Budget Officers shows that state spending rose steadily between 1987 and 2009 at an average rate of 6.3 percent a year.

Figure 8.1: Total state spending by funding source, fiscal 1987 to 2014

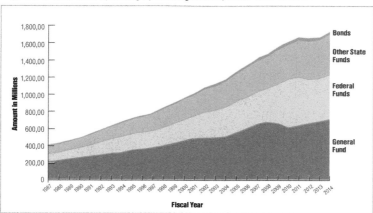

Every state, except Vermont, has balanced budget rules written into their state constitutions or in statute. They are required to balance their budgets, but can borrow to finance capital expenditure. As well as raising local taxes and revenue from charges and user fees to cover their own expenditure, states and local authorities also receive funding from the Federal Government for a variety of programmes and locally administer federal programmes such as Medicaid.

In Fiscal 2014, 41.1 percent of state expenditure was financed from state general funds with money raised from taxation and charges, 30.1 percent from federal government transfers, 26.9 percent from 'other state funds' – which are mainly hypothecated taxes ear-marked for specific purposes – and 1.9 percent from revenue raised from bond issues.

Figure 8.2: Total state expenditure by funding source, fiscal 2014

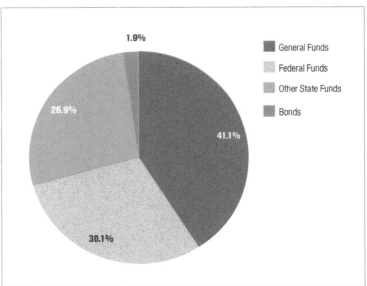

State budgets have historically been vulnerable to economic disruption. Many states are heavily dependent on a relatively narrow range of economic activity and have tax bases that are therefore vulnerable to adverse economic developments. In recessions, tax revenue falls, spending rises and budgets are unbalanced – but states are not allowed to run budget deficits. The result is that state and local authorities undergo draconian fiscal squeezes during recessions and then enjoy periods of rapid growth in tax revenue budget surpluses that then results in fiscal expansion until the next downturn. Many states try to offset this cycle of feast and famine with rainy-day funds, but they have not been accumulated on a scale to offset the impact of the economic cycle.

State and local authorities carry out the principal functions that are necessary in any modern community – highway building and maintenance, street lighting, the provision of parks, policing, schools, colleges and universities. Almost a third of state budgets are spent on education, over 25 percent goes to healthcare and income security programmes, 7.9 percent is spent on transport and 3.2 percent on correctional facilities. The problem is not so much the spending and functions that they undertake, but the costs they incur to carry out these functions and the efficiency and productivity of the services that they provide.

Overall spending state spending since the Great Recession has been principally driven by federal government transfer payments. These rose between 2009 and 2012 and then fell back as the fiscal stimulus package came to an end. In 2009 and 2010 federal funding for states rose by 19.3 percent and 21.4 percent as a result of the American Recovery and Reinvestment Act 2009. The winding down of the stimulus package reduced federal transfers to states by 9.8 percent and 2.6 percent in 2012 and 2013. Federal funding then rose by 4.7 percent in 2014 as some states began to implement the Affordable Care Act. The Affordable Care Act has increased federal support for Medicaid programs administered by the states. National Association of State Budget Officers estimate that in Fiscal 2015 federal funding for state Medicaid programs increased by 22.5 percent

Figure 8.3: Total state expenditure by function, fiscal 2014

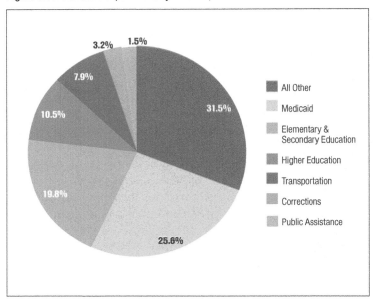

States have long-established employment practices and costs that reflect historic pay and pension arrangements, often distinguished by strong public sector producer interests and trade union interests. Wages and benefits of state and local employees are often not only higher than comparable private sector wage levels, but significantly above a realistic idea of efficiency wages.

State and local governments also have substantial pension liabilities. The terms and conditions of the pension liabilities are generous from the perspective of the public sector employee, but expensive for the employer. Most of these liabilities are funded by assets accumulated and invested on actuarial assumptions intended to ensure that the pensions can be paid in the future. The difficulty is the combination of generous pension liabilities and uncertain investment returns is toxic, with the result that apart from having immediate fiscal problems that arise as a result of the recent recession, many states have what appear to be longer-term structural financial problems.

The state government and the Great Recession: fiscal crisis

State governments underwent a fiscal crisis as a result of the Great Recession, and the effects of that fiscal crisis has been protracted. The Centre on Budget and Policy Priorities showed that the combined budget gap that the states faced in fiscal 2009 was $110bn, around 15 percent of total state general fund budgets. The gap identified in fiscal 2010 was even larger at $200bn, some 30 percent of state budgets. In *Fiscal Crises of the States: Causes and Consequences* published in 2010, Jeremy Guest and Daniel Wilson showed that the causes and severity of the state fiscal crises vary. They identify two main factors that have affected every state to a greater or lesser extent.

First, the macroeconomic shock affected the country as a whole, with a fall in real GDP of over 5 percent, a fall in non-farm employment of 6.1 percent and a doubling of unemployment from 5 percent to over 10 percent in October 2009. While the economic distress was general, its impact on state finances was not uniform. Many states, particularly those in the west, had greater exposure to the housing down turn and experienced greater contractions in their economic activity.

Second, such a deep recession had a severe impact on state tax revenue. Receipts fell as GDP contracted, and in 2009 real state and local tax revenue fell by over 10 percent on a year-on-year basis. During recessions tax revenue always declines or grows more slowly. In the Great Recession between 2007 and 2010, the fall in revenue was the greatest since 1947 when the data was first collected. In addition, in 2010 and 2011 revenue collection in many states was weaker than the forecasts used in budget planning.

As revenue has fallen, states have not fully matched lower tax receipts with lower spending. States made some discretionary changes, but this was been dwarfed by the fall in revenues. The capacity of state governments to respond to economic difficulty is constrained by institutional arrangements – they have to balance their budgets. Many states entered the recession with modest or non-existent savings, or rainy-day funds. Many states are legally restricted in how much they can put aside in such reserve funds. There are also important countervailing pressures that make it difficult to control spending in recessions. Demand for many state government programmes increases in periods of weak economic activity. Unemployment insurance benefit claims increase with higher unemployment. Job losses also increase demand for use of Medicaid. Many state programmes are tied to complex rules about federal matching funds that make it expensive for them to reduce spending in those areas of activity. States receive reimbursement of 50-80 percent of their spending on Medicaid from the federal government. The American Recovery and Reinvestment Act 2009 increased each state's matching funding by 6.2 percent. This meant that if a state cut spending on Medicaid by one dollar, it would have secured a net public expenditure saving of only between 12 and 44 cents. For that saving, its residents would have experienced a full dollar's worth of reduction in Medicaid services.

Differences in the scale of budget gaps or deficits among state governments are explained both by variations in the severity of the economic shock and in differences in the political institutions that regulate fiscal policy. In 2009, ahead of the fiscal year starting in July 2009, California had a fiscal gap of 37 percent, while Oregon had a deficit of 7 percent. Economists at the Federal Reserve Bank of San Francisco concluded that the difference was largely explained by the two states' different constitutional procedures for making tax and spending decisions. If both states had kept their per capita state public expenditure constant between 2007 and 2009, both the Oregon and California budget gaps would have been about the same – around 20 percent.

However, in 2008 Oregon reduced growth in spending, increased taxes and drew down rainy day reserve funds to reduce the budget gap. California broadly maintained growth in expenditure, with only modest discretionary reductions in its planned growth, enacted only limited tax increases and had nothing in its rainy day reserve fund as it entered the recession. California's modest policy response to a very significant adverse economic shock reflected the institutional constraints on policy- and lawmakers to change fiscal policy. Tax increases, for example, in California must be approved by two-thirds of the legislature. In addition, voter propositions approved in statewide referenda in the past, such as, the famous Proposition 13 passed in 1978 cutting property taxes, limit the legislature's scope to curtail spending and raise taxes in many areas.

The *Economic Report of the President* in 2016 drew attention to the weakness of spending and the problems in state finances. The report pointed out that state and local share of nominal GDP fell from its historical peak of 13.0 percent in 2009 to 10.9 percent in 2015, a level not seen since the late 1980s as State and local governments cut their purchases in the face of budget pressures years. Years. In the present economic recovery growth in State and local purchases has been the weaker than in any other economic recovery since 1945. The *Economic Report of the President 2016* showed that during the four quarters of 2010, State and local purchases subtracted 0.5 percentage point from GDP growth, and then subtracted about another 0.3 percentage point in both 2011 and 2012. Spending stabilized in 2013 and contributed modestly to GDP growth in 2014 and 2015. State and local governments also cut jobs early in the recovery. From 2013, this trend was reversed and state and local government employment rose by 210,000. Employment in this part of the public sector remains 528,000 below its previous peak in 2008. Some 40 percent of the fall in jobs was concentrated in education services provided through state and local authorities.

Figure 8.4 Real State and Local Government Purchases During Recoveries, 1960–2015

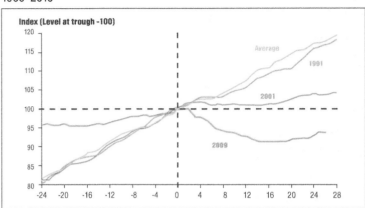

Source: *Bureau of Economic Analysis, National Income and Product Accounts, National Bureau of Economic Research, CEA calulations.*

The Pew centre analysis *States' Fiscal Health* illustrates how difficult the Great Recession was for state revenues. Nationally total state tax receipts only recovered in 2013. In the middle of 2015 states were collecting 5.6 percent more in tax revenue than they did at the previous peak in the third quarter of 2008. Among the 50 states this overall improvement masks a mixed performance. In five of the 29 states that enjoyed increased revenues receipts in the second quarter of 2015 were fifteen percent higher than their inflation adjusted previous peak before or during the recession. Twenty one states were still collecting less revenue than at the peak of the economic cycle in 2008, after adjusting receipts for inflation and in three states receipts were down 15 percent in real terms. This difference in performance reflects varying economic circumstances and the different policy responses of states to the economic crisis. California took discretionary measures to raise taxes that added to the recovery in receipts arising from higher levels of economic activity. The increasing number of states reporting higher tax revenue shows that the effects of the Great Recession are receding, albeit slowly.

It has been a long and slower process than in previous economic cycles. Following the recession after the 'Techwreck' in 2001 that was shorter and less deep, for example, tax receipts rebounded in all states with the exception of Michigan within six years

State government debt

The US Census Bureau's *State Government Finances Summary 2013* reports that state governments' total debt at the end of fiscal year 2013 was $1,137.4 billion, down 1.0 percent from 2012. States have smaller debt burdens than local governments. In 2012 total debt of state and local governments was $2,945.7 billion, 39 percent belonged to state governments and 61.0 percent to local governments. The *Economic Report of the President 2016* points out that until 1990 state and local governments only ran deficits during recessions. 'Since then, State and local governments have frequently run deficits. State and local governments continue to spend more than they collect in revenues and their aggregate deficit during the first three quarters of 2015 amounted to nearly 1 percent of nominal GDP'. 49 out of 50 states have constitutions or statutes mandating a balanced budget and many local governments have similar provisions. This does not prevent them from running deficits. Many of those balanced budget statutes apply only to the operating budget, while deficits may be allowed on their capital accounts. Spending from 'rainy day funds' is scored as a deficit on the government balance sheet in the national income and product accounts. This deficit has narrowed however, during the recovery.

Figure 8.5 State and Local Government Surplus as Percent of Normal GDP, 1947–2015

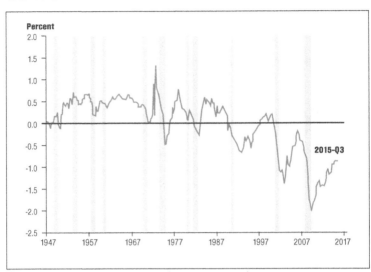

Source: *Bureau of Economic Analysis; Haver Analytics.*

Federal government assistance to states

Federal government provides substantial assistance and grant aid to the states and has a major role in funding state government functions. The rudiments for federal assistance to states developed during the Civil War when the Morrill Act was passed establishing land-grant colleges. Conditions were attached to federal funding, requiring states to meet minimum standards. Federal grants were later introduced for agriculture, highways, vocational education and rehabilitation, forestry and public health. The Great Depression resulted in an extension of federal aid to assist with income maintenance and social welfare, but assistance to states did not become a significant part of the federal budget until after World War II.

Figure 8.6: Federal Government Expenditure, Per Capita Amounts by State, by Major Agency, Fiscal Year 2010

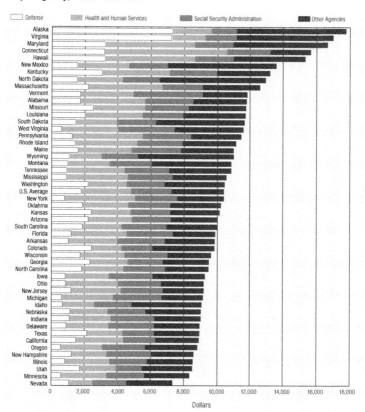

Source: US Census Bureau, "Consolidated Federal Funds Report for Fiscal Year 2010"

Total federal grants to states in 2016 were $666.3bn. They have risen from 7.6 percent of federal spending in 1960 to 17.6 percent in 2010 in the depth of the recession. In 2016 they represented 16.9 percent of estimated federal outlays. As a share of GDP, these transfer payments have risen from 1.4 percent to 4.1 percent in 2010. In 2016 the US Budget Fiscal 2017 estimated that these transfer payments would account for 3.6 percent of

GDP. In 1960 these transfers financed 14.3 percent of state government spending, in 2015 the figure is closer to 30 percent. The composition of the spending has also changed significantly. In 1960, 35.3 percent of the Federal grant went on transfer payments to individuals. In 2016, this had increased to 74 percent of the grant. In 1960, 47.3 percent of all federal grants went toward capital investment as part of the federal infrastructure project to help states build the Interstate Highway System. Transport spending now only accounts for about 12 percent of federal assistance to states. There has been a significant rise in the proportion of the grant spent on education, training and social services, which accounted for 16 percent of federal assistance in 2010. Federal grants for health services – principally Medicaid – have increased more than six-fold over the past two decades. Federal support for state health programmes accounts for 58.9 percent of the federal grant to states. Before the Great Recession, about 20 percent of state expenditure was financed through federal grants to state and local government programmes, covering most areas of domestic spending such as income support, infrastructure, education and social services. Since the recession, federal assistance has risen. By 2010, it was $608.4bn and financed almost 30 percent of state spending.

Figure 8.7: Composition of total state expenditure by function, fiscal 1987 to 2014

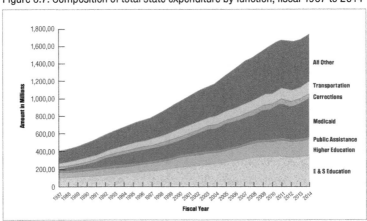

The reason states need significant federal assistance in a recession is the pro-cyclical character of their budget rules. Eleven states restrict their legislators' ability to increase taxes, by requiring more than a simple majority vote for any legislation that would go beyond a statutory or constitutional limit. States, while having balanced budget rules, can issue short-term debt to fund operating deficits and long-term debt to fund capital investment and contributions to pension and healthcare funds.

The amount of debt that can be issued in most states is limited by law or the state constitution. Historically, states have approached the federal government for assistance during periods of fiscal stress. The Congressional Budget Office paper *Fiscal Stress Faced by Local Authorities*, published in December 2010, estimates that from state fiscal year 2008 to state fiscal year 2009, federal aid as a share of total state spending increased from 26 percent to 30 percent. The American Recovery and Reinvestment Act provided $71bn to states in additional Medicaid grants and $36bn through the State Fiscal Stabilisation Fund. Ignoring the additional assistance provided under the Act, the federal government made $453bn in payments to states for Medicaid between 2009 and 2010. To restart loan purchases by housing finance authorities facing high interest costs on their debt because of market turmoil and the failure of several municipal debt insurers, the US Treasury Department provided $24bn to states. This assistance consisted of new debt and credit support to increase the liquidity of outstanding debt, significantly reduced the debt service costs of state housing authorities, enabling them to purchase new mortgages and to support lending to first-time and low-income house buyers.

Historically, the recovery in state finances lags the recovery in the national economy. The recovery in output that began in 2010 did not translate itself into significant improvement in state finances until 2012. The Center on Budget and Policy Priorities estimated that significant gaps would remain in state budgets, and the Rockefeller Institute found most states were uncertain about when revenue will recover and indicated fiscal problems would extend beyond 2012.

Gerst and Wilson explained that the condition of state government finances would deteriorate before it improved. Grants made to state governments as part of the Obama administration's fiscal stimulus helped states cover budget gaps. From 2011, this stimulus assistance was diminished and was originally planned to be withdrawn in 2012. States would then had to deal with their own budget gaps without federal support. State budget problems were also aggravated by the depletion of rainy day reserve funds, because those states that had them largely exhausted them.

Some states that avoided exposing the full scale of their budgets gaps by using accounting devices that have the effect of delaying fiscal adjustment are finding such devices and accounting tricks are exhausted and the 'end of the road is in sight'. The macroeconomic impact of the states' fiscal crises in terms of demand is relatively small, because state budget gaps account for only around 1 percent of US GDP. The combined state budget gap, for example, calculated by the Center on Budget and Policy Priorities, totalled less than the cost of the federal stimulus package in 2009.

Can states go bankrupt?

Like most sovereign entities, state governments cannot go bankrupt and are not subject to conventional insolvency procedures in the manner of other public authorities or private sector corporations. The federal government cannot take control of a state's fiscal operations, given that the US Constitution protects the states from infringement on their sovereignty by federal authorities. Under federal law, states cannot file for bankruptcy. But there is nothing to stop a state under great fiscal stress from defaulting on its debt. The last occasion when a state did so was Arkansas, in 1933. And of course the Commonwealth of Puerto Rico that is not a full US territory has for all practical purposes twice defaulted on its debt recently.

Local government in the US

Local governments in the US vary in size, purpose, scale of spending and revenue sources. There are about 3,000 counties, 36,000 municipalities – cities, towns, villages and boroughs –37,400 special districts and 14,600 public school systems in the US.

Figure 8.8: Sources of Revenues for Local Governments, 2008

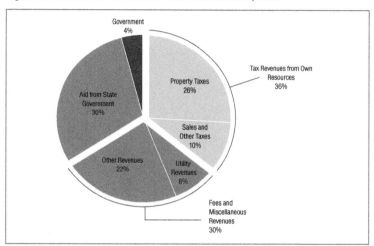

Source: Congressional Budget Office based on data from the Department of Commerce, Census Bureau

Figure 8.9: Types of Spending by Local Governments, 2008

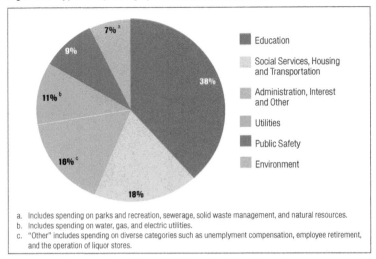

a. Includes spending on parks and recreation, sewerage, solid waste management, and natural resources.
b. Includes spending on water, gas, and electric utilities.
c. "Other" includes spending on diverse categories such as unemployment compensation, employee retirement, and the operation of liquor stores.

Source: Congressional Budget Office based on data from the Department of Commerce, Census Bureau

County and city governments tend to be larger and have bigger budgets and more staff. They provide services such as police, transportation, welfare payments and employment training. Special districts tend to be the smallest entities and have a single purpose, such as providing water or treating waste. Collectively, local governments spend more on education than on any other category of expenditure, followed by spending on social service, housing and transportation, administration debt interest, public safety and the environment.

Congressional Budget Office research has shown how local government authorities face fiscal pressures. It also shows that state governments have experienced more financial stress during the recent economic crisis than local authorities. This is partly because state governments are more dependent on volatile sources of revenue such as receipts from income and sales taxes. Local government collection of tax revenue grew in real terms in each year for the 20 years to 2010, and grew by 9 percent from fiscal year ending June 2008 to fiscal year ending June 2010.

State collection of tax revenue fell in real terms during the past two decades, and fell 13 percent from the fiscal year ending June 2008 to the fiscal year ending June 2010.

Local governments obtain one-third of their revenue income from state aid, about a quarter from property taxes, one-tenth from sales and other taxes and most of the remainder from fees and other revenue receipts. Only 4 percent of local government funding is directly from the federal government. Counties and cities rely heavily on property and sales taxes. While water and sewer districts are funded by utility fees and as a result have suffered less fiscal stress than the cities and counties.

Local authorities have experienced fiscal stress as a result of several factors. They have faced increased demand for their services during a period of economic distress at a time when growth in their tax revenue was weakening and state government assistance fell because of the fiscal crisis experienced by state governments. Local authorities' reliance on property taxes that make up a quarter of their revenue income helped, because during the contraction of economic output, property taxation was a relatively stable source of income. On average, collection of property tax revenues lag changes in property prices by around three years. This meant that in a period when property prices fell by 27 percent nationally between fiscal year ending June 2006 and fiscal year ending June 2010, revenue from property tax collections actually increased by 31 percent. However, the decline in house prices implies that in future years, as local authorities update property tax assessments to reflect their lower market values tax collections will fall. Even a small fall in property tax revenue could cause significant difficulty for local governments at a time when their spending is rising.

In 2008, state governments provided 30 percent of local government revenues. As a result of plummeting tax revenue, the state governments reduced the assistance they provide to local authorities. Given that state and local government fiscal stress tends to coincide with when state grants to local government fall, state assistance to local authorities falls when it is most needed. After the recession in 2001, total transfers to cities fell by 9 percent between 2002 and 2004. The *Fiscal Survey of States* published by the National Governors Association and Association of State Budget Officers in June 2010 found 22 states reduced aid to local governments in fiscal 2010 and 20 proposed further cuts in fiscal 2011. Almost 40 states cut spending for K-12 education in fiscal 2010 and 31 state governors proposed to cut such funding in their 2011 budgets.

Local government investment and financial risks

As well as increasing demand for public services such as employment training, use of public hospitals and other social welfare services, economic contractions may also result in investment losses. When investment losses are large they can be extremely disrupting for local government budgets. In the main, these fiscal challenges arise out of transitory economic shocks and will dissipate over time. There have been unusual instances where investment losses cause severe fiscal distress for local authorities.

In 2003, Jefferson County in Alabama attempted to lower the cost of debt incurred to finance its sewer system by replacing its fixed rate debt with variable rate debt. To protect itself against adverse movements in interest rates, the county simultaneously entered into agreement with an investment bank where the county would provide fixed payments to the bank in exchange for variable rate payments that the county would pay to its bond-holders. The arrangement was flawed because the two variable rates were tied to different indices and the payments on them eventually diverged, causing the county to default in 2008.

Another example is Orange County, California, in the 1990s. In 1994, Orange County's investment pool lost $1.7bn, about 22 percent of its assets. The losses of the pool, which was created to manage the revenues of about 200 local authorities, occurred because its fund manager invested heavily in assets whose value would fall if short-term interests rates rose. A the beginning of 1994, the Federal Reserve Board increased short-term interest rates, causing the value of the of the pool's investments to drop and triggering withdrawals by local governments and calls by private banks for collateral held by the pool to back loans.

Long-term structural budget challenges in US local government

Long-term structural budget imbalances arise out of a variety of sources that are often difficult for economists and budget analysts to separate out. Several features of local authority behaviour have provoked structural or permanent budget gaps in US local government.

Some local authorities have a political culture where fiscal good practice is difficult to achieve or exposes the authority to disproportionate financial risk. The failure of a local authority to agree a budget, particularly where legislative and executive bodies are dominated by different political parties, creates the conditions for deficits. Institutional pay and other employee compensation arrangements such as those agreed with public sector unions can be a significant factor.

When Vallejo, a town in California, filed for bankruptcy in May 2008, the inability of its town council and mayor to control labour costs was the main reason. When its debts were restructured, its labour contracts had to be restructured as well. Three out of four unions accepted healthcare obligations to retired employees being cut by 75 percent, from $135m to $34m. The employment costs for the police service were cut by 18 percent from the level specified by the contract in place before the bankruptcy order. That saved a total of $6m in financial years 2009 and 2010.

Demographic shifts, such as so-called 'suburban flight' can also create structural deficits for local government. When high- and average-income households leave a locality, the community's tax base is eroded but basic services such as roads and police still have to be provided. Over time, the need for public services will rise as personal incomes fall and unemployment rises as business move out to follow customers into the surrounding suburbs.

Lax financial and budgetary controls also create the circumstances where chronic budget deficits can emerge. The Congressional Budget Office paper *New York City's Fiscal Problem: Its Origins, Potential Repercussions, and Some Alternative Policy Responses* published in October 1975 spells out how these factors played a big part in New York's problems in the 1970s. It shows how officials masked growing deficits over several years with the result that eventually the deficit was so large the markets would not finance it. Budgetary controls –including balanced budget requirements, debt limits, and tax and expenditure limits – were all put in place to restrict the ability of officials to spend more on operating expenses than they received in revenue. The extent to which states require local authorities to comply with budgetary controls varies from state to state.

Borrowing by local government can be a response to and a cause of fiscal stress. Where an operating deficit is caused by temporary weak economic conditions, issuing short-term debt can alleviate transitory fiscal pressures. Local authorities that spend more than they collect in tax and other revenue for a number of years usually reach a limit on their ability to postpone balancing budgets. When it reaches this stage, budget balancing often involves even more awkward decisions.

Local government default and bankruptcy

Local authorities experiencing acute fiscal stress can default or file for bankruptcy.

A default takes place when a municipal government fails to make interest or principal payment to bondholders. Municipal bankruptcy is a process established by federal law that allows local authorities to restructure debt and other obligations under the supervision of a federal court. Both municipal default and bankruptcy are rare.

Between 1970 and 2009, 18,400 municipal bonds were issued and rated by Moody's. Of these, only 54 bonds defaulted. The majority of these defaults came from local government entities that were special districts issuing debt to support housing or healthcare facilities. Only six counties, towns or cities defaulted. In most instances, the investors recovered most or all of their money eventually. In recent years municipal default has increased, with over $4bn worth of defaults in 2010.

Local authorities that suffer large and sudden losses of revenue or an increase in the cost of debt service sometimes default. Good examples are Jefferson County, Alabama and Orange County, California. Both defaulted when interest payments would have required them to make large payments they could not afford. A municipal default often leads to a local authority seeking bankruptcy proceedings to protect itself from lawsuits or courts' orders related to the default.

Chapter 9

The solvency and efficiency of state and local government

Over the last 70 years, 600 governmental entities have filed for bankruptcy. Some 170 of these filings occurred between 1988 and 2005.

A pattern has emerged where an unusual event since World War II has now become more common. Organisations attempting to file under chapter 9 of the federal bankruptcy code have to meet certain specific criteria. They must be a political subdivision of a state, state law must authorise a governmental entity to use chapter 9 of the code, the entity must be insolvent and it must negotiate in good faith with its creditors to restructure its debt outside of the bankruptcy to any extent that is practical.

Twenty-six states authorise local authorities to use chapter 9. Of those states, 12 impose no restrictions on the ability of municipal entities to file, while 14 require them to seek state approval – such as approval from the governor, the attorney-general or a board or commission – before doing so. The other 23 states have passed no law making provision for use of chapter 9 and local authorities in them cannot use the bankruptcy code unless the state passes a special law authorising them to so.

The exhaustion of reserves, scope to reduce spending and raise taxes, borrow and manage or postpone debt payments on pay obligations are used by a judge to determine a local government's insolvency under chapter 9. The court applying the bankruptcy code is prohibited from interfering with the municipality's property, revenue or political or governmental powers. The courts will not, for example, remove officials from office. Unreasonable behaviour such as refusal to use taxing powers could violate the municipal entity's duty to act in good faith. If a court decided that duty was breached, the municipality may be disqualified from the protection of assets that bankruptcy offers.

Use of the federal bankruptcy code offers local governments an 'automatic stay' that stops creditors from taking action against them and their officials without the approval of the court. Without such a protection, a local authority in difficulty may incur additional legal costs and be distracted by multiple legal claims while attempting to sort out a difficult set of budget issues. The payment of claims as they arise may also divert funds needed to maintain public services and make debt service payments.

While the stay is in place, bondholders cannot force local authorities to raise taxes to service debts. Bankruptcy also enables the court to implement a coherent plan to restructure a local authority's debt without needing the consent of every creditor. For the approval of the court, a restructuring plan has to secure the consent of two-thirds of each class of creditors whose interests would be affected by the plan. The process also can allow other long-term contract and costs issues that are unsustainable to be adjusted, such as financially unrealistic employment, pension and healthcare costs.

Bankruptcy proceedings come at a cost: Orange County

Bankruptcy proceedings may offer some assistance in dealing with a series of difficult decisions, but it does not automatically offer an easy way forward for a community that has got its affairs into a fiscal mess. Given that two-thirds of creditors have to consent to any restructuring, a local authority may emerge from the process with only a marginally improved balance sheet. For example, if new debt is issued to alleviate part of a cash flow problem, its debt problems may be aggravated rather than eliminated. Such a restructuring would constrain a municipality's operations for many years after the plan is approved.

A good example of this is California's Orange County. In the 1990s, Orange County debt restructuring reduced investors' claims by over 20 percent so that bondholders were only paid out at a rate of 77 cents on the dollar. For Orange County this was a great help. Bondholders would not normally accept a reduced payment on that scale outside of bankruptcy. But it came at a long-term price. Orange County is still making debt service payments on a portion of the $1.2bn worth of bonds issued between 1995 and 1996 to exit the bankruptcy regime. Servicing that debt has limited the county's scope to meet the increasing costs of existing services and to develop new services where they are needed. In addition, some of the financial benefits of restructuring will be absorbed by the administrative and legal costs incurred in the process.

No administrative or insolvency regime can overcome political institutions and a political culture that is fundamentally defective. An electorate that will not vote for the taxes to pay for the services it demands will not have its affairs sorted out by filing for chapter 9. Orange County has, for example, proposed a measure to increase its local sales tax on the ballot and this has been rejected. State laws limiting property taxes and requiring local authorities to contribute to certain pension costs likewise limit the ability of local governments to resolve their entrenched structural fiscal challenges.

Structural fiscal challenges in state and local government budgets

While states and local authorities face an immediate fiscal challenge because their principal sources of revenue contracted during the recession, their balance sheets are in a better condition than that of the federal government. This is because their balanced budget and other fiscal rules have constrained their behaviour. State governments have been obliged to take action to manage their budgets in a manner the federal government has not been subject to. Nevertheless, states face structural fiscal challenges that will be difficult to manage.

Since 2007, the General Accounting Office has published long-term simulations of fiscal policy for state and local governments and these show that, like the federal government, the state and local sector face persistent and long-term financial challenges. The General Accounting Office's *State and Local Governments' Fiscal Outlook*, published in April 2011, confirms that states face unprecedented fiscal challenges as a result of lower tax revenue and those challenges will increase over time.

The long-term structural fiscal gap

Most state and local governments are required to balance their operating budgets. The General Accountability Office's analytical simulations suggest state and local governments need to make substantial policy changes to avoid growing deficits, projected to rise from rough balance in the five years to 2010 to deficits of over 3.5 percent of state GDP by 2060. Without policy changes, there would be an increasing gap between receipts and expenditure.

Health costs

Long-term decline in the operating balance of state and local authorities is principally driven by rising health-related costs. State spending on Medicaid and on employee and retiree health insurance benefits is projected to grow at a faster rate than state GDP, rising from around 3.7 percent of GDP in 2010 to 8.3 percent in 2060. Other areas of spending such as wages and salaries and investment in capital goods are expected to grow slightly less than GDP. Non-health costs will be 10.9 percent of GDP in 2011 and 7.1 percent in 2060. State and local revenues, excluding Medicaid transfer payments from the federal government, are projected to fall as a percentage of GDP.

Employee pension liabilities

The long-term fiscal position of the states is also affected by their pension liabilities. While pension fund assets recovered in value and were worth $3.2trn at the end of 2009. In April 2011, the General Accountability Office estimated the sector's required actuarial contribution rate to their pension funds rose to 11.8 percent of the its wages, which is higher than the sector's actual 9.8 percent of wages contributions in 2009.

The General Accountability Office's findings raise important questions about the long-term sustainability of both state and local government spending and budgets. Given the structural budget deficit that the federal government has, Washington DC will not be in a position to assist the states. It is more likely to legislate to cut assistance over and above the withdrawal of emergency help given in the fiscal stimulus package of 2009, and to ask states to make a greater contribution to both Medicaid and Medicare.

The General Accountability Office analysis – and that of the Congressional Budget Office – is confined to examining state and local government fiscal stress and the extent that budget gaps or deficits are manageable. It has little or nothing to say about how efficiently state and local authorities deploy their resources, the implications of the deadweight costs arising from spending or the opportunity costs it represents. Like so much of the fiscal argument and analysis surrounding the federal government's budget, it is essentially a mechanical analysis of the extent to which spending and taxation are sustainable under present law. The result is that the wider, and in many respects more important, issues – such as the economic consequences of spending and taxation for economic welfare – are missing in American public policy discussion.

General Accountability Office looked again in its *State and Local Governments' Fiscal Outlook 2014* update at the fiscal gap in state budgets five years or more after the Great Recession and broadly confirmed the analysis laid out in 2011. A primary driver

of the decline in the operating budget balance of state governments in the long term is the rising health-related costs of state
and local expenditures on Medicaid and the cost of health
care compensation for state and local government employees and retirees. Given that most state and local governments
are required to balance their operating budgets, the declining
fiscal conditions indicated by the GAO's simulations continue to
suggest that there would need to be substantial policy changes to
avoid fiscal imbalances that would grow in the future. As well as
the challenge generated by health related expenditures state and
local government pension face long-term problems in financing
their pension liabilities. Most state and local governments have
sufficient assets to cover benefit payments to retirees for a decade
or more, but pension plans have experienced a growing gap
between assets and liabilities. In response to this gap, state and
local governments are taking steps to manage their pension obligations, including reducing benefits and increasing employees'
contributions. Unless there are significant policy changes, state
and local governments are facing, and will continue to face, an
increasing gap between receipts and expenditures in the coming
years. Declines in state and local pension asset values stemming
from the 2007 to 2009 economic recession could also affect the
sector's long-term fiscal position. Using real dollars, pension
asset values increased about 6 percent from 2012 through 2013,
from approximately $2.67 trillion in 2012 to $2.83 trillion in 2013.
By 2013, asset values had not recovered to match or exceed the
2007 value of $2.91 trillion. GAO simulation, looks at state and
local sector expenditures over 50 years and they rise considerably as a percentage of GDP to a gap of almost 4 percent of GDP.
The GAO calculated that closing the fiscal gap would require
action to be taken today and maintained for each year to engineer an 18 percent reduction in the state and local government
sector's current expenditures. Closing the fiscal gap through
revenue increases would require action of similar magnitude
through increases in state and local tax revenues. In the GAO

judgment closing the fiscal gap would involve some combination of both expenditure reductions and revenue increases.

Are state fiscal problems exaggerated?

Concerns raised by the General Accountability Office and the character of the media debate stimulated by credit rating agencies and investment services assessing the long-term credit position of state and local governments provoked the Center on Budget Policy to publish *Misunderstandings Regarding State Debt, Pensions, And Retiree Health Costs Create Unnecessary Alarm*, by Iris Lav and Elizabeth McNichol, in January 2011. Lav and McNichol assert that much of this media debate has conflated the problems of state and local governments resulting from the recession and economic cycle with longer-term issues relating to pensions, debt, and retiree health costs. The result is that there is a 'mistaken impression that drastic and immediate measures are needed to avoid an imminent fiscal meltdown'.

While Lav and McNichol recognised most states projected large operating deficits for fiscal year 2012, in many states these would be dealt with in the annual budget process. Closing these deficits through revenue-raising decisions and spending cuts would cause severe problems, but they are essentially cyclical problems and will ease as the economy recovers. There is a separate set of structural issues that relate to pension, debt and retirement healthcare over the longer term, and should not be exaggerated.

What the paper offers is a guide to many of the issues involved. The first point is that state and local government balance sheets are in a much better condition than that of the federal government. Their balanced budget rules mean that they simply do not have a stock of debt comparable to that of the federal government. Unlike the federal government, state and local governments maintain separate operating and capital budgets. Almost all state and local debt is therefore long-term debt incurred to pay for capital expenditure, not to cover current or operating spending. Most state debt is issued for infrastructure spending to finance roads, bridges, and water systems. There have, however, been a few instances where proceeds from debt issues have been used for current spending, including Louisiana in 1988 and Connecticut in 1991. In 2009, Connecticut again sold a bond to cover its operating budget with a seven-year maturity.

Revenue anticipation notes are issued by a small number of states. These are short-term debt instruments used to match the timing of revenue collections with the timing of expenditure in state operating budgets. Revenue anticipation notes have to be repaid during the same financial year. A state that has used this method often is California. In 2008, it could not find investors willing to buy its debt and asked the federal government for financial assistance. In the end, California managed to sell the notes without federal help, as did Massachusetts when it encountered similar problems.

During the Great Recession, although state budgets were under intense pressure their levels of debt only rose modestly. This was because as part of the fiscal stimulus measures, the federal government gave states help through the Build America Bonds (BAB) programme to maintain and increase spending on infrastructure to create jobs. Suggestions emerged, such as those appearing to originate on a Reuters blog post, 'the lack of a BAB programme would make it harder for states to borrow to cover a $140bn budgetary shortfall next year, as estimated by the Center for Budget and Policy Priorities.'

This view confuses capital borrowing and operating deficits, and articles such as 'Mounting debts by states stoke fears of crisis' by Michael Cooper and Mary Williams in the New York Times (December 2010) probably exaggerate the scale of state borrowing. The states have not used new bonds to finance their current spending because they can only be used to finance infrastructure. The stock of state and local government debt in the second quarter of 2010 stood at 16.7 percent of GDP, compared to a cyclical low of 12 percent in 2000, and is similar to average levels from the mid-1980s to mid-1990s. State and local authorities spend between 4-5 percent of their budgets on debt service. There are two sources of information about this. Census data suggests that in 2008, debt service was 4 percent and data provided by the Federal Reserve Bank Flow of Funds Data for debt services and total expenditures from the Bureau of Economic Analysis suggested it was 5.4 percent. In its *Taxable Municipal Market Commentary 2011*, Barclays Capital concluded 'despite frequent media speculation to the contrary, we do not expect the level of defaults in the US public finance market to spiral higher or even approach those in the private sector. We hold this view in large part because of the steps taken thus far by the preponderance of municipalities and the control that public entities can exert over the expense and revenue proportions of their balance sheets'.

Lav and McNichol argue that bondholders should be assured that state and local governments can 'make good on their bonds', because 'they have many options from raising taxes or fees to reducing spending'. This certainly should reassure bond investors, but it does not answer the broader questions about the economic efficiency of their activities and the deadweight and opportunity costs involved in their spending and taxation.

State and local authority pension liabilities

Since the 1970s, state and local authorities have made annual contributions to their pension funds. The intention was that each year, a sufficient amount of money would be deposited in a trust fund to equal the future pension liability that their employees earned that year. On average, states pay 3.8 percent of their general or operating budgets into their pension funds. State and local authorities have used an 8 percent discount rate, which means their pension liabilities are fully funded if their investments return the yield achieved on pension fund assets over the previous two decades.

During the two recessions since 2000, some states and local authorities have reduced or failed to make the necessary pension fund payment to meet the 8 percent discount rate necessary to fully fund them. Given the cyclical character of their tax bases, in order to balance their budgets they cut pension fund contributions.

In addition, the recessions were associated with significant investment losses. In 2008, state and local pension funds in aggregate were funded at 85 percent of their liabilities. The Center for Retirement Research at Boston College, in the paper *The Funding of State and Local Government Pensions 2009-2013*, published in April 2010, by Alicia Munnell, Jean-Pierre Aubry and Laura Quinby, estimated that in 2010 these pension funds were funded for 77 percent of their liabilities and that funding would decline further to 73 percent by 2013. The Centre for Budget and Policy Priorities recognises that funding at around 70 percent of liabilities is a significant problem, but 'not an imminent crisis'. Quoting the US General Accounting Office paper *State and Local Government Retirement Benefits: Current Funded Status of Pensions and Health Benefits*, the Centre takes the view that an 80 percent funding level is sufficient for public sector organisations, because bodies with tax-raising powers can use tax revenue to make the pension payments if there is a shortfall in the fund. In that sense, public sector pensions are in a different position from private sector pensions, where a company can go out of business. That is why federal law under the Pensions Protection Act 2006 generally requires private companies to be 100 percent funded, so that the federal government does not have to make up any shortfall through payments into the Pension Benefit Guarantee Corporation.

A number of states have either skipped or reduced contributions to their pension funds. These include Illinois, New Jersey, Pennsylvania, Colorado, Kentucky and Kansas, and to a lesser extent California. Each of these states has either failed to make payments, reduced them or increased future pension liabilities without a commensurate increase in funding. They will have to make difficult policy choices to stabilise their future pension liabilities.

Are public sector pension fund liabilities and assets properly measured?

There is a difficult and complex debate about whether the actuarial rules used to design state and local government pension funds are appropriate and take full account of the character of the liabilities they have.

The argument turns on the discount rate used. This is important because 60 percent of pension fund revenues come from investment returns, and the discount rate helps decide how much money a state should put into the fund each year. The discount rate used and currently recommended by the Governmental Accounting Standards Board is 8 percent, reflecting the return on state pension funds invested in a mix of equities, bonds and property over the last 20 years or more. Some economists have started to question whether this is the appropriate discount rate.

Joshua Rauh of Northwestern University and Robert Novy Marx of the University of Rochester argue in their paper *Public Pension Promises: How Big Are They and What are They Worth?* published in October 2010 that a significantly lower discount rate would be more appropriate. Given that the pension is guaranteed, they argue the assumed growth of assets – that is to say the discount rate used – should also be similar and that of a so-called riskless rate, based on the returns available from US Treasury securities. Such a rate would be between 4-5 percent. In cash terms, the unfunded pension liability is $3trn when using a discount rate based on risk free assets. In contrast, using the current discount rate of 8 percent the unfunded liability is $700bn.

What public sector pension fund discount rate and what contribution rate?

If states were to use a risk-free discount rate, they would have to make a greater annual contribution to their pension funds. They currently allocate 3.8 percent of their budgets to pension funding, and to meet the 8 percent discount rate contribution they would have to devote 5 percent of their operating budgets to pension contributions. In states that have grossly underfunded pension funds or agreed retroactive benefits without funding them – such as Illinois, New Jersey, Pennsylvania, Colorado, Kentucky, Kansas, and California – they would need to make significantly greater additional payments. For California it would be 7.3 percent, Illinois 8.7 percent and New Jersey 7.9 percent of their budgets. If all states and local governments were to fund pension funds at the risk-free discount rate of 5 percent, they would have to allocate 9 percent of their operating budgets.

The Center for Budget and Policy Priorities regards the unfunded pension liabilities to be long-term issues and state and local authorities have thirty years to manage these liabilities. Alicia Munnell et al point out that 'even after the worst crash in decades, state and local plans do not face an immediate liquidity crisis – most plans will be able to cover the next 10 to 20 years'.

Over 20 states have made changes to reduce the costs of pensions. The length of services required for a full pension has been extended. The factors that determines the ratio of salary an employee receives as a pension payment for each year of service has been reduced. The Center recognises that other issues, such as the retirement age, ought to be looked at. In general, it takes the view that changes to things such as the retirement age are long-term in that it should only be applied to newly hired employees. Some states have already increased employee contributions, particularly where state government employee contributions were low.

The main point that the Center makes is that there are awkward long-term funding issues in state and local pension arrangements and there are features of the systems' generosity and abuses that must be addressed. But these problems do not represent any kind of immediate fiscal crisis. Some states are already addressing these problems and more states will do so later in the economic cycle when governments are better placed to increase their pension contributions to tackle unfunded pension liabilities.

The core conclusion is: 'The evidence does not support the claim that states and localities are on the verge of bankruptcy because of unfunded pension liabilities.'

While this may be true, it does not address the important issue of the economic desirability of devoting such resources to public sector pensions – that is another question.

Public sector employee healthcare costs

An expensive part of state and local authority spending that is rising and is projected to rise further without discretionary action on the part of state and local authorities is spending on healthcare insurance for retired employees. Some public sector employers give their employees continuing health insurance when they retire. Usually, they try to bridge the gap between retirement and the eligibility for Medicare at 65 years of age. State and local governments, with a few exceptions, have made no provision for this expense by setting aside investment funds to finance it in the way they try to do for pensions.

The Governmental Accounting Standards Board in 2004 brought in rules that obliged public sector employers to estimate their future retirees' health insurance liabilities. While states have to estimate them, the Governmental Accounting Standards Board has no power to compel them to follow its recommendations. Most states still fund their health insurance on a pay-as-you-go basis from their general budgets. Robert Clark and Melinda Sandler Morrill in *Retiree Health Plans in the Public Sector: Is there a Funding Crisis?* published in 2010 estimate that the aggregate unfunded liability for retiree health insurance is $500bn.

Whereas state pension plans are roughly comparable, public sector retirement health insurance varies from state to state. In 2006, 14 states – Idaho, Indiana, Iowa, Kansas, Minnesota, Mississippi, Montana, Nebraska, Oregon, South Dakota, Washington, West Virginia, Wisconsin and Wyoming – only provided an implicit subsidy by allowing retirees to remain part of the health insurance plan, but required them to pay the full premium. The implied subsidy arises from the fact that the ability to participate in an insurance pool with younger and healthier members and pay lower premiums than if they had to buy individual insurance in market is a benefit in itself. Another 14 states – Alaska, California, Hawaii, Illinois, Kentucky, Maine, New Mexico, New Hampshire, New Jersey, North Carolina, Ohio, Pennsylvania, Rhode Island and Texas – paid the entire insurance premium for their retirees. The remaining 32 states had arrangements that fell somewhere between these. The pattern of benefit generosity does not appear to coincide with regional traditions, political tendency or degree of unionisation. States have a lot of discretion over the rules they choose to apply and can easily modify them.

Healthcare costs have risen faster than GDP and they are projected to continue to do so. This means states that pay most or all of their retirees' health insurance premiums will either have to make significant cuts to service budgets or will have to raise taxes substantially.

The General Accountability Office, in a paper *State and Local Government Retiree Health Benefits: Liabilities Are Largely Unfunded, but Some Governments Are Taking Action* published in 2009, projected the costs of retirees' health benefits would rise from 0.9 percent of total operating revenues to 2.1 percent on average in 2050. Given that some states do not provide much in the way of health benefits in retirement, the proportion of operating budgets that will need to be allocated to financing them in states that are more generous will be significantly higher than the average figure suggests.

Unlike pension costs that are perceived to behave in a predictable manner based on actuarial tables, the future cost of health insurance is subject to much greater uncertainty. The Affordable Care Act 2010 adds to the uncertainty surrounding estimates of this future cost, given that it could lead to significant changes to insurance markets. The Center on Budget and Policy's judgement is that states should reconsider the healthcare benefits they offer retired employees and suggest that it may be better to modify their generosity, rather than to embark on pre-funding them and moving away from pay-as-you-go arrangements. What distinguishes this part of public sector employee compensation and benefits is that states have greater flexibility to ensure this aspect of public spending remains affordable.

Education spending growth and educational results

Education spending has been increasing as a share of national income since the 1980s. US Census Bureau data show that in constant (2009-2010) dollars, real spending on schools more than doubled, from $267bn in 1985 to $620bn in 2010. Historically, the US had the world's best education system. Secondary schools were free and generally accessible from the early part of the 20th century. In the 1950s, 80 percent of 15- to 19-year-olds were enrolled in secondary schools, compared to 40 percent in Western Europe. The US spends more on education than other developed economies. Overall spending is about 11 percent higher than the OECD average and spending on higher education is twice that.

For level of resource allocation, the results appear disappointing. Attainment by age for each new cohort joining the labour market has failed to keep up with the demand for educational skills. The *Economic Report of the President 2006* shows how the proportion of residents who had completed high school with a diploma had risen from 36 percent of the workforce in the middle of the 20th century to over 85 percent in 2005.

Table 9.1: Educational Attainment by Age, 1947–2004

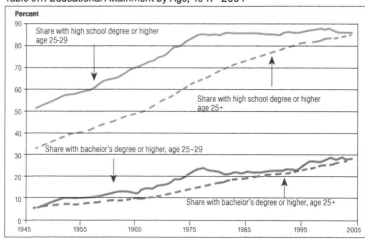

Source: *Department of Commerce (Bureau of the Census)*

Figure 9.2: Educational Attainment by Birth Cohort, 2007

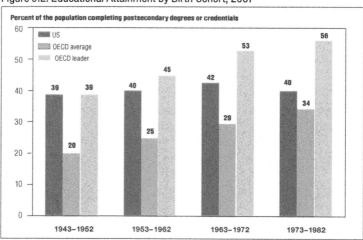

Note: Postsecondary degrees or credentials include only those of normal duration of two years or more and correspond to the Organisation for Economic Co-operation and Development (OECD) tertiary (types A and B) and advanced research qualifications US data reflect associate's, bachelor's and more advanced degrees.

Source: *OECD (2009)*

Table 9.1: Rankings of Selected Advanced Countries by Average Score on International Tests

Age 9		Age 13		Age 15		Last year of secondary school	
Math	Science	Math	Science	Math	Science	Math	Science
Hong Kong	Japan	Hong Kong	Hong Kong	Hong Kong	Japan	Netherlands	Sweden
Japan	Hong Kong	Japan	Japan	Netherlands	Hong Kong	Sweden	Netherlands
Netherlands	USA	Netherlands	Netherlands	Japan	Australia	Norway	Norway
USA	Netherlands	Australia	USA	Canada	Netherlands	France	Canada
Italy	Australia	USA	Australia	Australia	New Zealand	New Zealand	New Zealand
Australia	New Zealand	Sweden	Sweden	New Zealand	Canada	Australia	Australia
New Zealand	Italy	New Zealand	New Zealand	France	France	Canada	Germany
Norway	Norway	Italy	Norway	Sweden	Sweden	Germany	France
		Norway	Italy	Germany	Germany	Italy	USA
				Norway	USA	USA	Italy
				USA	Italy		
				Italy	Norway		

Note: The last year of secondary school is 12th grade in the United States but varies in other countries. In countries that track students, students in all tracks were tested in their last year of secondary school; the last year may differ within countries for students on different tracks. Students who dropped out of school before the last year of secondary school were not tested. Data are for 2003 except for last year of secondary school (1995).

Source: Department of Education (National Center for Education Statistics

Figure 9.3: Long-Term Trend Math Performance

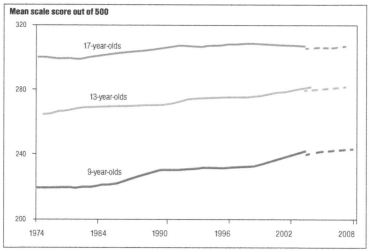

Note: In 2004 and thereafter, accomodations were made available for students with disabilities and for English language learners, and other changes in test administrtion conditions were introduced. Dashed lines represent data from tests given under the new condition.

Source: Department of Education (National Center for Education Statistics, National Assessment of Educational Progress (NAEP)

The proportion of residents with a bachelor degree rose to 29 percent of 25- to 29-year-olds. Until the 1980s, there was a consistent improvement in educational attainment from one generation to the next. Older workers with less education retired and younger, better-educated workers took their place.

Over the last 30 years the position has changed. The share of US residents aged 25 to 29 who have completed high school remains 85-88 percent. The composition of people completing high school, however, has changed. The proportion of them scored as completing high school by passing the general education development (GED) certificate, as opposed to the regular diploma, has made up a higher proportion of the people scored as high school graduates. Between 1988 and 1999, among 18- to 24-year-olds the ratio doubled to 11 percent. GED recipients experience lower levels of earnings and find it harder to get post-secondary education than conventional high school graduates.

Unlike high school graduates, the proportion of 25- to 29-year olds with a bachelor degree has continued to grow, but at a slower rate than 30 years ago. Between 1979 and 2004 the proportion of 24- to 29-year-olds with a bachelor's degree increased from 23 percent to 29 percent, a change of 6 percent. In the 25 years before 1979 it increased by twice that rate, by some thirteen percentage points. In 2002, half of young people in Canada and Japan had a bachelor degree. In contrast, in the US only 39 percent held one. Many students enter university, but fail to obtain a degree. In 2004, a quarter of adults had attended a post-secondary educational institution but not completed a bachelor degree.

The US Federal Department of Education conducts tests on maths, science and reading ability to assess how the US compares to other countries. Older students appear to perform worse relative to other developed countries than younger students do. By the age of 15, they are outperformed by most of their international peers. The US has conducted its own national testing of reading and maths since the 1970s for 9-, 13- and 17-year-olds as part of the National Assessment of Education Progress. These show the scores of elementary school students have increased, but the math and reading scores of 17-year-olds are largely unchanged. This was part of the reason why President George W Bush proposed the No Child Left Behind Act in 2002 to improve school performance. Under the act, states set standards to measure the progress made and schools must meet annual overall performance goals and specific objectives for different categories of students such as racial, ethnic and income groups.

Yet when President Obama's economists looked at these issues in the *Economic Report of the President* in 2010, little progress had been made. If anything, the National Assessment of Education Progress scores of 17-year-olds appear to have fallen slightly on a changed methodology. The report is particularly concerned about the poor performance of the US in terms of science, technology, engineering and mathematics (STEM). It notes that employers are not able to recruit Americans with the required skills for technical jobs and are forced to recruit abroad.

The report comments: 'Indeed, international comparisons show that other countries achieve higher outcomes in STEM skills than we do. In 2006, US 15-year-olds scored well below the OECD average for science literacy on the Programme for International Student Assessment, and behind most other OECD nations on critical skills and competences such as explaining scientific phenomena and using scientific evidence.'

It set out a clear analysis of what was wrong and how the US education system under-performs, but it is not clear that additional federal spending on specific programmes will remedy the issues. The states and local authorities are the government bodies with principal responsibility for education, and it is in the secondary schools that the problem is most acute. It appears that much of the American problem of relative international under-performance turns on matters such as teaching method and testing, not a lack of resources. If anything, the slowing rate and deteriorating quality of high school and university level graduation, in the context of high and rising spending, illustrates diminishing returns.

State tax systems

The principal source of state tax revenue is from sales taxes. State revenue systems were largely developed 40 or 60 years ago and have developed little since. In contrast, the structure of the economy has changed a great deal. The role of services now dominates the economy.

The Internet and telesales have made taxes bases more mobile. State tax policies have not adjusted to these changes. There is no comprehensive expenditure tax similar to the value-added tax regimes in place in the European Union at state or federal level.

Few states tax services adequately or on an equal basis with the taxation of tangible or physical goods. Internet sales are untaxed. The tax base of states has been narrowed because they have chosen to carry out a significant proportion of economic and social policy through tax expenditures instead of direct public expenditure. Good examples of this are the relief and tax breaks given to encourage economic development and to provide large tax exemptions for elderly and retirement income regardless of the level of this income.

State tax expenditures are expensive, yet spending through the tax code is rarely scrutinised with the care that conventional programme spending receives. Unlike most tax systems in developed economies where there is fiscal drag where tax revenues tend to be buoyant and rise faster than the increase in GDP, when the economy expands state tax revenue lags behind economic growth.

Economic forecasting and a pro-cyclical tax base

Most states do not have revenue or expenditure forecasts that can reliably project spending and revenue adjusted for inflation over a four- or five-year period. Given that state budgets are highly cyclical, this is a significant weakness.

Too often, policymakers at state level do not have the information they need to properly inform measures that will have a budgetary impact over several years. The Center on Budget and Policy Priorities believes that 'moving to accurate multi-year budgeting is one of the most important reforms that states can adopt'. *States' Revenue Estimating: Cracks in the Crystal Ball*, a joint report published in March 2011 by the Nelson A Rockefeller Institute for Government and the Pew Center on the States, analysed 23 years of data on personal income, sales and corporate tax estimates and revenue collections. States regularly make mistakes with their revenue forecasts and those mistakes are significantly greater in periods of fiscal stress.

There is a long-term trend where the revenue forecasting error has become greater and has increased during each of the last three recessions, and more states have made errors. In fiscal year 2009, the states overestimated revenue by over 10 percent. All three of the major sources of tax revenue were overestimated – personal income taxes by 9.7 percent, corporate incomes taxes by 19 percent and sales taxes by 7.6 percent.

Illinois exemplifies inefficient tax collection and poor fiscal practice

The Center on Budget and Policy Priorities has used Illinois to exemplify what can go wrong.

Illinois has a flat low rate of income tax that does not capture growth in incomes, and income tax rates often lag behind economic growth. Illinois relies heavily on a state and local sales tax that applies almost exclusively to goods and excludes almost all services. It is one of the states that exempts the largest share of income received by elderly people regardless of their income level from state income tax. It fails to examine its tax expenditures, its budget only considers the next fiscal year and policymakers make decisions without a consideration of their longer-term implications.

The result is that the state is chronically short of revenue. Payments of invoices on purchases are delayed. Pension fund contributions are either not made or funded through borrowing. Assets have been sold or securitised. As a result of the decline in revenue during the recession, a fiscal deficit for the financial year

2012 was initially projected equal to half of its general fund and the state has a large overhang of longer-term debt and unfunded liabilities.

The core problem of Illinois in the judgment of the Center of Budget and Policy Priorities is not spending, but a revenue system in need of modernisation. The state has chosen a level of expenditure but not put in place the tax system necessary to finance it. There have been a succession of attempts to sort out Illinois's well-known budget problems, but gridlocked political institutions have prevented progress on them. In January 2011, Illinois increased personal and corporate income tax rates to close a portion of its budget deficit. Yet it still planned to borrow to make its pension contributions and has not tackled the fundamental mismatch between its revenue system and its spending programmes. It is a textbook example of public sector mismanagement.

It is not clear that all Illinois' financial problems are located in a defective and inefficient tax collection system. In common with state and local government as a whole, there are issues in Illinois concerning public spending and its efficiency that would not be resolved by a more efficient tax system. There are issues around the level of public expenditure, its affordability and efficiency and value for money in state and local government across the US. There are significant issues in public sector pay and benefits. There are also issues about the efficiency and productivity of the public sector.

Education and public school systems have, for many years, been subject to a debate about their quality and effectiveness that has centred on a discussion about the role of the teaching unions. It is part of the stimulus behind the charter school movement. Healthcare costs may be difficult for state governments to contain, but they cannot be seen as representing an efficient use of resources and value for money.

Conclusion

State and local government authorities in the US are distinguished by the range of institutions, agencies and polices that they carry out. There is scope for interesting policy experimentation and many examples of it. Both state and local governments exhibit interesting examples of direct democracy. This includes the direct election office holders, such as state attorney-generals, judges, auditors and sheriffs, as well as plebiscites on specific policies and decisions. They also have significant challenges in terms of efficiency, economy and effectiveness. There are particular problems with pay and public sector employee health and pension benefits and unrealistic pension investment provision. The requirement to balance budgets means that most states do not have the kind of borrowing and debt challenges that the federal government has, but there is growing evidence of state and municipal debt accumulation. The problems of Detroit, Orange County, and Illinois are egregious. They illustrate how fiscal mistakes have been made in many local communities. The refusal of the administration and the Congress to assist Puerto Rico initially to help avoid a potential $72 billion default on its General Obligation Bonds in 2016 was been interpreted as a signal from federal policy makers in both the executive and the legislature as a warning that Washington DC would not necessarily provide assistance to heavily indebted states such as California and Illinois.

Chapter 10

Public sector employment in the US

The traditional picture of public sector employment in the US is one where public sector employees may enjoy greater job security, but pay a price in term of lower wages and salaries, albeit slightly enhanced by good pension arrangements. As Lise Valentine and Richard Mattoon put it in *Public and Private Sector Compensation: What is Affordable in This Recession and Beyond* published in May 2009: 'For many years, the conventional wisdom held that public sector wages were lower than private wages so generous ancillary benefits were needed in order to attract and retain skilled workers.'

There is now evidence from the Bureau of Labor Statistics that suggests that total compensation averages now exceed those in the private sector. Over the past 25 years, there has been rapid change in the US labour market. The returns for certain skills have changed and some job categories have contracted or disappeared entirely. Manufacturing jobs have contracted, trade union densities in the private sector have fallen and with them identifiable trade union wage mark-ups have all but gone. The public sector throughout the US has been touched much less by these wider labour market changes. In the federal, state and local government, American public sector workplaces have experienced less change than in the private sector. Valentine and Mattoon show 'private sector benefits have gone through significant restructuring over the last several decades, while public sector benefits have largely remained the same.'

A strong trade union presence remains in the American public sector at all levels. The US Census Bureau's *Current Population Survey 2008* showed before the Great Recession that 40 percent of public sector workers were represented by a union, compared with 10 percent of private sector workers. A trade union wages mark-up or pay premium is observable and a range of defined pension and health benefits remained in place. The traditional picture of public sector pay may have been an example of misleading conventional wisdom even 25 years ago.

The Congressional Research Service published *Selected Characteristics of Private and Public Sector Workers* by Gerald Mayer in March, 2014. The note recognised that for both the federal and state and local governments the question of whether the pay and benefits of public workers are comparable to those of workers in the private sector is an issue. Among the ways budget deficits can be reduced, policy makers are considering the pay and benefits of public sector employees. The number of people employed in both the private and public sectors has increased steadily as the U.S. economy has grown. However, after increasing to 19.2 percent of total employment in 1975, the percentage of all jobs that are in the public sector fell to 15.7 percent in 1999.

Figure 10.1: Private and Public Sector Employment, 1955–2013 (in millions)

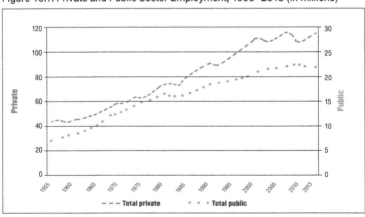

Source: Bureau of Labor Statistics, Current Employment Statistics survey

In 2013, public sector jobs accounted for 16 Percent of total employment. The recession that officially began in December 2007 and ended in June 2009 affected employment in both the private and public sectors. From 2007 to 2010, the number of jobs in the private sector fell by an estimated 7.9 million, while the number of jobs in the public sector increased by almost 272,000. As output recovered from 2010 to 2013, private sector employment grew by approximately 6.7 million jobs, while public sector employment fell by about 626,000 jobs. Reflecting the effects of the Great Recession between 2007 and 2009 on state and local governments the budgets, from 2010 to 2013, public sector employment as a share of total employment fell from 17 percent to 16 percent.

Figure 10.2: Public Sector Employment, by Level of Government, as a Share of Total Employment, 1955–2013

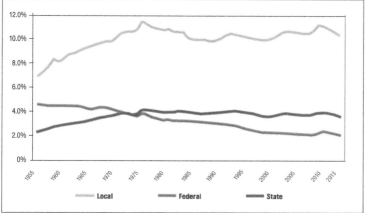

Source: Bureau of Labor –Statistics, Current Employment Statistics survey

The number of workers covered by a collective bargaining agreement is greater in the private sector than in the public sector. The percentage of workers covered by a union contract, however, is greater in the public sector. In 2013, 38.7 percent of all public wage and salary workers were covered by a collective bargaining agreement, compared to 7.5 percent of private sector wage and salary workers. Since 1983, the percentage of workers represented by a union has fallen in both the private and public sectors. In the private sector, union coverage fell from 18.5 percent to 7.5 percent of all wage and salary workers, a fall of 11.0 percentage points. In the public sector, union coverage fell from 45.5 percent to 38.7 percent of workers (a fall of 6.8 percentage points). In the public sector, the largest fall in union coverage was in the Postal Service, where coverage fell from 83.5 percent of workers in 1983 to 67.2 percent of workers in 2013, a fall of 16.3 percentage points. In the rest of the federal government, coverage fell from 29.4 percent to 22.4 percent, a fall of 7.0 percentage points. Coverage fell from 51.0 percent to 44.1 percent among employees of local governments, a fall of around 6.9 percentage points and from 35.9 percent to 33.8 percent among state government workers, a fall of 2.1 percentage points.

Today, it is plain there is a premium in public sector pay and benefits and it is provoking debate. During the Great Recession this led to an argument about whether American public sector workers are now the 'pampered' segment of the US labour workforce. Some economists associated with think tanks such as the Heritage Centre, the American Enterprise Institute and the Manhattan Institute have looked at the differences in the employment experience, levels of pay and benefits and the growth of pay during the recession and have drawn a stylised picture of the sharp difference between people who work for the private sector and people who work in the public sector, concluding that by every labour market measure, public sector employees have done quite well and as a whole the public sector has expanded during a time when the private sector contracted. An expanded public sector during a deep and protracted recession is to be expected as a result of the operation of automatic stabilisers and the use of fiscal stimulus measures. But a permanently expanded public sector raises important structural challenges. As Michael Jahr of the Mackinac Center said, recent public sector policies could lead to the 'long-run hollowing out of the private sector, in other words we could be in the early stages of the "Detroitification" of the economy.

Figure 10.3: Union Membership Rates by Industry, 2002

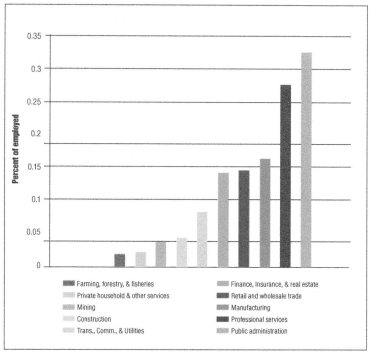

Source: Calculated by CRS from the monthly CPS

Figure 10.4: Union Membership Rates by Level of Government, 2003

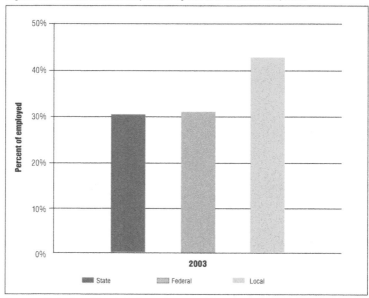

Source: Calculated by CRS from the monthly CPS

The assertion of a public sector pay premium is highly contested, particularly by public sector trade unions. President of the NTEU Colleen Kelley has challenged it, citing federal government statistics on pay produced by the Office of Personnel Management. These suggest that federal employees earn 22 percent less than private sector workers doing comparable jobs, a figure very much in line with the traditional perception of public sector pay.

Comparing like with like

Public sector employees are likely to have characteristics that are different from the labour market average. Public services throughout the world have to employ people with above-average levels of skill and education to carry out their functions, such as senior administrators, scientists, teachers and social workers.

The *Occupational Employment Survey and the National Compensation Survey* published by the US Bureau of Labour Statistics in 2007 showed that two-thirds of public sector jobs are professional and administrative compared with 51 percent in the private sector. Some 20 percent of private jobs were in low-paid, often part-time sectors such as retail sales and food services compared with only 2 percent in the public sector. So it is important to ensure that comparisons of pay are made on a like-for-like basis that adjusts for skill, education, experience and age. Crude comparisons that suggest that average federal employee pay is double that of the average private sector employee are misleading.

Federal pay comparison

Andrew Biggs and Jason Richwine have looked at public-private sector pay differentials and, using different datasets and methodologies, draw similar conclusions from the statistics about pay. When adjustment is made to ensure that comparable occupations are being compared, federal employees earn significantly more than they would get in the private sector. James Sherk of the Heritage Foundation found that after making adjustments for observable skills and other characteristics, average hourly cash earnings are 22 percent higher in the public sector. When other employee benefits are included, the average public sector compensation package is 30-40 percent higher than in the private sector. Federal pay rises automatically with seniority, irrespective of performance. President Obama's suspension of annual cost of living adjustments does not affect these pay increments.

Among the benefits that federal employees receive are more expensive health benefits, both a defined benefit and a defined contribution pension plan and full retirement at 56. Health benefits continue in retirement. Significantly more paid leave is taken by federal employees than by private sector workers. A federal employee with three years on the job receives all 10 federal holidays, 20 paid holiday days and 13 sick leave days a year. Federal employees enjoy greater job security than private sector employees, something exemplified by an increase in federal employment – not including the postal service – of 231,000, around a 12 percent increase in the federal labour force. Private sector employees are five times more likely to get laid off than federal workers. Turnover among federal employees is lower than among private sector employees. As well as greater job security, federal employees leave their jobs at one-third the rate of private employees.

The pay differential between federal and private sector workers is not uniform. In general, the pay premium is concentrated at the bottom end of the skill distribution and is quite large for low-skilled workers. For highly skilled workers it is negligible or negative. High-level skills are under-rewarded, and because of this the pay level for certain senior federal government and specialist positions is below efficiency levels in order to attract and retain appropriate employees.

Each year the federal government makes an assessment of the relative pay of its employees compared with the private sector. The President's Pay Agent compares wages in various occupations and at different levels of responsibility. On average, federal positions pay 22 percent less than the private sector. That does not mean that federal employees earn less than they could in the private sector. Andrew Biggs shows that federal employees often hold a grade or position higher than they would in the private sector. He uses the example of an accountant – for example, a senior federal accountant might only qualify as a junior accountant in the private sector, because in the private sector they would be under-qualified for the job. The Congressional Budget Office concluded the average federal employee is placed two-thirds of a pay grade above a similar private sector employee. One academic study identified a larger gap of three-quarters of a grade.

In 2008 the President's Pay Agent's report recognised the limitations of its approach: 'We continue to have major methodological concerns about the underlying model for estimating pay gaps'.

The first report on pay made by the Obama administration omitted this rider. The Office of Personnel Management has stuck to the figure that federal government positions underpay 22 percent compared to the private sector, which is clearly implausible. It has, however, indicated it will now look at the way federal salaries are determined.

Some federal employees do not receive Social Security on retirement. At a glance, this might appear a disadvantage, but it is balanced by the fact that just as they receive no Social Security benefit they are not obliged to pay payroll Social Security taxes. There is a high degree of progression within the US federal Social Security system so that someone on average earnings pays more taxes into it than they get back out in benefit. For an employee to not participate in Social Security is a benefit, because they will retain a greater proportion of their lifetime earnings.

In 2012 the Congressional Budget Office published a study of federal government pay *Comparing the Compensation of Federal and Private-Sector Employees*. It concluded that after accounting for identifiable differences in the characteristics of the workers being looked at that the federal government paid two percent more in total wages than it would have if average wages had been comparable with those in the private sector. On average for workers at all levels of education, the cost of hourly benefits was 48 percent higher for federal civilian employees than for private-sector employees with certain similar observable characteristics.

Table 10.1: Average hourly compensation of Federal Employee relative to that of Private-sector Employees, by level of Educational Attainment

	Difference in 2010 Dollars per Hour			Percentage Difference		
	Wages	Benefits	Total Compensation[a]	Wages	Benefits	Total Compensation[a]
High School Diploma or Less	$4	$7	$10	21%	72%	36%
Bachelor's Degree	About the same	$7	$8	About the same	46%	15%
Professional Degree or Doctorate	-$15	About the same	-$16	-23%	About the same	-18%

Note: CBO compared average hourly compensation (wages, benefits, and total compensation, converted to 2010 dollars) for federal civilian workers and private-sector workers with certain similar observable characteristics that affect compensation–including occupation, years of experience, and size of employer–by the highest level of education achieved.

Positve numbers indicate that, on average, wages, benefits, or total compensation for a given education category was higher in the 2005–2010 period for federal workers than for similar private-sector workers. Negative numbers indicate the opposite.

a. The differences shown for total compensation may not equal the sum of the differences for wages and benefits because of rounding to the nearest dollar and because of the composition of the samples used by CBO.

Source: Congressional Budget Office

The most important difference between the federal government and the private sector is the generosity and cost of the pension arrangement that employers makes available to the employee. The most important factor that determines differences between the two sectors is the cost of the federal government's the defined-benefit pension plan that is available to most federal employees. This sort of pension plan is becoming less common in the private sector. CBO's estimates of the costs of benefits are more uncertain than its estimates of wages, primarily because the cost of defined-benefit pensions that will be paid in the future is more difficult to quantify and because less-detailed data are available about benefits than about wages

The CBO study shows that after adjusting for education all levels of federal employees are paid higher wages than in the private sector, apart from the very top of the government service. Among people whose education culminated in a bachelor's degree, the cost of total compensation averaged 15 percent more for federal workers than for similar workers in the private sector. Among people with a high school diploma or less education, total compensation costs averaged 36 percent more for federal employees. Among employees with a professional degree or doctorate, total compensation costs were 18 percent lower for federal employees than for similar private-sector employees, on average. The federal government paid 16 percent more in total compensation than it would have if average compensation had been comparable with that in the private sector, after accounting for certain observable characteristics of workers.

Table 10.2: Federal and Private-sector Wages, by level of Educational Attainment

	Average Wages (2010 dollars per hour)		Percentage Difference in Average Wages between Federal and Private Sectors
	Federal Government	Private sector[a]	
High School Diploma or Less	23.50	19.40	21
Some College	27.10	23.60	15
Bachelor's Degree	35.30	34.80	2
Master's Degree	41.20	43.40	-5
Professional Degree or Doctorate	48.50	63.20	-23
All Levels of Education	32.30	31.60	2

Note: wages are measured as an average hourly rate and include tips, commissions, and bouses.

a. Average wages for private-sector workers who resemble federal workers in their occupations, years of work experience, and certail other observable characteristics likely to affect wages.

Source: Congressional Budget Office

The earning premium that federal and state and other public sector workers enjoy is not a recent phenomenon. It has been apparent for more than two decades. There is a body of academic literature on the subject of federal pay being higher than in the private sector. Alan Krueger, who served as assistant secretary for economic policy at the US Treasury Department and chair of the Council of Economic Advisors in the Obama administration, made a seminal contribution to it in his book '*Are Public Sector Workers Paid More than their Alternative Wage? Evidence from Longitudinal Data and Job Queues*' in *When Public Sector Workers Unionize*, published in 1984, comparing wages of similar private sector workers who had joined the federal government and looking at how their wages workers changed after joining.

State and local government pay and benefits

In December 2009, the Bureau of Labor Statistics reported that state and local government paid on average $39.83 per hour worked for total employee compensation. Some $26.24 was paid for wages and $13.60 was spent on employee benefits. In the private sector, average employee compensation was $27.49 per hour – $19.45 for wages and $8.05 for benefits. These figures imply a public sector compensation premium of 45 percent relative to the private sector. These figures are headline raw data comparing the private and state and local government public sectors. While the scale of the premium should be treated with caution, it is plain that this part of the public sector enjoys a pay and benefits premium of between 10-20 percent.

During the Great Recession, public sector employment compensation grew more rapidly than that of the private sector. Between 2006 and 2009, the employer cost index for state and local government employees rose by 9.8 percent whereas for the private sector it rose by 6.9 percent. In the Manhattan Institute paper Two Americas: Public Sector Gains In Recessions, author Josh Barro shows how public sector pay and benefits have increased and explores some of the reasons why. Strong compensation growth is partly explained by public sector contracts negotiated before the recession. In New York, state employees were scheduled to receive a 4 percent wage increase each April under a contract signed in the middle of the previous decade.

In December 2015 the U.S. Bureau of Labor Statistics published is regular report on *Employer Costs for Employee Compensation*. A research product generated out of the National

Compensation. It suggests that since the Great Recession state and local government employers have taken steps to reduce the generosity of their employment packages, but a significant identifiable public sector premium remains. The survey, measures employer costs for wages and salaries, and employee benefits for nonfarm private and state and local government workers. Total employment compensation that scores wages as well as benefits, such as pension entitlements, health insurance and paid leave was 33.8 percent higher for state and local authority employees than in the private sector. Wages in state and local government were around 20 percent higher than in the public sector. Employer costs for employee compensation for civilian workers averaged $33.37 per hour worked in September 2015. Wages and salaries averaged $22.88 per hour worked and accounted for 68.6 percent of these costs, while benefits averaged $10.48 and accounted for the remaining 31.4 percent. Total employer compensation costs for private industry workers averaged $31.53 per hour worked in September 2015.

State and local government employers spent an average of $44.66 per hour worked for employee compensation in September 2015. Wages and salaries averaged $28.45 per hour and accounted for 63.7 percent of compensation costs, while benefits averaged $16.21 per hour worked and accounted for the remaining 36.3 percent. Total compensation costs for management, professional, and related workers averaged $54.02 per hour worked. This major occupational group includes teachers, averaging $60.92 per hour worked. Total compensation for sales and office workers averaged $30.83 per hour worked and service workers averaged $34.02. The role that benefits plays in enhancing the total employee compensation of state and local authority employees is illustrated in BLS's table.

Table 10.3: Relative importance of employer costs for employee compensation, September 2015

Compensation component	Civilian workers	Private industry	State and local government
Wages and salaries	68.6%	69.7%	63.7%
Benefits	31.4	30.3	36.3
Paid leave	7.0	6.9	7.3
Supplemental pay	2.8	3.3	0.8
Insurance	8.9	8.2	12.0
Health benefits	8.5	7.7	11.6
Retirement and savings	5.2	4.0	10.4
Defined benefits	3.2	1.7	9.5
Defined contribution	2.0	2.2	0.8
Legally required	7.6	7.9	5.9

Most of the national debate in the US has concentrated on federal government pay and pensions, but the perception that pay and benefits are more generous in the public sector than the private sector goes further. Similar comparisons are made about the employment compensation packages of state and local government employees and about their pension arrangements in particular. Biggs argues that it is not simply that public sector pensions are more generous in terms of their benefits, but also in terms of the contributions that public sector employees have to make to get those pension benefits. In the private sector, employees generally receive pensions based on defined contributions, but in the public sector they receive defined-benefit pensions. A public and private sector employer contributes $5,000 towards the pension of an employee every year. In the private sector it goes into a 401(k) account and the individual either gets a low-risk and low-benefits return, or by investing in government bonds gets a higher expected return with a larger risk. In the public sector, the government promises a high return and takes all the risk. As Biggs said: 'A public sector worker with the same amount of money going into pensions, gets higher benefits. That is how a public employee can get benefits twice as high for each dollar of contribution as a private sector worker.'

In 2015 the BLS reported that trade union density in the US is much greater than in the private sector. In its annual report Unions Members 2015 published in January 2016 uses data on union membership collected as part of the Current Population Survey (CPS). The CPS is a monthly sample survey of about 60,000 eligible households that obtains information on employment and unemployment among the nation's civilian non-institutional population age 16 and over. There are some 14.8 million union members in the US. Union density varies significantly among the states. New York continued has the highest union membership rate 24.7 percent, while South Carolina had the lowest at 2.1 percent.

Public sector workers had a union membership rate of 35.2 percent. That is more than five times higher than that of private sector where 6.7 percent of workers were unionised. Public sector is more unionised than the private sector. Trade union density in the public sector is 37 percent, while it is only 7 percent in the private sector. Public sector employees are also more likely to have their pay regulated by multi-year contracts.

Some public sector employers, however, chose as a matter of discretionary policy to agree substantial pay awards as the economic crisis began to become apparent. The day after Lehman Brothers filed for bankruptcy in September 2008, the Mayor of New York Michael Bloomberg announced agreement on a new contract that gave 4 percent annual pay increases for city employees. Government agencies subject to binding arbitration arrangements for settling pay disputes have also faced higher employment costs. Mass transit agencies in New York and Washington DC have recently been obliged to enter into new employee contracts that had significant wages increases, aggravating the budgetary positions of both those organisations.

Andrew G. Biggs and Jason Richwine published an American Enterprise Institute study of state employment compensation *Overpaid or Underpaid? A State-by-State Ranking of Public-Employee Compensation* in April 2014 Their analysis found that the average US state pays salaries that are around 12 percent below those paid by large private-sector employers for similarly-skilled workers. This confirms the traditional belief that public employees receive lower salaries than private-sector workers. They point out that single national average obscures the considerable variation from state to state. They identified a 23 percentage point gap between the lowest paying state – New Hampshire, with a public-employee wage penalty of 21 percent – and the highest-paying state, Connecticut, with a wage premium of 2 percent.

In the average state, state government employees receive a total compensation premium of around 10 percent relative to private-sector employment. Biggs and Richwine found that because the most populous states pay larger premiums, the average state government employee receives a slightly larger compensation premium. There is substantial state-to-state variation means that national averages do not yield meaningful information. For instance, they point out that pay differentials range from a compensation penalty of 6 percent in Virginia to a premium of 42 percent.Biggs and Richwine's research found that state government employees in most states receive greater total compensation than similarly educated and experienced private-sector employees, who work for large employers. Public-employee wages in nearly all states fall below those paid in the private sector, but fringe benefits – in particular health and retirement benefits – are significantly more generous in government than in the private sector. In addition, public employees in every state have greater job security than they would likely enjoy outside of government. The compensation premium is not uniform across the nation. Many states pay government employees at market levels. Others were found to pay 'huge premiums, and still others fall somewhere in the middle'. Large differences between the states makes 'broad generalizations and national-level analyses' awkward and 'are not especially useful' to the policymakers. In Biggs and Richwine's judgement policy makers ought to make budgetary decisions based on an understanding of the circumstances in their own states. They make the point that analysis can inform those decision public employees such as teachers do not always value the expensive benefits and may prefer to trade some portion of their very expensive benefits for higher cash salaries and that there may be scope to negotiation a more cost effective public service in state governments that is more closely aligned with the preferences of state employees.

Employee pension and health benefits and long-term concern about cost pressures

The cost of public sector pensions represents a central part of the concerns about the long-term fiscal viability of much of state and local governments' present spending and tax law. The central argument is that state and local government provide their employees with pension and healthcare benefits and have not made sufficient actuarial provision to match the future costs of those benefits. This lack of realism has partly been exposed by the loss of financial assets during the crises between 2008 and 2009. Concern over unfunded pension liabilities has provoked a debate about the extent to which states and local government in the US do not just face an immediate fiscal crisis that is a product of the Great Recession, but also face chronic budget problems representing a substantial structural problem rooted in state and local government pension liabilities.

Valentine and Mattoon's paper summarises conference papers presented at the Federal Reserve Bank of Chicago's conference on public sector pay and benefits. These papers and presentations illustrated the extent of modern public sector pensions and health benefits. For example, 60 percent of part-time state and local government employees receive pension benefits and two-thirds receive automatic cost of living adjustments – now unusual in the private sector. The recent financial crisis has shown the value of a defined-benefit pension plan that transfers investment risk from the employee to the employer. A presentation by Allen Steinberg of Hewitt Associates illustrated the dramatic erosion of private sector pension provision. In 1998, 68 percent of Fortune 500 firms had some form of pension plan – by 2008, this had fallen to 42 percent. In the same period, privately provided retiree health insurance before Medicare eligibility at 65 fell from 88 percent to 27 percent. In contrast, 80 percent of public sector employees have a defined benefit pension plan and 75 percent receive some kind of retiree medical subsidy.

There are good reasons to take the view that the funding challenges of public sector pension funds are essentially longer-term challenges than an immediate fiscal crisis. This is very much the view of the Center for Budget and Policy Priority. Its paper *Misunderstanding State Debt, Pensions, And Retiree Health Costs Create Unnecessary Alarm* recognises there needs to be reform of state and local pension provision and that abuses within the system need to be corrected. The central feature of the public sector system that needs to be looked is the retirement age. The Center argues: 'It is difficult to defend a system where public employees can retire at age 55 with a pension after 25 or 30 years of service, particularly if their work is not physically arduous, while the age for receiving full Social Security benefits is set to increase to 67'.

The paper also identifies specific abuses all state and local governments need to address. These include the scope that employees and managers have to inflate the pay of employees in the year or two before retirement, so that on retirement the employee receives a bigger pension. Likewise, a number of states need to look at the provision of disability pension benefits 'to ensure only employees who are appropriately qualified can retire on a disability pension.' These are not the major source of financial stress to the system, but are recognised as abuses that are frequently publicised and undermine public confidence in the fairness and administrative efficiency of public sector.

The Center also recognises there are difficult funding issues that need to be managed, although it regards them as essentially longer term matters that are tractable. Probably a more radical agenda both to curb cost and to ensure greater equity between the public and private sectors is needed to improve the performance of the US economy. One obvious area to look at would be to consider moving away from a defined benefit final salary scheme to either benefits defined in relation to a career average or a move to defined contribution arrangements of the sort that the private sector increasingly uses.

A radical reform of state and local government pensions would be contentious. Even examining the retirement age would provoke intense political controversy. It would also raise arguments about the balance of compensation between wages and salaries and pensions and other benefits. While the raw data may suggest that public sector employees are paid over 45 percent more, once adjustments are made for skill, education and experience the disparity is not so large. Overall, some academic studies suggest public sector workers are, in terms of wages and salaries, paid between 4-11 percent less than private sector workers with similar education, job tenure and other benefits. This research includes work by Keith Bender and John Heywood in *Out of Balance? Comparing Public and Private Sector Compensation over 20 Years*, Center for State and Local Government Excellence April 2010 and John Schmidt's *The Wage Penalty for State and Local Government Employee*, published by Centre for Economic and Policy Research in March 2010. Higher-paid public sector employees appear to be paid less than their counterparts in the private sector, while low-wage state and local workers enjoy a pay premium. Taking account of more generous benefits and security does not eliminate the disparity between public and private sector compensation for all comparable jobs. Bender has referred to this as the 'double imbalance' where the public sector is over-paying for low-skilled workers and under-paying high-skilled workers

Most public sectors inevitably employ people with a range of specialist skills, which means the average earnings of public sector worker are likely to be higher than for that of the economy as a whole. In the US federal government and in state and local authorities, however, there appears to be a structure of pay, benefits, and pensions that do not reflect reasonable notions of efficiency pay. The greater presence of effective trade union power in the public sector means that public sector terms and conditions of employment have not adjusted to a changed labour market where there is a wider dispersion of earnings. Instead, pay and benefits have continued to reflect labour market conditions that prevailed more than a generation ago.

At the lower end of the skill distribution scale there appear to be significant earnings premiums, and overall within the public service at both the federal and state level there is a compression of pay differentials that mean higher-skilled positions are not consistently rewarded in a manner best suited to recruiting and retaining people.

Politics of public sector employment reform

Achieving reform is necessary, but will be difficult. The federal government's methodology for measuring and assessing the pay of its employees is plainly flawed. The Bacon-Davis Act that requires businesses receiving federal government contracts to pay the local union rate for the job makes federal programmes unnecessarily expensive and contributes to the channels through which federal spending crowds out local private sector spending. In addressing the details of the cost of pension benefits, state governments are highly constrained by their state statute law and constitutional procedures. Achieving effective reform in the states would be contentious and difficult. In most states, pension benefit entitlements for public sector employees require legislation to change the statutes setting out their details.

In Illinois, they are entrenched in the state constitution. Several Republican state governors facing substantial budget gaps and identifying structural defects in the details of pension contribution rates and wage bargaining procedures have embarked on ambitious and radical programmes of public sector employment reform. They have been highly contentious because they have focused on the fundamentals of state employee collective bargaining rights. Governor Chris Christie of New Jersey swiftly became a highly controversial figure and acquired a national political following in his own Republican Party.

Wisconsin's Governor Scott Walker's legislation proposed to raise employee contributions to pension and health benefits by 8 percent and was estimated to save $300m over three years. Collective bargaining rights would be limited and the right to strike would be removed except for wage bargaining. The Democratic opponents of the legislation, although a minority and unable to vote the legislation down, used a series of procedural devices to obstruct its passage. This included the need for a quorum in the legislature, to cast doubt on its legitimacy and lawfulness. The legislation was then subject to judicial review proceedings and was struck down by the court of first instance, on the grounds that its passage breached the state's legislative procedures for open meetings. That court decision was then overturned by the Supreme Court of Wisconsin. Democrats and unions then set about using the state constitutional procedures that allow voters to demand the recall of office holders who have displeased them after a certain period from their election date. Six Republican state senators who voted for Governor Walker's legislation were subject to recall elections, of whom two were removed from office. Governor Walker, who was elected in 2010, was subject to a recall election that he survived in 2012 and was re-elected as Governor in 2014. This was only the third gubernatorial recall election in U.S. history and the first and only recall that failed. Walker won the recall, his second face-off with Barrett, by a slightly larger margin 53 percent to 46 percent than in the 2010 election 52 percent to 46 percent and became the first U.S governor win a recall election.

Similar collective bargaining proposals were put to the ballot in a referendum proposed by Republican Governor John Kasich in Ohio in November 2011. These would have limited strikes and collective bargaining rights for all public sector workers and required state public sector employees to pay at least 15 percent of their healthcare premiums and 10 percent of their salaries as pension contributions. The Governor's proposals were defeated, with 61 percent of voters rejecting them. There was a national resonance to the Ohio result because of the state's swing role in presidential elections, Governor Kasich's high national profile and the national effort that organised labour made to mobilise voters against the measure. John Kasich is known for having been a former Republican chair of the House of Representatives' Budget Committee in the 1990s, the author of a book that was on the *New York Times* Best Seller List in 1998 and as a Fox television presenter. The response of union leaders was triumphant. Richard Trumka, president of AFL-CIO, was blunt in his appraisal of the situation: 'Ohio sent a message to every politician out there – go in and make war on your employees rather than make jobs with your employees and you do so at your peril'.

Harold Schaitberger, president of the International Association of Fire Fighters, called the vote 'absolute momentum-shifting victory for the labour movement'.

President Obama 'congratulated the people of Ohio for standing up for workers and defeating efforts to strip away collective bargaining rights, and commends the teachers, firefighters, nurses, police officers and other workers who took a stand to defend those rights.' Kasich accepted the result gracefully and later had little difficulty in being re-elected as governor in 2014 taking 64 percent of the vote and carrying 86 of Ohio's 88 counties.

Conclusion

The scale of public spending and the level of pay benefits means these issues cannot be avoided in relation to ensuring American public expenditure is financially sustainable and economically efficient. Much of the detail of the problems turn on traditional practices and entrenched trade union power in the public sector.

The principal objective should be to save money and increase efficiency, that does not necessarily require a direct assault on employees fundamental collective bargaining rights. What is required is greater realism about what is affordable. Public sector employment needs to reflect the wider changes that have taken place in the labour market over the last 35 years. The practical politics of managing and sustaining consent for the necessary reform agenda are difficult. Governors Christie, Kasich and Walker each acquired a national conservative following within the Republican Party and ran in the 2016 presidential primary cycle. Despite the fact that public service as a state governor with direct executive experience is widely perceived as a better preparation for holding the office of president than serving in the Congress, none of them obtained traction with the Republican primary selectorate. The US is not alone in these difficulties with public sector pay and pension costs – most of the advanced economies of the OECD, particularly the European economies have comparable structural problems in the public sector and similar practical political constraints.

Chapter 11

Healthcare

Spending on healthcare has risen dramatically over the past 40 years and is at the heart of America's long-term fiscal challenge. Healthcare spending is central to the federal government's unsustainable fiscal position and it is also central to the long-term fiscal challenges the states face. It also has implications for the performance of the US economy as a whole.

The challenges of health care go far beyond the contentious debate stimulated by the passage of the Affordable Health Care Act in 2010 and what a Republican administration and congress might do to replace that legislation. The cost of medical care imposes directs costs on the private sector through the costs employers face in making provision for employee medical benefits. Healthcare also imposes costs in terms of taxation to finance Medicaid and Medicare, along with the wider costs businesses face that arise from a population of working age that does not have comprehensive access to affordable healthcare and a public health environment that does not match contemporary best practice among advanced economies.

The level of healthcare spending, its growth and the dispersion of access to healthcare, combined with healthcare statistics in terms of morbidity and mortality, suggest that the US healthcare market is inefficient. It exhibits high levels of rent-seeking and other distortions. The principal feature of the system is third-party payments. Public policy, by providing tax expenditure subsidies to employer-based health insurance, encourages over-consumption of healthcare. This arises where a patient is advised by a doctor on a course of action and a third-party, such as an insurance company or a government-financed insurance programme such as Medicare, then pays the bill.

There are also fundamental issues that go to the heart of how a profession should conduct itself and how it should be regulated to secure an appropriate service for the public. Medicine is different from other goods and services. There are asymmetries of information that make the user of the medical service in the US vulnerable to financial and other exploitation. The differences between medicine and the basic flaws in conventional market-based insurance for medical care were summarised by Kenneth Arrow in his seminal article 'Uncertainty and the welfare economics of medical care', published in the *American Economic Review* in December 1963.

Many of the questions involved are beyond the scope of a book focusing on the performance of the American economy. They swiftly stray into complex arguments about clinical governance, how best to manage complex health conditions towards the end of life and go to the very fundamentals of medical ethics, technology and what it means to be human. As Garry Gensler once said when he was under-secretary for domestic finance at the US Treasury Department these 'questions are above my pay check'. This book will only touch on them where they raise questions about efficiency, productivity and equitable and practical access to the kind of healthcare that is normally readily available in a developed economy.

No easy public health policy choices

Many people writing about US healthcare and analysing its deficiencies are often motivated by distaste for the use of the price mechanism, and can be starry-eyed about other healthcare models such as the National Health Service (NHS) in the UK. Throughout the OECD, different approaches have been taken to the provision of healthcare.

In the UK, a fully socialised system based on a centrally planned and controlled budget is at one end of the spectrum. The US is at the other end, making extensive use of private doctors, hospitals and insurance for the bulk of health provision. With European countries such as France, there are publicly arranged and managed social insurance system making use of private doctors and clinics.

There is no easy ideal model. All developed economies face difficult financial pressures and rising healthcare costs as a result of improving technology and an ageing population. Rising patient expectations also play a role in these fiscal challenges. Each system has merits and claims on the attention of open-minded policymakers. The outstanding achievement of the UK's NHS was to provide good public health and better than average outcomes in term of the management of morbidity or illness and mortality, while spending about one-third less on healthcare than total spending in most other comparable advanced economies and roughly half that in the US.

Other countries, operating with a social insurance model that makes greater use of private provision, offered patients' greater choice, higher standards of convenience, faster access to treatment and new technology. This was in marked contrast to the explicit rationing of access to healthcare in the UK. The NHS has traditionally controlled costs by rationing through waiting times. Patients with non-life threatening treatments, often with painful and uncomfortable conditions that are difficult to manage without significant clinical intervention, would wait. Certain expensive treatments that offered little clear benefit in terms of patient comfort or life expectancy were simply not funded.

In countries such as France and Germany, waiting times were lower, access to care was easier and the choice and variety of treatment was more extensive. This came at a price – with about two or three extra percentage points in GDP being absorbed by government spending on healthcare. There were higher levels of patient satisfaction, but it was not clear that 'hard' clinical outcomes were significantly better in terms of morbidity and mortality than in the UK. Whatever defects the NHS may have, it has provided good-quality healthcare to the whole of its population at a relatively low cost. In terms of the resources it used, it was very efficient.

Planned health care systems such as that in the UK have found it increasingly difficult to adjust to change and respond to changing patient expectations and the opportunities presented by new technology. They have also often exhibited clinical vested interests that can have unexpected outcomes for a publicly funded health service. The UK's NHS, for example, has a bias towards acute medicine of the sort practiced by surgeons in a major hospital environment. Services directed at chronic conditions such as mental illness and services for elderly people have been relatively neglected and have acquired the term 'Cinderella services'.

While NHS care is provided freely at the point of use or 'delivery' and there are no co-payments – apart from a limited drug or prescription charge of $12 per item – there are still significant health inequalities. These are partly because of much wider social issues that relate to lifestyle, but many of them still directly relate to the inability of low-income households to have consistent access to good NHS General Practitioners (GPs) physicians based in the community and being able to access timely and good-quality diagnoses and specialist medical treatment.

The reason why it is necessary to set out some of these international comparisons of health care systems is to make clear there are no easy solutions to the complex challenges thrown up by healthcare. Technical progress offers a huge range of expensive potential interventions, with sometimes ambiguous results, and these have to be accommodated within limited resources. These limited resources are unevenly distributed, and also distributed in a way which has little correlation to either need or the capacity to benefit from medical intervention.

A trenchant critique of the defects of American healthcare should not lead to some kind of rose-tinted idea of what alternatives might look like, or that simply expunging the price mechanism or the profit motive would solve all the issues. Rationing will remain the central issue. The only question is the manner in which it is rationed. The removal of the use of prices from a healthcare system may offer a variety of benefits such as equity and improved access to treatment, but it would also involve a loss of some elements of efficiency. An administrative regime for allocating the use of resources outside the price mechanism would create its own distortions, losses of X-efficiency and cost inflation.

To say such costs would not result is mistaken. It is not impossible, but it would be a significant challenge to maintain productive efficiency in a setting where market prices and the disciples of bankruptcy are not present. The present role of profit, however, in American healthcare is its central problem. Medicine should not be practiced in a profit-maximising setting.

American healthcare does not appear to offer an optimal model. It exhibits true strengths, but these are more than exceeded by its flaws. It has an over-reliance on a private healthcare insurance model – model American policymakers too readily replicate and supplement when resources and policy are used to correct the market failures that healthcare markets inevitably exhibit.

Market failure in healthcare and the limitations of insurance markets

A critical market failure in the American healthcare market arises from the fact that income and wealth are unevenly dispersed. Many people who need healthcare do not have the money to pay for it when they need it. Insurance is a help in smoothing payment for health care over a working life, but insurance markets have limitations. Adverse selection means people who are ill or have a history of illness in their or their families' lives choose to buy it. People in rude good health often choose to forgo it. Insurance companies run the risk of insuring a pool of people that will exhibit greater than average morbidity or illness than the population as a whole. In addition, once people have bought insurance they will often exhibit a determination to use it. In short, there is a moral hazard.

They have got their insurance and may deliberately seek a more extensive procedure where a simpler one or none may have done just as well, or they opt for the most expensive physician or hospital the insurance will pay for. It may take a more remote form – a kind of confidence that the combination of medical technology and an insurance company to pay any bills may mean a person incurs greater risks with diet and other habits.

There is an asymmetry of information between the customer and the insurer. The insurer cannot accurately assess the behavioural risks of each person it insures no matter how hard it tries. These factors mean that insurance companies have to charge more for the healthcare they are offering. To control their costs and to prevent patients from exploiting the system, insurance companies must limit the benefits they offer and the payments they make. They avoid insuring medical conditions a person already has and limit the amount of care that they will pay for. Large catastrophic health events may not be fully insured and insurance will not properly cover long, protracted chronic diseases of the sort associated with old age.

Private health insurance can cover limited, discrete and clinically uncomplicated events such as a broken leg, a cataract operation and a hip replacement. What private insurance cannot cover is continuous medical treatment of the sort people need towards the end of their lives. Or to be more precise – insurance companies cannot offer such cover at an affordable price to all households. All but the richest households would probably find such premiums a problem in very old age.

Unfortunately, we tend to need medical care more when we are older. At precisely the time when insurance companies begin to exclude many of the conditions people start to encounter – or alternatively, price premiums so high that they are unaffordable to most people – is when these services are needed by the individual the most. The need for medical care no longer takes the form of the limited discrete episodes that private insurance can deal with at a reasonable cost as age progresses. Most of the healthcare people consume is needed in the final two years of their lives. In the US, three-quarters of all healthcare provided through Medicare is consumed in the final 18 months of life.

Doctors are different

Medicine is different from other goods and services, not just in the pattern of its consumption and the challenges it presents in terms of how a person pays for it, but in terms of how it is supplied. There is a fundamental asymmetry in knowledge and understanding between the doctor and the patient, which is much more pronounced that in most other market transactions. This is further aggravated by the fact that the patient is ill and less able to make an informed judgment than normal, and they and their families and friends are likely to be emotionally and psychologically vulnerable – prepared to try anything that is suggested to them.

This provides clinical practitioners with the scope to both over-prescribe treatment and charge heavily for their services, with the result that doctors can extract an economic rent. There is incentive and opportunity to prescribe frequent, complex tests and treatments that are expensive and may not yield benefits to the patient that are comparable to their cost. The patient is not in a position to properly assess the clinical judgment being made. The public, of course, are well aware of this. Bernard Shaw described the medical professions as conspiracies against the public and it is an old axiom that 'doctors bury their mistakes'.

Historically, modern medicine recognised it is a service that cannot be sold like other products or services, because the public have to be protected from unscrupulous practitioners. That is why in the 19th and early 20th century rigorous professional rules were established. These had two purposes. The first was to ensure that doctors were properly trained, knew what they were doing and carried out their work to a high and reliable standard.

The second was to ensure they did not impose charges and interventions that were unreasonable.

One of the most important things was to ensure operations or drugs were not prescribed unnecessarily, so that the patient was protected against over-payment and inappropriate clinical intervention. Special professional rules were constructed to protect the public from doctors. These rules overrode any sense of caveat emptor or conventional market considerations, even at the high point of laissez-faire liberalism, because it was recognised that medicine was different.

Healthcare provision has to be an area where governments intervene. Public action is necessary to ensure proper standards of care. Medical practitioners should not be allowed to exploit the asymmetry of information between them and their patients. Public policy and money is needed to ensure people have access to healthcare over their lifecycle, given that it is needed at times when people may not expect or may not be able to work at the end of their lives. And low-income people and households must to be given access to it.

The result is large-scale public intervention in terms of both regulation and public spending, and often direct public organisation of health provision. Governments in different developed economies set about these challenges in different ways, but they all exhibit high levels of public intervention, regulation and expenditure. America is no exception.

US public spending on healthcare

The *Budget of the US Government Fiscal Year 2017* shows that in 2016, total federal government outlays for health programmes were estimated to be $1,236.8bn. This accounted for 31.3 percent of the federal budget and 6.7 percent of GDP. It included $685.1bn spent on Medicare, $367.2bn on Medicaid, $47.9bn on defence medical programmes, $67.7bn on medical care for veterans and other spending on health programmes, such as medical research, training and consumer and occupational health and safety.

Figure 11.1: Projected Increase in Health Care Spending Until 2030

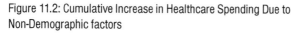

Sources: European Commission (2009), US Congressional Budget Office, IMF, and IMF staff estimates

Figure 11.2: Cumulative Increase in Healthcare Spending Due to Non-Demographic factors

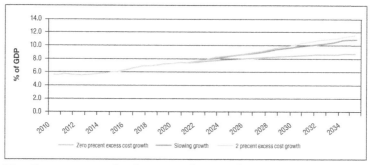

Note: Excess cost growth refers to growth in spending per beneficiary above GDP per capita growth.

Sources: Congressional Budget Office, "The Long-term Budget Outlook", June 2010

Figure 11.3: Projected Federal Health Spending as Percent of GDP Under Various Assumptions about Excess Cost Growth, 2010–2035

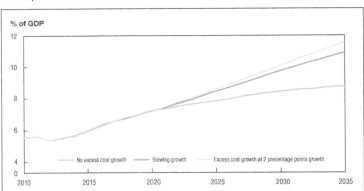

Note: Excess cost growth refers to the extent to which the growth rate of annual health care spending per beneficiary is assumed to exceed the growth rate of normal gross domestic product per capita.

Sources: Congressional Budget Office

In addition, the federal government engages in tax expenditures that significantly subsidised the provision of private employer-based health insurance for employees. *Budget of the US Government Fiscal Year 2017 Analytical Perspectives* document identifies twelve individual income tax expenditures. Health-related tax expenditures amounted to over $300bn in 2016. The federal government pays for about two-fifths of all healthcare. A further fifth is paid for by state government in their contributions to match the funding of federal government programmes such as Medicaid. Overall, the public sector in the US funds around two-thirds of US healthcare.

Through the public and private sectors, America spends some $2.9trn – 17.4 percent of GDP – on healthcare in 2013, 3.6 percent more than in 2012. The main problem is its expense. This is closely followed by efficiency, overall outcomes that are disappointing and a lack of access to good health care for many households.

The system has inadequate control over professional standards and insufficient government regulation to control costs. The acute problem of doctors' fees, which have steadily been increasing over the last 30 years, is a relatively recent phenomenon. It emerged in the 1970s and was given a powerful fillip by litigation over the regulation of professional fees of lawyers practicing at the Virginia state bar in 1975. Arnold Relman, in *Second Opinion 2007*, explained how this case, eventually decided by the Supreme Court, fundamentally changed American medical practice and drove a coach and horses through the framework of rules for professional conduct that had previously governed medical costs and operated to restrain them.

In *Goldfarb v Virginia State Bar* 421 US 773 (1975), the Supreme Court held that lawyers and by extension doctors were a profession engaged in interstate commerce and should therefore be subject to antitrust or competition law, which until then they had largely been exempted from. In late Arnold Relman's judgment, the decision did not initiate the commercialisation of American medicine – but it accelerated it and gave it legal justification.

After medical organisations lost some other competition law cases, in 1980 the American Medical Association (AMA) changed its guidelines and announced that medicine is both a business and a profession. The AMA began to allow doctors to participate in any legal profit-making business arrangement that did not harm patients. This turns on its head the proposition that patients need to be protected against professionals in a unique position to exploit their vulnerability. This was exacerbated by a market where the patient would normally be passing the bill for care on to a private insurance provider or government arranged insurance such as Medicare.

Medical industrial complex

In the 1960s, America increasingly turned to insurance-based healthcare solutions. The federal government established Medicare. At the same time, employer-based insurance was developing because of the tax relief that it had enjoyed since the 1940s. The combination of large-scale publicly funded insurance programmes and extensive private employer-provided medical insurance, created in response to the tax subsidy and often 'gold plated' in its coverage, provided huge opportunities for private investors in health care.

The private health insurance system covers some 170 million people under the age of 65. The health insurance industry is estimated to have revenues of between \$700 and \$750bn. Its profits and management costs absorb between 15-25 percent of this. In contrast, the Medicare insurance programme run by the federal government has administrative expenses of about 3 percent. Where insurance cover is provided for Medicare patients by private insurance companies, such as through the Medicare Advantage plan, the cost to the federal government is about 13 percent higher than standard Medicare coverage. A much lower ratio of private insurance is spent on actual provision of care, and the cost of providing an appropriate level of care for people under 65 is probably higher than if the same cover were provided through a publicly provided social insurance scheme.

Both private insurance and the publicly organised insurance programmes provide huge opportunities for medical providers and hospitals to make profits. There are few effective constraints on clinicians' billing, either in terms of the level of charges or the number of tests, treatments and therapies. If anything, there are powerful incentives that act as a stimulus to both medical activity and cost.

Hospital-employed specialist doctors are in a position to prescribe tests and therapies, confident that the bill will be met by third parties in the form of publicly or privately financed insurance. The system lacks regulation to check excessive costs and is fuelled by the moral hazards that accompany insurance, whether it is social insurance or private insurance, and further aggravated by an expensive and highly distorting tax subsidy. The result is that American healthcare delivery is dominated by a complex web of business, insurance and hospital and doctor interests that exhibit high degrees of rent-seeking.

Normally, public policy attempts to curb such behaviour. In the US, public policy not only aggravates it, but is a significant cause of it. Arnold Relman invoked the memory of President Eisenhower's famous television warning about the dangers of an *Industrial Military Complex* and describes this as the *medical industrial complex.*

Tax subsidy for employer-provided insurance

The Tax subsidy for employer-based insurance goes back to the 1940s. During World War II, the federal government imposed controls on prices as a wartime emergency measure. As part of that framework of inflation control, it also introduced wage controls. Inevitably, employers tried to find ways around the wage policy and started to compensate their employees with enhanced nonwage benefits and began to set up health insurance plans for their employees.

The War Labour Board ruled that wage and price controls did not apply to fringe benefits such as health insurance. This led many employers to set up such schemes. In the late 1940s, the National Labour Relations Board ruled that health insurance and other employee benefits were subject to collective bargaining. In 1954, the Internal Revenue Service (IRS) decided that health insurance premiums paid by employers were exempt from income tax. The origins of this tax relief can be traced back to the way the IRS treated a group of teachers in Dallas who contracted with a hospital to cover inpatient services for a fixed annual premium. In the post-war period this tax relief acted as a powerful stimulus to developments in employer-provided health care insurance. By the 1970s, it had become a central feature of the compensation package that went with corporate America.

The US Census Bureau report *Health Insurance Coverage in United States 2014*, published in 2015, shows that 175 million people have employer-sponsored health insurance. It dominates private medical insurance, accounting for over 83 percent of the private health insurance market.

The tax relief on employer-provided health insurance is a poorly focused subsidy, as Professor Jonathan Gruber, an MIT economist who has advised the Obama administration, pointed out in a *New York Times* article 'End a health insurance subsidy' in 2012. In terms of the distribution of income, it is regressive as the households that pay the most in income tax gain most from it. Three-quarters of the benefit is received by people in the top half of the earnings distribution.

Like many narrowly focused tax expenditures, it has had a highly distorting impact on economic behaviour. First, it created the incentive to establish insurance plans that are unnecessarily generous in their range of benefits, resulting in over-consumption of scarce resources and increasing overall healthcare costs. Second, it created serious distortions in the labour market, contributing to the creation of internal and segmented labour markets by making it harder to change jobs once a person worked for a company offering healthcare benefits – not least because a person with existing conditions would not get new cover from another employer's plans. As a result, people found themselves locked into employment contracts. Third, it made it more expensive for an individual to take out personal insurance over their lifetime until they reached 65 and then coverage through Medicare and increased the opportunity cost of doing so.

There are several reasons why people do not have health insurance. It is expensive and they cannot afford it. There are good reasons to have reservations about the extent to which it will pay out in the event of an expensive or protracted condition. People may not obtain coverage because of pre-existing conditions even when they want health insurance and are willing to pay for it. Young people who are not working for an employer that provides health benefits often do not have coverage, especially if they live alone and do not have children. Many young people up to the age of 26 will be effectively covered by their parents' health insurance. And older people who have lost their jobs and with it their health insurance often cannot afford or cannot obtain coverage until Medicare kicks in.

As well as the egregious issues of obtaining coverage for existing conditions from insurance companies and the unilateral cancellation of existing health insurance policies when a person becomes ill, there are a broader set of issues that relate to value for money that deter people from taking out insurance. As well as high premiums, the combination of exclusions, matched payments, and limits on payment create uncertainty about what kind of insurance a person is getting. Co-payments are not necessarily a bad thing and can play an important part in preventing over consumption of health care, but they are often exploited to make insurance bad value for money for individual consumers. These are, of course, the kind of issues that go to the heart of the limitations and defects of a private insurance markets.

Work by Jonathan Gruber modelling the effects of tax subsidies suggested that at any one time some 16 percent of people below the Medicare entitlement age would not be eligible for a tax subsidy for health insurance. What is interesting is that as wealth and incomes have increased, far from the proportion of the population without health insurance falling it has risen. This probably reflects long-term changes associated with the contraction of large manufacturing employers with high unionisation, exemplified by the Detroit motor manufacturers. Employer provision of health insurance correlates closely with the size of the firm. Ninety-seven percent of corporations employing over 100 people offered health insurance, but only 40 percent of firms with fewer than 25 employees offer it. But it also reflects the expense and limitations of insurance market and the perception that it was not worth the money. In *Is Health Insurance Affordable to the Uninsured?*, Kate Bundorf and Mark Pauly showed, before the passing of the Affordable Healthcare Act, that while a significant proportion of uninsured adults between 25 and 65 years of age could afford cover, it was affordable for between a quarter and three-quarters of them. They concluded 'that for a large proportion of uninsured people, health insurance is a matter of choice'.

Thomas Buchmueller and Alan Monheit in *Employer-Sponsored Health Insurance and Health Reform* (NBER Working Paper 14839) looked critically at employer-based changes and explore why workers choose to purchase their healthcare through their employers rather than the individual market, given that workers pay for health benefits through reductions in wages. They show how employer-provided schemes can partly overcome some of the defects of insurance, such as the problem of adverse selection, by pooling risk over more people. There are economies of scale and of course the tax subsidy. Small firms find it more expensive and harder to control costs.

Relative efficiency of US healthcare

America devotes over 17 percent of its GDP to spending on health. In 2006, healthcare expenditure was 15 percent of GDP compared with 11 percent in France and Germany, 10 percent in Canada and 8 percent in Japan and the UK. The US spends almost 50 percent more per person on healthcare than the next highest-spending country. This spending does not appear to buy better health outcomes than in other countries.

Samuel Preston and Jessica Ho explore this in their paper *Low Life Expectancy in the US: Is the Health Care system at Fault?* (NEBR Working paper 15213). Life expectancy lags behind that in other developed economies. Life expectancy, for a 50 year old is 3.3 years lower than Japan and 1.5 years lower than in Australia, Canada, France, Italy, Iceland, Spain and Switzerland.

They point out that the association of disappointing outcomes and high spending should be treated with caution, given that health outcomes depend on a much wider range of personal behavioural issues such as diet, exercise, smoking and so on. They assess two diseases, cancer and cardiovascular disease. What they establish is that these diseases are more aggressively tested for and treated in the US than in Europe. And there are better outcomes that follow from those aggressive interventions in terms of patient survival prospects. A reduction in mortality from prostate and breast cancer have been exceptionally rapid in the US compared to other comparable societies. They conclude that the system works well to reduce mortality from important causes of death such as cancer, but that it is 'possible that the US healthcare system performs poorly in preventing disease in the first place'.

They also recognise there could be great inefficiencies in the system resulting from misallocation of doctor and patient incentives and the practice of defensive medicine. Medicine and healthcare face a slightly more challenging hurdle than other comparable care systems in advanced economies. Healthcare outcomes tend to be worse for low-income households and the US has a wider dispersion of earnings and incomes than other countries.

Not all studies conclude that the more aggressive treatment of diseases such as prostate cancer result in improved outcomes that match or justify the spending. David Cutler in *Where are the Health Care Entrepreneurs? The Failure of Organisational Innovation in Health Care* (NBER Working Paper No 16030) explores the causes of inefficiency and why it has not been eliminated by market forces. He shows how productivity has been much slower than in other sectors of the economy.

In most sectors of the American economy, productivity has come from new ways of organising production, distribution and sales. There has been little organisational innovation in healthcare. Most success has been associated with more intensive care or interventions to treat more severe patients. Cutler shows how 'flat of the curve medicine' has increased where the provision of additional Medicare and intervention results in little to no health benefit. He points out that in the US when treating heart attacks, patients are 10 times more likely to receive coronary bypass surgery or balloon angioplasty than patients in Canada – but have no better outcomes.

A second source of inefficiency is poor co-ordination of care. Many conditions need to be managed by a non-specialist GP, with period visits to a specialist and regular tests and management of a medication regime. There are poor guidelines on how this should be planned and co-ordinated. Where there are such regimes, such as for the treatment of diabetes, fewer than half of patients with diabetes receive the recommended treatment plan – leading to greater future complications and expense. Cutler concluded that one-third or more of US health expenditure does not result in improved health outcomes. This translates into excess spending of over $700bn each year.

US healthcare appears to be no better in its overall outcomes than other systems. Alan Garber and Jonathan Skinner in *Is American Health Care Uniquely Inefficient* (NBER Working Paper 14257) distinguish two forms of efficiency.

The first is productive efficiency that addresses the amount of health produced from a bundle of doctors, nurses, hospital beds and other inputs. The paper found that productive efficiency is relatively poor because similar outcomes are produced with much higher spending in the US than in other countries. The production care function appears to be flat, meaning that consuming extra healthcare services yields little or no benefits.

The second is that the US may also be on lower healthcare production than other countries. Identifying production functions in healthcare is difficult because so many factors, such as genetics and behaviour, affect international variations of outcome. Four proxies are used to make comparisons in the paper – the proportion of elderly people receiving immunisation against flu, the ratio of primary healthcare physicians using electronic medical records and administrative costs per capita. The US is average on influenza vaccination, but has the highest proportion of chronically sick elderly people skipping vaccination on grounds of cost. The country lags behind in the use of electronic records and per capita administrative costs. The cost of administration cannot explain differences in spending between the US and other countries because they are not sufficiently large, nor do they explain why health spending is growing more rapidly in the US.

The concept of allocative efficiency enables economists to explore the extent to which Americans may consume 'too much healthcare'. The US is average for number of acute hospital beds, practicing doctors per capita and use of prescription drugs. But it has much greater access to certain investigative technology than other countries. The number of MRI machines per capita is five times as that in other advanced economies. The rate of invasive and expensive treatments such as heart procedures and the intensity of care per day of hospitalisation is higher in the US than in other countries.

Garber and Skinner look at the literature on the cost effectiveness of health spending to form a judgment about whether American spending represents value for money. They conclude most of the gains in survival in recent decades have come from improvements in health behaviours and from low-cost interventions, such as use of aspirin and beta-blockers in heart disease. Improvements in health outcomes in the US have increased life expectancy at roughly the same rate as in other countries. The diffusion and use of new technology is fuelled by favourable reimbursement rates from insurance programmes and 'are the most compelling explanation for the more rapid rise in healthcare costs in the US'.

There are dramatic inequalities in the US healthcare systems in use of resources by region, social and economic status, and race and insurance coverage status. If care were provided uniformly, health outcomes would be vastly improved. The adoption of better electronic record keeping and more comprehensive insurance coverage could also improve health outcomes for the population as a whole. Such changes would save some additional lives and enhance productive efficiency, but they would not reduce expenditure overall.

To address the central cost problem will require improvements in allocative efficiency. What sets the US apart is a combination of incentives for the over-use of some services and under-use of others in a predominately fee-for-services system, coupled with few supply–side constraints.

Tort and health ligation costs

The high cost of healthcare is aggravated by the effect of the wider litigious character of American culture. Costs are particularly increased by the way courts award damages in civil tort cases. The issue of the operation of tort law in the US is a much wider problem than the way it impinges on the practice of medicine and spending on healthcare.

The potential costs of litigation are widely perceived to encourage so-called defensive medicine, where doctors send patients for additional tests and treatments that may not be necessary in terms of strict patient treatment but protect the doctor from an allegation of negligence. The rules governing tort damages vary from state to state. Ronen Abraham, Leemore Dafny and Max Schanzenbach in *The Impact of Tort Reform on Employer-Sponsored Health Insurance Premiums* find that where states have introduced measures to cap non-economic damages and tort reform there is a reduction in treatment intensity and healthcare expenditures generally.

Arnold Relman's judgement in *A Second Opinion* was certainly correct – American healthcare costs are not centrally driven by litigation costs, although litigation aggravates costs at the margin. He pointed out that litigation costs amount to $7bn. In the context of public and private spending on health, that totals $2trn. Even if the full indirect costs coming from 'defensive medicine' are between $50-$80bn, the tort and litigation system cannot be identified as the principal driver of cost or potential source of control. That observation does not in any way diminish public interest in reforming tort law and litigation procedures to contain its cost.

The Affordable Health Care Act

In March 2010, two significant pieces of legislation were passed that significantly modified and will shape future healthcare in America.

The Patient Protection and Affordable Health Care Act and the Health Care and Education Reconciliation Act required every resident in the US to have health insurance from 1 January 2014. Failure to comply when the legislation was fully implemented in 2016 carries a financial penalty. Single people on a low income will have to pay $695, while a high-income household will be fined up to $12,500.

There are three features to the legislation that intended to broaden access to healthcare in the US. There was a substantial expansion of Medicaid and new tax credits to subsidise the cost of health insurance premiums for low- and middle-income families and small businesses. In each state, exchanges will be established to facilitate the purchase of health insurance and the delivery of subsidies. Where companies do not provide insurance and their employees have recourse to the subsided care, they could be fined. Existing health insurance will be regulated to guarantee access to health insurance regardless of pre-existing conditions. The Congressional Budget office estimated that after 10 years the number of non-insured, non-elderly people will fall by more than 30 million, from 54 million to 23 million. Overall, this expansion in coverage costs is estimated to cost $900bn.

Jacob S Hacker, in his 2012 article *'Health care reform 2015'* in *Democracy a Journal of Ideas*, describes President Obama's healthcare legislation in comparative terms: 'Medicare was a model of simplicity – a single national programme automatically enrolling a defined population and dealing with a few key stakeholders, most notably hospitals and doctors whose main interests were higher reimbursements. By comparison, the ACA looks like a Rube Goldberg contraption. Its basic structure mixes state and federal responsibilities, competing administrative centres of authority and public and private activities in a manner that can be charitably described as complex'. He argues the best way of describing it is as three pillars of coverage, supported by a foundation of regulations and spending.

The first pillar is an upgrade to Medicaid, the state-run programme of healthcare for low-income households. Medicaid will be expanded to most non-elderly residents of the US with an annual income below 138 percent of the federal poverty guideline, often called the federal poverty level. In 2009 the federal poverty level was $10,830 for a one-person household. The states will need to identify the people who are eligible for the expanded benefit and ensure coverage, which means finding doctors and hospitals prepared to take on patients that cannot pay. Many states already have difficulty in doing this and deliver these services poorly. They will continue to perform poorly after the reform is fully implemented.

Individuals that do not have health coverage through Medicaid, other federally funded insurance such as Medicare or employer-provided health insurance will have to take out insurance or pay a fine. This is a particularly contentious aspect of the legislation that some Republican state attorney generals have challenged in the federal courts as unconstitutional.

There are a significant number of people exempted from the fine, and these include households with low incomes below the federal poverty level, people who have been offered insurance that is considered unaffordable (if the premium exceeds 8 percent of a worker's salary), someone experiencing hardship in obtaining cover, where a lacuna arises in cover such as when changing jobs (provided it is no more than for three consecutive months) and all Native American tribes. The Congressional Budget Office and Joint Economic Committee of Congress estimated that 13 to 14 million of the 21 million non-elderly people who will still be without health insurance will fall into in these categories of exemption. There is also be an exemption for religious beliefs.

The second pillar is the creation of new health exchanges that will allow small employers and people without employer-based coverage to choose among regulated private insurance plans, with much of the premium for low- and middle-income people financed by federal government subsidies. Individuals and families with incomes between 138 percent and 400 percent above the federal poverty level are be eligible for a new health insurance premium assistance tax credit.

The intention was that state governments would set up these exchanges by 2014. If they did not establish them, the federal government would set them up directly. States can work co-operatively to set them up, which may help small and rural states. And the federal government will establish at least two private health plans, one of which should be not-for-profit, to provide coverage on a nationwide basis which will be offered through the exchanges.

The third pillar is employer-provided insurance. People will be covered by regulated and subsidised private employer-based insurance. Large employers with more than 50 employees will have to provide minimum cover for their employees or pay a penalty or fine. The terms of the employer-based insurance will be regulated and eventually the tax subsidy going to them will be limited. The Affordable Care Act, in Hacker's judgment, 'gradually transforms the present voluntary, regulated and subsidised system of workplace insurance into a less voluntary, more regulated and less subsidised system'. The Affordable Care Act relies on states to expand coverage and to regulate the insurance market with the result that the act is in 'essence not one reform law, but a framework within which as many as 50 could blossom – or wilt'.

The assumption of the Congressional Budget Office that an additional 30 million people will be insured at a containable cost to the federal government that is modest in the context of US healthcare costs relied heavily on the assumption that all existing employers carry on providing their present insurance benefit for their employees, even if their plans are subject to new rules. The improvements in insurance benefits envisaged by the regulation will raise the cost of insurance premiums, which may reduce the willingness of employers to provide insurance at all. Employers could simply opt out and pay the $2,000 penalty for not offering insurance. This is why many existing employer plans that may not meet future regulation standards have been 'grandfathered' in.

Most employer insurance plans including plans offering limited coverage for low-wage employees, such as the coverage offered by Wal-Mart, passed the regulatory test and were grandfathered in. Provided a plan covers 60 percent of a person's health costs, it will meet the test of the regulation. The current average coverage of medical costs is 80 percent. This means that under the regulations, an employee could be expected to meet 40 percent of a medical bill as well as a share of the insurance premium contribution.

The grand bargain

At the height of the debate surrounding the extension of health insurance, President Obama called a meeting of the main players involved at the White House and a 'grand bargain' was struck. The meeting was described as a 'watershed' moment. The health insurance industry would reduce costs by $2bn over a decade. Health insurance companies would face more regulation and greater competition, but in exchange would get access to millions of new customers as a result of federal subsidies and the legal requirement to hold health insurance. A few days later, however, the health insurance industry and the American Hospital Association told the *New York Times* that a specific level of savings had not been promised and that any savings would be more gradual. Arnold Relman in a 2009 article in the *New York Review of Books* entitled *'The health reform we need and are not getting'*, describes the Grand Bargain as an episode 'best described as part of the industry's strategy to appear supportive, more by words than action, hoping thereby to fend off legislation that would seriously threaten health interests'.

Hacker also makes the point that costs may not be controlled by increased competition, because if anything the medical industrial complex is getting more concentrated. There appears to have been a consolidation of both the demand health insurance side of the market and a consolidation of the provider or supply side in terms of hospital ownership and large physicians groups.

Affordable Care Act Implementation

The provisions of the Affordable Care Act took effect in 2014. The US Census Bureau's *Health Insurance Coverage in United States 2014* published in September 2015 reports an expansion in the number of people covered by health insurance. The percentage of people without health insurance coverage decreased sharply between 2013 and 2014 by just under 3.0 percentage points, specifically, by 2.9 percentage points. After several years of a relatively stable uninsured rate between 2008 and 2013. The percentage of the US population who had no health insurance coverage during the entire year, changed from 13.3 percent in 2013 to 10.4 percent in 2014. The passage of the Patient Protection and Affordable Care Act (ACA) in 2010, included several provisions that have taken effect at different times. For example, in 2010, the Young Adult Provision enabled adults under age 26 to remain as dependents on their parents' health insurance plans. Many more of the main provisions went into effect on January 1, 2014, including the expansion of Medicaid eligibility and the establishment of health insurance marketplaces (e.g., healthcare.gov). Fall in the uninsured rates between 2013 and 2014 were consistent with the intended purpose of the ACA. In 2014, people under age 65, particularly adults aged 19 to 64 years, may have become eligible for coverage options under the ACA. Based on family income, some people may have qualified for subsidies or tax credits to help pay for premiums associated with health insurance plans. In addition, the population with lower incomes may have become eligible for Medicaid coverage if they resided in one of the 24 states (or the District of Columbia) that expanded Medicaid eligibility. During 2014, the state with the lowest percentage of people without health insurance at the time of the survey was Massachusetts (3.3 percent), while the highest uninsured rate was for Texas (19.1 percent) Six states (Massachusetts, Vermont, Hawaii, Minnesota, Iowa, and Connecticut) and the District of Columbia had an uninsured rate of about 7.0 percent or less. Three states, Florida, Alaska, and Texas, had an uninsured rate of about 16.0 percent or more.

Between 2013 and 2014, all 50 states and the District of Columbia experienced a fall in the rate of people without health insurance coverage in 2014. The fall in the uninsured rate between 2013 and 2014 ranged from 0.4 percentage points in Massachusetts to 5.8 percentage points in Kentucky. In states that expanded Medicaid eligibility "expansion states", the uninsured rate in 2014 was 9.8 percent, compared with 13.5 percent in states that did not expand Medicaid eligibility "non-expansion states".

The Congressional Budget Office and the staff of the Joint Committee on Taxation (JCT) projected that in 2016, the average premium for an employment-based insurance plan was about $6,400 for single coverage and about $15,500 for family coverage. Although premiums for private insurance have grown relatively slowly in recent years, they have usually grown faster than the economy as a whole and thus faster than average income. Over the period from 2005 to 2014, premiums for employment-based insurance grew by 48 percent for single coverage and by 55 percent for family coverage. Analysis of early regulatory filings by the McKinsey Center for U.S. Health System Reform reported in the New Times in 26 October 2014 found that insurers were proposing a median increase in premiums of 4 percent in 21 states for 'silver plans' health insurance plans. A 'silver plan' is a category of health insurance within the ACA. The different levels of cover are categories determined by the percentage the plan pays of the average overall cost of providing essential health benefits to members. The category of plan a person selects determines the total amount they are likely spend for essential health benefits during the year. The percentages the plans will spend, on average, are 60 percent (Bronze), 70 percent (Silver), 80 percent (Gold), and 90 percent (Platinum).

Some of the innovations of the legislation have not worked smoothly. The computer access to the on-line health insurance exchanges was initially overwhelmed and collapsed. The process of application was complex for many applicants. The attempt to bring in new players in the market by providing federal subsidies has also been problematic. Co-ops, an acronym for Consumer

Operated and Oriented Plan, were launched as part of the 2010 Affordable Care Act to help spur competition, increase consumers' options and lower premium prices for health insurance. Non-profit health insurance companies were intended to provide low-cost, high quality policies to individuals and small businesses. The rationale was that without the requirement to yield a return on investment, these enterprises would be able to compete against the major generally for-profit players in the market. In places where competition was limited the co-ops would help the market deliver better value for all consumers. They also had a political purpose in demonstrating the benefits of a public funded not for profit option within a policy. The federal government allocated $6 billion in loans to help these start-ups to get established. The amount of federal funding was eventually reduced to $2.4 bn. The co-ops were intended to create networks of doctors and to attract consumers by providing lower cost insurance. Providing insurance requires a strong balance sheet and capital that can absorb unexpected losses and meet the complex demands of insurance regulators.

The co-ops mainly sold their health insurance plans through the exchanges created by the Affordable Care Act. These often attracted customers who had not previously had health insurance. Some of these people had pre-existing medical conditions and were therefore expensive to insure. New customers with no history of health insurance are hard to asses in terms of risk. The start-ups cop-ops found it difficult accurately to cost the risk and how much to charge their customers. Their principal purpose was to offer more competitive and cheaper rates than existing insurance companies. As a result they frequently charged too little and did not have high enough revenue from insurance premiums to match their costs. Twelve of 23 co-ops set up collapsed having been estimated by Melissa Quinn in the Daily Signal (9 November 2015) to have received more than $1.2bn in federal subsidy. Department of Health and Human Services inspector general reported in June 2015 that 21 of the 23 co-ops lost money in 2014.

Since the passage of the Affordable Care Act in 2010 there has been a moderation in health cost pressures in the US. The legislation contained provisions to contain spending within Medicare and to limit tax relief given to expensive premium health insurance plans provided by employers to senior executives. There appears to have been a concerted response to the Great Recession that resulted in governments and employers trying to moderate health care costs. The demand for new medical services fell and individuals when faced with co-payment bills avoided elective procedures. Health cost pressures have moderated throughout the OECD economies. It is probably premature to attribute this moderation in cost pressures to the ACA.

There is some disappointment about the cost of health insurance coverage for low income households that do not qualify for Medicaid. In a Commonwealth Fund survey conducted in 2014, found that 44 percent of adults with incomes above 250 percent of the poverty level, or $29,175 for individuals, reported that they found it difficult to pay their premiums for market place plans, compared with 33 percent of those with incomes below that level. They receive subsidies to buy health insurance, but find that the subsidy is withdrawn as their income rises. Moreover, the insurance plan will often be quite basic with an initial high co-payment before any health care is paid for. Some people have decided to pay the penalty because the overall cost is less than that of an inadequate insurance plan they cannot afford. The ACA also has wider implications for labour market participation and labour supply. The CBO estimates that once it takes full effect and overall economic output nears its maximum sustainable level, the ACA will reduce the total number of hours worked, on net, by about 1.5 percent to 2.0 percent during the period from 2017 to 2024. This reduction in labour supply will almost entirely result workers will choosing to supply less labour in response to the new taxes and other incentives they will face and the financial benefits some will receive. The largest declines in labour supply will probably occur among lower-wage workers, the reduction in aggregate compensation (wages, salaries, and fringe benefits) and the impact on the overall economy will be proportionally smaller than the reduction in hours worked. CBO estimates that the ACA will reduce aggregate labour compensation over the period between 2017 and 2024 by around 1 percent period, compared with what it would have been. These effects are will continue after 2024 the end of the CBO current budget forecasting horizon and the CBO has not estimated the magnitude or duration of these effects over a longer period.

Health costs in increasingly concentrated markets

Hacker points out that the American Medical Association has found 99 percent of metropolitan areas have highly concentrated insurance markets. A single private insurer has more than 70 percent of the market in 24 out of the 43 states examined. A similar consolidation has taken place in relation to medical provision – hospital systems and group doctor practices are acquiring the monopoly power to raise prices even when they are dealing with large insurance companies.

In California, one study shows that payment rates to hospitals and powerful doctor groups approach and exceed 200 percent of the price Medicare pays. The rates have risen in double-digits in recent years. There currently appears to be little active use of regulatory power to control dominant health provider organisations or the concentrated health insurance market.

The Federal Reserve Bank held a conference on healthcare that it wrote up as part of its Chicago Fed Letter series as *New perspectives on health and health care policy* in July 2010. Among the papers presented, two provided evidence that corroborates Hacker's concern about increased insurance market concentration. Leemore Dafny of Northwestern University showed how mergers had consolidated insurance markets between 1998 and 2008. The Herfindahl-Hirschman Index increased by 31 percent. Dafny was careful to note that the role increased market concentration plays in raising insurance premiums is not clear. It can, for example, yield increased efficiency. Looking at the Aetna-Prudential merger in 1999 and using data on 10 million insurance premiums paid between 1998 and 2006, she concluded that overall insurance premiums rose 3 percent as a result of greater market concentration. James Hilliard of the University of Georgia looked at the effects of health insurance market concentration on stock market performance. Looking at data for 36 mergers between 1999 and 2007, he found that stock market prices rose in the sector as investors expected greater profits in a more concentrated sector. Hilliard's evidence confirms the anticompetitive effects of such mergers.

Containing administration costs

The Affordable Care Act has brought in rules to contain administrative costs. These are aimed at reducing the medical loss ratio (MLR) – the proportion of insurance that goes on administrative and marketing costs and costs other than medical care. Insurers will be required to ensure that at least 80 percent of premiums are spent on medical care and will have to pay rebates to consumers where the ratio is below 80 percent. The MLR has been falling since the 1990s, but on average the ratio is still 81 percent. Many insurers, however, spend less than 80 percent of premiums on care, particularly in individual and small markets where the ratio can be as low as 60 percent.

Hacker quotes the campaign pressure group Health Care for America Now that asserts that the six largest for-profit insurance companies would have had to provide $2bn in rebates. Limiting administration costs through this rule may offer a one-off reduction in one aspect of health insurance costs, but it is unlikely to stop the overall rise in health costs and over-consumption of healthcare. The insurance companies themselves will obviously 'game' the rules and already have started to. Functions that were historically scored as administration such as policing claims and denying them – loss adjustment expenses, fraud prevention and so on – are now being reclassified as 'care'. Some state regulators have said that they will exempt certain categories of insurers or alternatively phase these requirements over an extended period. It is likely the effective implementation of the final MLR rules will be much softer than the rhetoric of the statute would suggest.

The provision of healthcare in the US is fundamentally flawed in several ways: it exhibits classic market failure, over-consumption and under-provision of certain necessary services that constrain costs. Those failures are in many respects aggravated rather than remedied as a result of the present public policy intervention.

The Affordable Care Act and the public debate that preceded it addressed an important dimension of the US healthcare market's flaws, namely the high proportion of non-elderly people who are not covered by insurance. It partially remedies this, although its complex interaction with existing employer-provided cover and its tax credit subsidies with the income tax system has almost certainly result in unintended negative consequences.

What the Act does not address are the fundamental flaws in US healthcare provision. As Arnold Relman put it, 'the central problem is expense'. Healthcare is about twice as expensive per capita as in other developed countries and accounted for nearly 17 percent of US GDP in 2008 – and its costs are continuing to rise. The main reason for this cost is 'ever expanding use of expensive kinds of diagnoses and treatment such as new drugs, diagnostic tests, imaging methods and surgical procedures. Doctors in most other advanced countries have access to virtually the same resources, but use them less. This difference is partly explained by a higher proportion of specialists in the US, who rely more than primary care physicians and expensive technical procedures for their livelihood, and in general are much more highly paid than primary care physicians – one reason why primary care doctors are now in short supply. The American College of Physicians attributes much of the high cost of the US health system to its relative excess of well-paid specialists and lack of primary care doctors'.

About 20 percent of non-public general hospitals, almost all specialist hospitals and most facilities for patients such as walk-in clinics and ambulatory surgical centres are privately owned. They are medical businesses operating on a fee-for-services basis that have to satisfy their investors and make a profit. They must market themselves, generate clinical activity and expand revenues. This results in medical businesses that concentrate on the provision of profitable services rather than clinically cost-effective healthcare. It is a system that favours patients in a position to pay over those who cannot. Although even those fortunate enough to pay may find they are given healthcare that is clinically inappropriate. This is made worse by defensive medicine, where tests and procedures are routinely carried out to protect the doctor or hospital from expensive litigation although the test may be detrimental to the patient. The over-use of CAT scans is a good example.

The cost flows in the Affordable Care Act are complex. The two principal increases in public spending are the subsidy for the purchase of health insurance, estimated to cost an additional $350m over 10 years, and the expansion of Medicaid, which will cost $434bn over 10 years. These costs are projected by the federal government to be offset by expenditure savings in Medicare, including a 1-percentage-point cut on the indexation of Medicare payments for clinical procedures and an assumption that doctors and hospitals will in future exhibit the same level of productivity growth that the rest of the US economy has managed in the past.

There is also an additional hospital tax and a tax on incomes over $250,000 that is expected to raise $210bn. There is considerable scepticism about these cost estimates and the potential savings to be made in Medicare. The extent to which healthcare insurance can be extended at a cost of only $434bn, given the pace of medical cost increase and the regulations of the Act, should work to increase the cost of insurance to existing holders by limiting the scope for loss adjustment.

The Affordable Care Act fails to deal with the central problem in American healthcare: systematic market failure arising out of a profession that is not properly regulated. If anything, public policy operates in a manner that magnifies this. There is both over-consumption of medical services and under-provision of services to many individuals and communities. Many cheap and effective medical interventions that prevent future cost are not used, while over-use is made of complex expensive investigations and treatments that may be inconsistent with patient welfare. The Act attempted to deal with one significant dimension of America's healthcare challenge – the fact that a significant proportion of people under the age of 65 do not have proper healthcare insurance. It is not clear that compelling people to take up what to them are often expensive and inadequate health insurance policies that will fail to protect them and their financial assets represents a step forward in improving healthcare.

What it offered was new business opportunities for the medical industrial complex. It does little to curb health costs or to develop a set of public policies that remedy the fundamental flaws and limitations of insurance markets. And it does little to ensure that doctors as a profession are properly regulated in the interests of patients and the people footing the bill for health care be they private individuals, employers, insurance companies or taxpayers.

Conclusion: health costs and the American economy

Medical costs are central to understanding the public sector problems that the US faces. Escalating healthcare costs are at the heart of the federal government's budget problem, and are central to the long-term budget gap faced by many state governments. Medical insurance costs as part of employee benefits also impose an increasing competitive handicap on American employers.

That handicap was, until the passage of the Affordable Care Act, largely the result of the distorting consequences of an expensive and poorly targeted tax subsidy for employer-provided health insurance. Employers with more than fifty employees were compelled to provide insurance cover or pay a penalty. The costs of providing employer-based cover is likely to rise given that some of the devices used by insurance companies to limit cost – such as not insuring people with pre-existing conditions – will no longer be available to them. This will mean an already expensive burden on employers will worsen.

In addition, the phasing in and out of federal tax credits to subsidise the purchase of health insurance will inevitably exacerbate the distortion created by the high net rate of withdrawal of benefit which is already a damaging feature of the federal income tax and benefit system. It could potentially add between 1-1.5 percent to the permanent or structural rate of unemployment. This has significant implications for labour market incentives and will contribute to a wider change in a US labour market that is becoming less flexible. In looking at all the federal spending programmes, state and local government budgets and the direct employment costs and burdens on employers, as well as the consequences for labour market incentives of the Affordable Care Act, is hard not to avoid concluding that the structure and cost of health provision is a central issue and cannot be ignored and remains a central structural economic problem in the US.

It is not clear what the health policy of the Trump administration will be. In the presidential election campaign higher insurance premiums, which rose by some 24 percent played a role in attracting support to the Republican ticket that was pledged to repeal 'Obamacare'. In his regular policy tweets Donald Trump has reminded Republican members of Congress that repealing the Affordable Care Act is a priority for them to concentrate on. He has also tweeted his concern about the cost of prescription drugs criticising pharmaceutical firms. This suggests an element of policy pragmatism. The increase in insurance premiums and the narrowness of insurance pools (where insufficient numbers of young healthy people take out insurance raising its cost) and the threat that insurance companies may withdraw from the market, illustrate the unstable and defective features of the Affordable Health Act. The Trump administration may have some interest in trying to identify direct controls on health costs. Public health systems with a high degree of 'command and control' such as the UK's NHS, exhibit impressive control of costs. OECD data, for example suggest that the NHS spends roughly half the amount that US health care system spends on drugs per capita each year.

Chapter 12

American higher education

The American dream in the decades of prosperity following the end of the World War II was often exemplified by home ownership, a university education and rising overall real living standards. The feeling that something had gone wrong, that the dream was fading and that young people and their families would not do as well as their parents had done began to surface in the early 1990s.

An important part of this perception was not just the overall functioning of the economy, but the fact that households increasingly found certain things more expensive, such as healthcare.

One of those increasingly awkward costs was higher education. In cash terms, between 1985 and 2009 the cost of a full year's tuition rose by 4.3 times for a private institution of higher education, to $23,201, and by 4.6 times in a public sector institution, to $4,544. Over the same period income per capita rose around 2.7 times.

More households need higher education

The importance of good undergraduate – and often graduate or professional – education was emphasised by almost all public policy and media comment on the issue. In the academic year 2012-13 there were 4,726 degree awarding, so-called Title IV institutions. That is institutions that have a written agreement with the U.S. Secretary of Education that allows the institution to participate in any of the Title IV federal student financial assistance programs. Of the 20 million students attending them 86 percent were undergraduates. The number of undergraduates studying increased from 7.4 million in 1970 to 17.8 million in 2012. Thirty-four percent of these institutions were public institutions, 14 percent were public four year degree awarding institutions and 20 percent were public two-year degree awarding institutions the issue. Thirty-five percent were not for profit private institutions, 33 percent being four year degree awarding bodies and 2 percent two year institutions. Thirty-one percent were private for profit institutions. The role of the private for profit institution in American higher education has grown dramatically over the last fifteen years. In 2002-03 there were 791 private for-profit degree awarding institutions, in 2012-13 there were 1,451. In 2012 public two-year and four-year institutions accounted for 76 percent of all undergraduate students, about the same percentage of students as in 1970. The proportion of students attending private not for profit institutions has fallen from 23 percent in 1970 to 15 percent in 2012. The proportion of undergraduates enrolled in private for-profit institutions grew from less than 1 percent of the total in 1970 to 9 percent of the total in 2012.

President Bush in 1988 had not wanted to become the 'education president' for nothing. He was responding to both a technocratic policy agenda and political pressure. Massachusetts Governor Michael Dukakis, his opponent in the 1988 election, based his main platform on the need to improve education and training to equip Americans for a high-tech, competitive world where they would provide value-added goods and services. The message for families was clear – their children needed a higher education to succeed in this new world. The problem was the cost.

And the cost was rising. By the 1980s a clear earnings premium in the labour market had been identified for graduates. What was less widely appreciated, although it was recognised by many economists at the time, is that America's best universities had been adapt at ensuring that they shared in that potential earning premium by charging high tuition fees. At a Rand Corporation conference in 1994, Barry Bosworth expressed the proposition that 'Harvard is very good at taxation through fees'.

University fees have risen faster than healthcare costs

America has the best universities and institutions of higher education and research in the world. Whether it has the most efficient and productive universities in the world is another and more complicated question.

Over the past 40 years, the cost of higher education for American households and taxpayers has risen much faster than the consumer price index, healthcare costs or household income. University tuition fees since 1978 have risen over five times on average and household income has increased by just over one and a half times in that period.

If the relationship between median incomes and tuition fees that persisted between 1976 and 1990 were in place in 2008, the average annual cost of college tuition at a four-year institution would be more than $5,000 lower than the $12,975 average level of fees. And if the trend rise in fees to income ratio between 1994 and 2000 had been in place in 2008, fees would have been $3,000 lower. An interesting feature of this data is that the main episodes of relative price change were during the recessions when the economy was contracting between 1981 and 1982, 1990 and 1991 and in 2001. *Money Magazine*, looking at it very much from the perspective of what a person would have to save and invest to pay for a university education, calculated that tuition fees increased by 439 percent between 1982 and 2007.

Following the Great Recession *Trends in College Pricing 2015* reported that published tuition and fees increased at about the same rate in current dollars in 2015-16 as in the preceding two years. However, because the Consumer Price Index increased by less than 0.2 percent between July 2014 and July 2015, the inflation-adjusted increase was larger in 2015-16. Average published tuition and fees at public four-year colleges and universities increased by 13 percent in constant 2015 dollars over the five years from 2010-11 to 2015-16, following a 24 percent increase between 2005-06 and 2010-11. Average published tuition and fees at public two-year colleges and universities increased by 14 percent in 2015 dollars over the five years from 2010-11 to 2015-16, following a 13 percent increase between 2005-06 and 2010-11. Average published tuition and fees at private not for profit four-year colleges and universities increased by 11percent in 2015 dollars over the five years from 2010-11 to 2015-16, following a 14 percent increase between 2005-06 and 2010-11.

The Pell Institute at the University of Pennsylvania revised edition of *Indicators of Higher Education Equity in the United States* published in 2015 examines trends in the cost and access to a university education over a forty-five year period. This shows costs are not only rising but also borne increasingly by students and their families, as the portion of bill financed by state and local authority support has fallen. For students in the bottom income quartile, average costs after all grant aid represented 84 percent of the average family income. Given this trend it is not surprising that both the percent of students who borrow to pay college costs and the amount they borrow have risen significantly since the 1990s. Low income recipients of bachelor's degrees (as measured by Federal Pell Grant receipt) on average borrow higher amounts than other recipients bachelor's degree. Average tuition and fees at colleges and universities in the U.S. more than doubled in constant dollars since 1970, rising from $9,625 in 1970 to $20,234 to 2012-13. Relative to the average cost of attendance, the maximum Pell Grant peaked in 1975 when the maximum Pell grant covered two-thirds (67 percent) of average costs. The maximum Pell Grant covered only 27 percent of costs in 2012, the lowest percentage since 1970.

America now spends twice as much on higher education than the OECD average. In 2014, it devoted 2.7 percent of GDP to it compared to 1.3 percent in the OECD as a whole. The story of US higher education is similar to that of US healthcare. It spends, overall privately and publicly, a third more than the OECD average on healthcare, yet has disappointing outcomes given its level of spending. If anything, the position in higher education is magnified.

In 2000, the OECD in *Education at a Glance* published in 2013, ranked the United States second internationally with 30 percent tertiary type A attainment, essentially the BA degree. By 2012, the United States ranked 12th, with a 34 percent tertiary type A attainment rate. Between 2000 and 2012, the U.S. experienced a 13 percent increase in tertiary type A attainment. This represented a significantly slower rate of growth than the 30 percent average increase reported across other advanced OECD countries.

When tertiary type A and type B attainment are examined, tertiary B includes shorter two year vocationally and technically orientated courses, the United States was ranked 11th on this indicator in 2012, with a 44 percent attainment rate. This was up from 39 percent in 2000, but the U.S. rate of increase between 2000 and 2012 of 13 percent, was lower than the 36 percent average rate of increase recorded for other OECD economies. The average rate of attainment for OECD countries was 40 percent in 2012, up from 30 percent in 2000.

Compared to the rest of the developed world, more than twice as much is spent, the variation in quality of institution is greater and the performance is significantly worse. In some respects it is possible to argue that American higher education is even less equitable than healthcare, because where healthcare has Medicaid and ensures care for the most vulnerable, higher education is able to step around such issues.

State budgets have been under pressure for more than a generation and previously generous state funding for public universities has been progressively reduced. Universities have made up for this by charging higher fees. These fees land on the classic middle-income household these universities were originally established to serve. As public funding has diminished, the need to attract applicants able to pay the fees has risen, as has the need to attract endowment and scholarship bursary funds from alumni and wealthy individuals and corporations. The result is universities have branded and marketed themselves and have slowly downgraded and displaced the objectives that were previously central to their mission.

The Pell Institute at the University of Pennsylvania revised edition of *Indicators of Higher Education Equity in the United States* published in 2015 examines trends in the cost and access to a university education over a forty-five year period. This shows costs are not only rising but also borne increasingly by students and their families, as the portion of bill financed by state and local authority support has fallen. For students in the bottom income quartile, average costs after all grant aid represented 84 percent of the average family income. Given this trend it is not surprising that both the percent of students who borrow to pay college costs and the amount they borrow have risen significantly since the 1990s. Low income recipients of bachelor's degrees (as measured by Federal Pell Grant receipt) on average borrow higher amounts than other recipients bachelor's degree. Average tuition and fees at colleges and universities in the U.S. more than doubled in constant dollars since 1970, rising from $9,625 in 1970 to $20,234 to 2012-13. Relative to the average cost of attendance, the maximum Pell Grant peaked in 1975 when the maximum Pell grant covered two-thirds (67 percent) of average costs. The maximum Pell Grant covered only 27 percent of costs in 2012, the lowest percentage since 1970.

Branding and the American higher educational bubble

Universities building their brand out of financial necessity. They try to attract attention and go out of their way to push themselves up institutional rankings such as the US News and World Report Best College ranking.

Sport and a celebration of an institution's distinctive history are devices that are frequently used. Both can be expensive and contribute little to contemporary academic performance, yet they inflate an institution's cost base. Some institutions have felt compelled to borrow to improve things such as student and sports facilities, and hired trophy staff from football coaches to Nobel Prize winners. There are increasingly institutions with balance sheets that will not be sustainable in the medium-term.

The notion of an American higher education bubble has two dimensions, and both relate to the fees that institutions charge. The first is that universities with high cost bases will not be able to attract enough students who can afford to pay the bill, with the result that a significant number of presently independent institutions will have to close and merge. The second is that individuals who borrow to finance the present projected future fees simply will not be able to afford to do so and will default on their loans.

Affordability is not the only economic issue involved in American higher education. There are important issues that relate to productivity, efficiency and use of resources. The full cost of higher education in America is not simply its cash cost or the share of GDP devoted to it by the public and private sectors, but the full economic opportunity cost.

For many years American universities, particularly the elite universities, have been highly effective at creating a brand. This brand has been as much about access to social status as it has been about education and scholarship. It has been reinforced by the 'preppy' fraternity hall caricature of the Ivy League tradition and has been immensely successful. So successful, in fact, it has given the senior faculty staff and administrators of elite universities the opportunity to engage in systematic and large-scale economic rent-seeking. This results in significant and unjustified losses in X-efficiency across the American system of higher education as whole.

Tenured staff at many of America's best universities are in a position where they are well paid and have to do relatively little direct teaching. This enables them to concentrate on research, private non-university pecuniary interests such as consultancy, making television programmes or leisure. This is possible because revenue from endowments is either directly spent on them or diverted through the creation of 'needs blind bursaries' to pay the inflated fees that such a set of incentives leads to. Not only does this make universities more expensive, it raises issues about the quality of teaching carried out by the university. If highly paid professors subcontract teaching to part-time assistants, there is an issue about the balance of spending between undergraduate and graduate teaching and research. It may well be that average-income American households are making a disproportionate contribution to the cost of American academic research on an involuntary basis.

This does not simply affect the first-division, Ivy League schools, but sets off a dynamic of incentives that runs throughout the American university system. Once the top tier is charging an inflated fee, often on the basis that it is 'needs blind', the next tier down is able to put up its fees. First because it is relatively cheaper and second because students are displaced by cost from the higher end university. This leads to a system where higher education institutions have to bid for star faculty, at the cost of raising tuition fees. Students then have to pay increasing fees, or be priced out of the best universities

Sixty percent of full-time students receive some form of grant aid and millions more benefit from federal tax credits and income tax deductions. The ability to pay has been enhanced by giving credit to students through federal government agencies. The Obama administration increased federal spending on student assistance by over $100bn over the next 10 years, mainly by making Pell grants more generous. There is extensive third-party payment from both state and federal public sector support. This has facilitated student access to credit, which in turn has helped drive up tuition fees. *The Economic Report of the President* in 2009 spelt out how, in response to higher tuition fees, federal government spending on the Pell Grant programme doubled from $8bn in 2000-2001 to $16.3bn in 2008-2009.

There is little ambiguity about earnings premium in the labour market. A degree retains a consistent premium, although there is considerable variability in earnings from different degrees. What is clear, however, is that the return on a degree itself is falling – because while there may be evidence that suggests the earnings premium is being maintained or may be increasing in the labour market, the cost of obtaining a degree has been rising significantly faster than the earnings premium, with the result that the rate of return on a university degree has been falling.

There are many bursaries and sources of needs blind student support, but about 40 percent of students pay the full university fee. This means that for the two-fifths of American households that seek a university- and college-based professional education, tuition has become a significant lifetime expense. It is not clear that higher education in the US is carried out in an efficient manner, or that the 2.7 percent of GDP spent on it represents an investment in the accumulation of human capital. A significant proportion of spending is lost in waste, renting-seeking and other losses of X-efficiency.

Chapter 13

US tort law

Over the past 30 years, there has been increasing concern about the impact on the American economy of costs that arise from court litigation, with Congress taking an increasing interest in this part of the American legal system. The concern about the economic cost of the US legal system is concisely summarised in a paper commissioned by the US Chamber Institute for Legal Reform with research undertaken by NERA, International Comparisons of Ligation costs published in June 2013. This study used data on all general liability insurance policies placed by Marsh, Inc., a major broker of commercial insurance, in Europe, the U.S., and Canada between 2008 and 2011. The data included the actual costs to companies of liability insurance policies they bought in particular countries in each year. Its conclusion, 'simply put, litigation costs affect the ability of companies to compete and prosper. But higher direct costs of doing business are just the tip of the iceberg: litigation also imposes indirect costs. These indirect costs stem from the uncertainty created by litigation, which may deter investment in high-cost jurisdictions'. The U.S. has the highest liability costs as a percentage of GDP of the countries in the survey, with liability costs at 2.6 times the average level of the Eurozone economies.

These legal costs cannot be easily explained away different countries making different policy and social choices in relation to matters such as regulation. Countries that have more comprehensive and effective regulations may reduce the occurrence of harmful liability events that result in expensive claims for compensation, such as traffic accidents, financial fraud or injuries caused by defective products, thereby liability costs are lower. Yet, survey evidence, suggests that the U.S. does not have a consistently lower regulatory burden than other Organisation for Economic Cooperation and Development (OECD) countries. The paper concludes that 'there is little evidence to support the hypothesis that liability costs in the U.S. are higher because of less effective regulation'. The study identified several features of the legal environments in each of the countries are highly correlated with litigation costs. The policy inference is that difference in the liability system may have a substantial role in explaining differences in effect costs. A common law, rather than civil law, traditions and a high number of lawyers per capita are strong indicators of higher litigation costs.

In 1996, the Joint Economic Committee published the study, *Improving the American Legal System: Economic Benefits of Tort Reform,* and in 2003 the Congressional Budget Office published, *The Economics of US Tort Liability: A Primer.* The George W Bush Administration took an interest in tort issues as part of its agenda to lighten regulation. The *Economic Report of the President 2004* contained a chapter providing a concise summary of the issues involved. As a result of this concern, the Class Actions Fairness Act was passed in 2005.

The concern over tort centres on the damages courts award in civil ligation for hurt done in matters such as personal injury. Tort is defined in common law as an injury to a person or a person's reputation or property. Tort law covers a range of matters that include trespass, slander and deceit, and are broadly outside the scope of economic activity. The boundary between tort and contract law is complex. Torts almost exclusively fall within the realm of state as opposed to federal law. The Supreme Court has periodically taken action in relation to tort law when a state's civil law system may conflict with the US Constitution.

The Supreme Court, for example, held in *State Farm Mut Automobile Inc Co v Campbell* (2003) that punitive damages should be 'both reasonable and proportionate to the amount of harm to the plaintiff and the general damages recovered', and suggested there may be rough limits on the ratio of punitive damages to compensatory damages in cases involving only economic losses. The Supreme Court was able to do this because of the Constitution's due process clause, which establishes limits on punitive damages.

Until the 1960s, the scope of tort law was largely confined to injuries resulting from events such as motor accidents. Injuries arising from a dispute where the people involved knew one another, such as a dispute between a doctor and a patient, tended to be regulated by a contract that a court could use as the basis for resolving the matter. Courts limited the application of tort to cases where no contract existed or where harm arose outside the terms of a prescribed contract. Where there was an action in tort, the court would determine if the defendant was liable or at fault and determine compensation from the victim or 'plaintiff'. In determining liability, courts would apply a test or standard of negligence. Under this test, the court would assess whether an injury had occurred because the defendant had failed to take proper care and exercised the caution of a reasonable person in the circumstances of the event that had taken place.

A series of changes have broadened the scope and application of tort law in America over the past 40 years. Product liability has developed as a form of strict liability. This means that defendants are liable for any product-related injuries even if they were not negligent. This has meant more injuries have fallen within the scope of compensation under tort and the number of cases litigated has risen.

Economics of tort: deterrence and its costs

The economic effect of the expanded tort system is greater than the direct cost of the expenditure involved. Resources that could be used for productive purposes are diverted into ensuring that firms and individuals are not exposed to tort liability and litigation. The tort system can yield potential benefits, by firms and individuals taking steps to reduce risks and to avoid accidents.

This would represent a societal benefit – it constrains behaviour and results in a higher level of economic welfare. But the key matter is if such benefits are produced by the system at a reasonable cost.

Table 13.1: Tort Costs as Percent of GDP

Year	US tort costs ($)	US GDP ($)	Tort costs as % of GDP
1950	1.8	294	0.62
1960	5.4	526	1.03
1970	13.9	1,038	1.34
1980	42.7	2,788	1.53
1990	130.2	5,801	2.24
2000	179.1	9,952	1.80
2001	205.4	10,286	2.00
2002	232.9	10,642	2.19
2003	245.7	11,142	2.21
2004	260.3	11,868	2.19
2005	261.4	12,638	2.07
2006	246.9	13,399	1.84
2007	252.0	14,078	1.79
2008	254.9	14,441	1.76
2009	248.1	14,256	1.74

Note: *Unadjusted or nominal GDP is used. Most news releases on GDP rely on inflation adjusted, or real GDP.

Source: Towers Watson

Figure 13.1: Tort Costs as Percent of GDP

Source: Towers Watson

Table 13.2: Tort Costs Relative to Population

Year	US population (millions)	US tort costs ($ billions)	Tort costs per capita	Inflation adjusted* tort costs per capita ($)
1950	152	1.8	12	106
1960	181	5.4	30	218
1970	205	13.9	68	374
1980	228	42.7	187	488
1990	249	130.2	522	857
2000	281	179.1	636	793
2005	296	261.4	884	972
2006	298	246.9	828	881
2007	301	252.0	836	865
2008	304	254.9	838	836
2009	307	248.1	808	808

Source: Towers Watson

Figure 13.2: International Comparison of Tort Costs, 1998

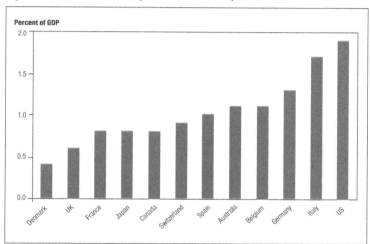

Note: Tort costs as a percent of GDP were higher in the United States than in other industrialised countries.

Source: Tillingham-Towers Perrin, February 2002

Table 13.3: Characteristics of State and Federal Tort Cases Decided by Trial, 1996

Tort cases by type	Cases won by plaintiff (percent)	Meridian award ($)	Percent of awards $250.000 or more	
			Total	$1 million or more
All tort cases				
State	48.2	31,000	16.9	5.8
Federal	45.2	139,000	38.1	14.6
Automobile cases				
State	57.5	18,000	8.7	3.4
Federal	59.7	100,000	37.4	11.6
Medical liability				
State	23.4	286,000	51.0	20.2
Federal	39.8	252,000	54.3	22.9
Asbestos				
State	55.6	309,000	50.6	12.1
Federal	40.0	465,000	50.0	0.0
Product liability other than asbestos				
State	37.1	177,000	41.2	16.3
Federal	26.6	368,500	62.0	24.0

Source: CBO

It is not clear that in general, such benefits accrue for the cost involved outside the narrow field of motor accident liability. The evidence from states that have opted for 'no fault 'accident insurance arrangements is that because a motorist has no personal long-term liability, driver behaviour changes for the worse and there is an increase in accidents. In other areas – for example healthcare and product liability – the benefits do not seem nearly as clear. In the example of doctors, the threat of losing their licence to practice medicine ought to provide an effective alternative.

Limiting liability in the aviation industry and Californian medical practice

In 1963, as a result of case law, strict liability was applied to the general aviation industry in America. This meant that a plane manufacturer could be held liable for accidents even if they were caused by defects not known or unknowable at the time of manufacture. By the mid-1970s, there was a big increase in the number of aviation-related tort cases and the costs of liability awards rose nine-fold in the 10 years to 1985. Most of the litigation did not relate to design faults of the manufacturer, despite the claims made.

Because of this, the litigation did not generate practical incentives for the manufacture of safer aircraft. There was little or no identifiable impact on aircraft accidents. But tort costs damaged the financial position of the sector and resulted in a sharp fall in the manufacture of smaller planes, which changed the composition of the mix of planes in use and may have made the overall fleet less safe. It discouraged the development of new planes and resulted in older designs continuing in service for a longer period.

When California imposed a cap on non-economic tort damages for medical lawsuits of $250,000, there was no evidence that suggested safety was undermined by the change. The experience of the Californian healthcare sector and the American aviation industry suggests that the much of the deterrence benefit can be achieved by other means at a much lower cost. There are strong conventional market incentives for firms to manufacture safe products and to develop and protect their brand and reputation. Regulation from professional bodies and legislation is more effective and has the merit of being there to protect people before something goes wrong rather than compensating them after the event.

Non-economic damages the aggravating factor in American tort

In the US, non-economic damages account for half the damages awarded in tort cases. These compensate the plaintiff for matters such as pain and suffering. In many other countries they are capped, as in Canada, or restricted, as they are in Germany. Compensatory damages are intended to make a successful plaintiff 'whole' after being damaged.

Punitive damages, in contrast, are intended to punish a party whose negligence caused the injury. Tort defendants may be liable for punitive damages if a jury finds they were malicious, oppressive, gross, wilful and wanton or fraudulent. The Department of Justice found in a study of 75 countries that punitive damages were only awarded in 2.5 percent of cases. In the US, the ratio was about 21 percent. These punitive awards averaged $40,000. High punitive damages encourage more tort litigation, and tend to be awarded against companies with long pockets. The Supreme Court has expressed concern that some of these punitive awards have been out of proportion to the harm done by the defendant. Capricious damages undermine the operation of deterrence. Deterrence from tort only works if it provides an incentive to avoid specific liability. When firms cannot identify actions that are likely to expose them to litigation risk, they cannot take steps to avoid them.

American court procedures also appear to aggravate the damages given in tort actions. They are more often decided by a jury than a judge, or panel of judges sitting without a jury, as is often the case in civil litigation in other countries. Whether this is the key determinant is less clear. Analysis of cases in the US does not offer a clear difference between the way courts decide cases – judges and juries appear to dispose of cases in a similar fashion.

Towers Watson has studied tort costs for more than a decade. Its *US Tort Cost Trends 2010 Update* shows that in 1950, tort costs accounted for 0.62 percent of GDP. By 1970 this ratio had risen to 1.34 percent, and in 1990 reached 2.24 percent. In 2003, the ratio was 2.21 percent. It then fell back to over 1.7 percent of GDP by 2007. Tort costs directly accounted for 2 percent of GDP on average over the last 20 years. In cash terms, tort cost peaked at $261.4bn in 2005 and has fallen to $248.1bn in 2009, roughly twice as high as in other developed economies. Uncertain damages and litigation influences all aspects of economic activity, from product design to healthcare and employment decisions. The full economic impact of America's tort arrangements is greater than its estimated cash cost.

The National Centre for State Courts data confirms the picture of the Towers Watson analysis that litigation relating to tort is diminishing. Less than two in 1,000 people filed tort law cases in 2015 compared to 10 per 1,000 in 1993. *The Wall Street Journal* for many years criticised the role of the legal profession and the courts in aggravating tort litigation. It reported in an article written by Joe Palazzolo *Court Room Surprise: Fewer Tort Lawsuits* (26 July 2017) that progress is being made in curbing the inappropriate use of court proceedings. The Conference of Chief Justices, the association of state judicial leaders has worked to modify court procedures so that cases proceed more swiftly and at less cost. Potential litigants are being put off by the cost and time consuming character of litigation. The US Chamber of Commerce's Institute of Legal Reform recognises that changes in state court procedures have weeded out some frivolous lawsuits, but considers that there is still too much litigation that imposes an inappropriate cost on the economy and absorbs scarce judicial resources. Tort cases now account for less than 5 percent of state civil litigation compared to some 20 per cent in the 1980s. National Centre fro State Courts data show that contract litigation and proceeding s to recover debt and litigation relating to housing and mortgages now account for around half of civil state legal proceedings. Tort litigation remains a matter for legal tribunals at the state level. In 2015 there were 15 million instances of civil proceedings in state courts compared to 281,608 cases in federal courts. States have capped damages that can be awarded and the costs of bringing litigation to court have increased. Some states, for example, require litigants medical cases to file expert witness statements with or soon after they file the case. These expert witness statements are expensive. Economic damages relate to loss of earnings and income for many retired people in medical litigation, such damages would make a case uneconomic given the costs and risks involved. And states have made progress in capping non-economic damages. These measures taken in some 30 states have helped to contain tort costs recently. National Centre for State Courts' data suggests that the Conference of Chief Justices and state legal authorities have · begun to get a purchase on constraining this source of cost and economic distortion.

Conclusion

It would be wrong to locate tort costs as the principal obstacle to US markets working properly. Yet the state court system over the past 50 years has evolved a clumsy and expensive form of liability that aggravates the cost of transacting business in the US. As well as aggravating medical costs and the costs of productive innovation, it also has a negative effect on the labour market. As the Congressional Budget Office points out, it is an area of law principally governed by state law. While federal involvement may be justified by the benefits that tort law might bring for interstate commerce, it is difficult for the federal government to offer effective comprehensive reform. What is required is further detailed and incremental modification to legal procedures in state legal systems.

Chapter 14

US Labour Market

The main challenge in the US labour market in the Great Recession was a lack of aggregate monetary demand. The deep shock to output, however, may have exposed accumulating structural labour market issues. The adverse employment shock in itself may also have created the conditions for future structural unemployment as a result of people being unemployed and detached from the labour market for extended periods.

Over the past 30 years one of the big differences between the performance of the American economy and European economies has been the performance of the labour market. Nothing shows the entrenched structural rigidities of the European economies more than the comparative inflexibility of their labour markets.

During most of the 'golden period' of post-World War II, between 1950 and the oil crisis in 1973, unemployment tended to be a little higher in the US than in other developed economies, such as those in Europe. From the late 1970s, the position began to change. European labour markets became less flexible and began to exhibit structural rigidities which meant that, however well they were doing in relation to the economic cycle, there was a permanent or structural level of unemployment that could not be shifted without the risk of price inflation. At best, macroeconomic policies directed at stimulating demand enough to reduce unemployment could only have a transitory effect on unemployment before they began to push up inflation. In contrast, the American labour market was a model of flexibility.

Employment has behaved differently in the US during the Great Recession. The *Economic Report of the President 2010* made it clear that the labour market responded differently to the fall in output in this recession: 'The normal relationship between GDP and unemployment has fit poorly in the recession. This relationship, termed Okum's law after former chair of the Council of Economic Advisers Arthur Okum who first identified it, suggests that a fall in GDP of 1 percent relative to its normal trend path is associated with a rise in the unemployment rate of about 0.5 percentage points after four quarters.'

The relationship broke down and unemployment rose much more steeply than it previously had. The Council of Economic Advisers estimated that at its peak, unemployment was about 1.7 percent higher than the fall in GDP would have normally implied.

The Congressional Budget Office in, *The Slow Recovery of the Labour Market,* published in 2014, attempted to disentangle some of the issues and illustrated how much slower the recovery of the labour market has been in this economic cycle. The CBO showed how some six years after the Great Recession the labour market remained impaired. It attributed most of this impairment to insufficient demand and the direct effects of the loss of output in the recession, but it did recognise that a structural element is involved as well. The CBO estimated that structural factors accounted for about one percentage point of the difference between the unemployment rate at the end of 2007 and at the end of 2013. CBO also estimated that the natural rate of unemployment was 5 percent at the end of 2007 and, reflecting structural factors, increased to 6 percent at the end of 2013. Structural factors in the CBO analysis account for that 1 percentage-point increase. These include the stigma of long-term unemployment, that makes employers reluctant to hire a person who has been out of the work force for a protracted duration; a fall in the efficiency with which employers filled vacancies, probably as a result of mismatches between the needs of employers and the skills and locations of those seeking work; one-tenth of a percentage point is attributable to the incentives generated in

2013 by extensions of UI benefits. They were extended from the usual 26 weeks to as much as 99 weeks.

Labour force participation rates are falling principally in the CBO's judgement because of the changing demography of the US with an aging population that is retiring. In the medium term the CBO expects the Affordable Care Act to exert a downward pressure on labour supply and labour participation. The ACA will reduce participation, the largest effect arises from subsidies that reduce the cost of health insurance purchased through exchanges. By providing subsidies that fall as a person's income rises and increase when incomes are lower and by making some people financially better off, the ACA will create an incentive for some people to choose to work less. The structure of the tax code, where rising incomes draw people into higher tax bracket, will also reduce labor force participation slightly.

The classic institutional rigidity – trade union power

Historically in market economies, the main source of inflexibility in labour markets has been the role of trade unions in setting wages.

Trade union power could prevent wages from adjusting over time to real changes in the demand for labour. When wages cannot adjust, it prevents the labour market from responding to an adverse shock, but it ensures that the necessary adjustment takes place as a quantity adjustment, rather than a price adjustment, where employment falls and unemployment rises. One of Lord Keynes's distinctive insights during the slump and unemployment in Britain in the 1920s and 1930s was that, because of what Keynes called 'institutional' factors – or trade union power – wages were unable to adjust and there was permanent unemployment. Because of this, Keynes wanted to engineer an increase in the price level to reduce the real value of wages and increase demand for labour. This source of labor market rigidity has significantly been reduced in the US labor market. Trade unions remain a presence in the public sector but are a much diminished influence in the private sector.

Modern policy rigidities that increase employment costs and reduce demand for labour

In addition to trade union power, other institutions can be created that make labour markets less flexible and permanently raise the cost of employing people. Some examples are fixed minimum wages set by regulation, payroll social security taxes, employment rights such as the right to paternal leave, and employment protection rules that make it more costly to hire and fire employees. These create a rigid system that makes employees more expensive and reduces the demand for labour, because its relative cost is increased.

Employers become increasingly careful about whom they hire because it can be expensive to let them go. This encourages discrimination in favour of people with education, training and experience. It entrenches so-called segmented and internal labour markets. It makes it difficult for people with a potential labour market handicap such as a lack of experience, few skills or a protracted period of unemployment to get work. These issues disproportionately affect young people entering the labour market, those who take time off to raise a family such as women, people who are unemployed or have an employment record with gaps through periods of unemployment or ill health, and minority groups.

These are features of institutional rigidity have permanently reduced the demand for labour in European economies. They result in capital being substituted for labour, because labour has become relatively more expensive. This can result in economies with entrenched structural rigidities appearing to show impressive levels of productivity per capita, because fewer people using more machinery produce at roughly the same level that would otherwise have been produced.

On careful examination this may also reflect higher labour costs, forcing firms to move to a more expensive mix of capital and labour as a result, leading to a more expensive production cost schedule. This then results in lower levels of employment, raising the level of unemployment and an overall production cost that uses capital and labour less efficiently. Such higher cost and less efficient capital output ratios make economies less competitive in international markets and work to lower output compared to what it would otherwise be. These structural rigidities have been influencing the labour markets in Europe for the past 30 years.

Structural rigidities that impede the supply of labour

High levels of public expenditure raising the tax burden, increasing marginal tax rates and social security benefits that replace employment earnings for protracted periods of time also make labour markets more rigid by reducing the supply of labour. The ratio of social security benefits to wages after tax – the replacement ratio – has a powerful influence on whether people choose to take a job.

These concerns mostly affect people with few skills and a low marginal revenue product. The level of marginal tax rates has an influence on both household decisions about labour market participation and the intensity of employment participation. High replacement ratios and high marginal tax rates at relatively low levels of earnings reduce the incentive to take work at all, or reduce labour supply by reducing the number of hours of labour that are supplied. These constraints on labour supply play a significant part in the structural rigidities of the European labour markets.

For 30 years, American labour markets outperformed Europe. In the 1980s and 1990s, they performed much better than their European counterparts.

There was less evidence of obvious structural rigidity and a much greater display of flexibility through wages adjusting to changing economic circumstances and in geographical mobility. Although the US enjoyed a higher level of labour productivity per capita, its productivity growth in the 1980s and early 1990s often appeared to be slower than other OECD economies that exhibited worse outcomes in terms of employment growth and unemployment. American labour markets performed better in terms of employment and unemployment, and this was reflected in more realistic wage and earnings growth. In the 30 years since 1979 real median earnings growth has been constrained.

The American labour market during the Great Recession

In the most recent economic cycle, something appears to have changed. A fall in output in the US that was smaller than that in the OECD as a whole has been associated with a larger fall in employment and rise in unemployment. As output started to recover, the labour market response has been more tepid than normal time lags would imply. There appear to be structural rigidities that were not present before.

Some of the weak performance of the US labour market in this economic cycle could have been explained by the cycle's particular features. These include that the Great Recession resulted from an asset price bubble that burst, causing a credit crunch, which ended a house price and construction boom. The collapse in house prices and the end of the construction boom have consequences that could worsen the rise in unemployment. It was also argued that a fall in output concentrated, in part, in an unusually sharp fall in construction activity will displace workers who will find it more difficult to get alternative work and transfer their experience and skills in an economy dominated by services. The fall in house prices could make labour mobility more difficult, because people cannot sell their houses and move to where their job prospects are better.

The combination of a lack of demand for houses, difficulty in remortgaging and negative equity combine to prevent people moving to take up new job opportunities and lock people into their local labour market for a longer period than would normally be the case. This was a particular feature of the contraction of output that took place between 2008 and 2009. It may have played a part in making this recession more difficult in terms of its impact on the labour market than would usually be the case. These constraints on the transfer of workers' employment and geographical mobility are characteristics of this recession and will improve as the economic cycle improves. So the present difficulties do not necessarily have implications for the future performance of the US labour market, apart from how they may result in longer periods in unemployment, itself contributing to structural unemployment through a process called hysteresis.

At least one of these arguments asserting that the poor labour market performance is an artefact of the character of the recession cannot be easily fitted with the facts. Negative equity disproportionately reducing the geographical mobility of home-owners does appear to be happening. In the Chicago federal letter *How much has house lock affected labor mobility and the unemployment rate?* From September 2011, Daniel Aaronson and Jonathan Davis show that between December 2008 and July 2010, state-to-state migration fell for both renters and homeowners. Additionally, the states most affected by house price declines exhibited smaller slumps in mobility than states that experienced less of a cut in house prices. They found no evidence that homeowner households with the head out of work were especially unlikely to move across states. Their conclusion is that state-to-state migration rates among homeowners fell 'roughly in line with those of renters during the latest recession and early recovery period, and roughly in line with previous recessions. There is little evidence that migration varied based on the magnitude of a state's recent house price decline'. In short, there is little empirical evidence that house prices have been an important influence on the high rate of unemployment during the Great Recession.

There are reasons, however, to examine the American labour market critically and to consider whether it now functions as well as it once did. It appears to now be exhibiting structural difficulties of the sort more normally considered to be an issue in European economies.

Extensions of benefits and unemployment duration

Part of the debate focuses on the George W Bush administration's and the Obama administration's decision to extend unemployment benefits to long-term unemployed people who would otherwise have exhausted them. Did this result in moral hazard that diminished the necessity and desire to look for work and increase the length of unemployment? Unemployment benefits have been extended from six months to 99 weeks. Elsby, Hobijn and Sahin in 'The labour market in the Great Recession' in *Brooking Papers on Economic Activity: Spring 2010* argue it helped raise the rate of unemployment by 1.8 percentage points.

Institutional and structural matters

There also appears to be a mismatch between unemployed workers and jobs that are available. Batini et al in 'US selective issues' in the *IMF Country Report 2010* suggest unemployment may have been increased by 1.75 percent as a result of unusual skill mismatches. This may simply be a short-term frictional matter, or it may reflect a more longer-term set of problems relating to the role of active labour market policies and the capacity of US public policy to train and re-deploy workers when they are displaced and do not have the skills to get different jobs in a changing labour market.

Other factors suggest that over the last 15 to 25 years, a series of factors – some purely policy-driven and some resulting from wider policy and institutional features in American society – have combined to increase the cost of employing people and reduce the incentives of households to participate in the labour market. The scale of the economic shock between 2007 and 2010 has exposed some of these issues.

The reflex among many economists is to argue that when an economy experiences the worst contraction in output since the Great Depression, the labour market is bound to perform badly and will take time to recover. They add that in this scenario, its performance offers little information about the effects of certain public policies and more about the scale of the economic cycle.

In many respects this was the view of the Obama administration's economists and policymakers during its first two years. It would have been persuasive if it were not for the fact that an economy that appeared to experience a smaller fall in output than other advanced OECD economies also experienced a much worse deterioration in its labour market conditions than the fall in output should suggest. What is more striking, is that historically this economy had normally experienced a more modest deterioration in labour market conditions for a given change in output compared to other OECD economies.

An international comparison of labour market performance in the Great Recession

When comparing the US with similar OECD figures for output and the labour market, a smaller fall in GDP has seen a larger rise in unemployment.

The US experienced a shorter period of falling output and that output fell by a smaller amount than any other G7 economy apart from Canada. The contraction in output started in the third quarter of 2008 and ended in the third quarter of 2009. In total, GDP fell by 3.7 percent in the US. This compares with an overall fall in OECD output of around 4.5 percent and a fall in GDP of:

- 6.8 percent in Italy
- 6.6 percent in Germany
- 6.4 percent in the UK
- 3.9 percent in France

The rate of unemployment between 2007 and 2010 rose from:
- 6.2 to 8.4 percent in Italy
- 5.3 to 7.8 percent in the UK
- 8.3 to 9.8 percent in France.

In Germany it fell from 8.4 to 6.9 percent. In the US, the comparable rate of unemployment increased from 4.6 percent in 2007 to 9.6 percent in 2010 (annual average unemployment rates for the calendar year).

What this suggests is that a smaller fall in output, during a contraction of slightly below average duration of four quarters, resulted in a disproportionately large impact on the labour market. A fall in GDP amounting to just two-thirds of the average fall in output experienced by other G7 economies during the Great Recession resulted in the rate of unemployment more than doubling. The unemployment rate rose by 5 percentage points in the US, increasing by 108 percent to 9.6 percent. Across the G7 the rate of unemployment rose by 2.8 percentage points, increasing by a half – just over 51 percent, to 8.2 percent in 2010. This adverse comparative labour market response to a rather smaller, but historically large fall in output, from an economy that had been distinguished in recent decades by its comparative labour market flexibility and much better performance in terms of apparent structural labour market rigidities before the recession, suggests something significant about the modern American labour market may have been.

The employment gap between the US and Europe narrows

Christian Grisse, Thomas Klitgaard and Aysegul Sahin describe in, *The Vanishing US-EU Employment Gap,* published in July 2011, how the performance of the US labour market has deteriorated compared with that of Europe over the past 10 years.

Figure 14.1: Okun's Law, Council of Economic Advisors

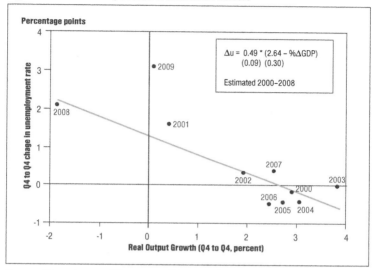

Source: *Department of Commerce (Bureau of Economic Analysis), National Income and Product Accounts*

Between 1980 and 2000, the employment-to-population ratio was on average 10 percentage points higher in the US than in Europe. Grisse et al attribute 'part of this difference' to 'higher labour taxes, higher minimum wages and better benefits for unemployed and retired workers in Europe'. This difference between the employment-to-population ratio in the US and Europe (defined by the first 15 EU member states) has fallen from 10.5 percent in 2000 to 4.8 percent in 2007. It narrowed further during the Great Recession and 'almost vanished at 1.7 percentage points in 2009'.

When they looked at differences in employment by gender, they found evidence that was 'consistent with the view that taxes and benefits are more likely to affect those with lower labour force attachment, like younger or older workers. The gap in employment rates for women, though, is wide across all age groups. Comparing changes in employment rates from 2000 to

2009, we see a significant narrowing of the gap between the US and Europe. US employment growth was weak even over the decade before the recession, which then accentuated the decline in employment rates relative to 2000.'

While some of the recent changes may have reflected periods of weak demand, US labour market institutions appear to have changed and have become progressively less able to adjust to market shocks over the last 20 years, narrowing the gap with Europe in employment rates.

Factors increasing employment costs and reducing the demand for labour

Historically, the main institutional impediment to labour markets responding flexibly to changing economic conditions were the unions. The power of unions in the workplace, particularly in manufacturing, prevented wage adjustment and instead resulted in quantity adjustments. While union power in the private sector has significantly weakened over the past 40 years in the US as it has in Britain, new sources of institutional rigidity have emerged affecting employment costs and the framework of incentives that shape labour supply.

Four main influences have emerged that, together, raise US employment costs.

The first is growth in the cost of employer-provided healthcare benefits. Large tax subsidies encourage employers to provide health insurance to their employees. These have contributed to a web of factors raising healthcare costs and imposing an expensive and rising burden on the person or organisation that ultimately foots the healthcare bill, whether it is a private household, the taxpayer or a corporation.

The second is direct federal regulation of employment imposing duties on employers that cannot be avoided by negotiation, such as the rules surrounding family and parental leave. These regulations often appear modest individually, but have a cumulative effect that raises employment costs, deters the hiring of employees and promotes a search for working practices where labour costs can be saved. The burden of federal employment regulation will be significantly increased as the Affordable Care Act is implemented. These will require employers to provide healthcare benefits or pay a fine of up to $2,000. The Act may ultimately raise unemployment by 1.5 percent if all provisions are put into effect. Regulation of this sort has a disproportionate impact on workers with limited skills, training and education who generate low levels of marginal revenue product.

The third source of rising employment costs is the operation of the system of civil damages (or tort) within the American framework of common law and federal court structure. Courts often award high levels of compensation for damages. These costs not only can be heavy, but are erratic and increase uncertainty about the costs any organisation or business may incur in their operation. The consequences of this have implications that go further than the operation of the labour market and impact on almost any activity where disputes can arise – not least in medical care. But there are specific effects on the labour market, and means any employment relationship can be exposed to litigation at potentially great expense. This has an effect comparable to that of extensive employment protection legislation in Europe, raising employment costs, making employers more selective about whom they hire and making employers examine working methods in to economise on locally employed labour.

The fourth factor is that relative cost of labour has risen at a time when the cost of an important element of the modern capital stock has fallen – the cost of computers. Computer cost has not only fallen, but over the past decade employers have learnt how to make greater use of them and to integrate them into their work routines to save money – and one economist working at the Joint Economic Committee of Congress has vividly said: 'A computer cannot sue you.'

These four factors have combined to raise the relative cost of hiring people in the US. They are likely to be permanent features of the country's labour market that are unlikely to change as the economic cycle evolves. In this way they represent a structural cost that will impede the performance of the market regardless of overall macroeconomic conditions.

Factors working to limit the supply of labour

Over the past 35 years, the US has evolved an extensive framework of transfer payments to reduce household poverty – in particular, poverty among households with children. In a market economy there is inevitably a wide dispersion of incomes and wealth.

A significant proportion of households will have an income from the market that is sufficient for their needs. Most advanced market economies have developed extensive tax and public expenditure systems to modify original incomes in order to raise those at the bottom to a socially acceptable level. The choice is between providing universal cash benefits or benefits in kind, such as free healthcare to all households, or providing targeted benefits to certain households which are withdrawn as income rises. Both approaches have strengths and weaknesses.

Universal benefits get to every household that needs them and do little direct damage to incentives – for example, saving and work – because they are not withdrawn as income rises. They do have an indirect and very powerful effect on incentives, however, through the tax burden necessary to finance them. By their nature, universal benefits are costly in public expenditure terms. This means that the amount of assistance that can be directed at households is less generous in order to be affordable.

In contrast, targeted benefits can be more generous – although there is the issue of the extent of take up. Targeting means benefits are phased out as income rises. This increases their affordability, in public expenditure terms, but directly damages the incentive to take work or to work additional hours, because the marginal rate of withdrawal of benefits can sometimes be as high as the sort of higher-marginal rates of income tax levied in a steeply progressive income tax system. The OECD has pointed out in the Economic Survey 2016 that the current disability insurance regime provides little incentive to re-enter the labour market for people with a health condition that has improved and would like to work, as earnings above a limit will lead to the disability benefit being withdrawn.

People qualifying for disability benefits also qualify for Medicare. Currently, there are some programmes that aim to help to return to the workforce, such as retraining, continuing cash benefits for a period of time, and that extend Medicare benefits for 102 months after a person resumes work. The OECD suggests that these programmes should be carefully evaluated and, if needed, the incentives should be strengthened to help people get off disability rolls to work and if they are capable of doing so. The number of disability benefit recipients, which exceeded 10 million in 2014, exceeds the number of unemployment benefit recipients, which dropped below 8 million in 2015. The previous *OECD Economic Survey* recommended encouraging greater labour market attachment, both by helping maintain labour force attachment during the claims process and by reducing the disincentives to work once receiving disability insurance.

Earned income tax credit (EITC)

Over the past 45 years, the US has developed a system of targeted benefits that provide cash benefits for general use or to fund the purchase of particular merit goods, such as university education. The centrepiece of this system of programmes is the EITC. This programme transferred some $56 billion in 2013 to 27 million households. The history of the credit offers an interesting perspective on the policy ambitions surrounding poverty relief and the difficult trade-offs policymakers encounter. In many ways, it also offers an unusual example of an academic idea floated by an economist that transformed public policy, and within 40 years became one of the central policy instruments used by governments in advanced economies attempting to tackle poverty.

Milton Friedman was the original author of the idea when he formulated the concept of a negative income tax. Friedman was convinced a negative income tax could replace a range of means-tested benefits and avoid high cumulative effective marginal tax rates. This coincided with the period in the 1960s that the Kennedy and Johnson administrations were formulating the Great Society programmes.

President Johnson took up the idea, but he was concerned about anyone having a guaranteed handout. A particular concern of his was to avoid policy that might deter people from taking a job, a concern shared by legislators. The Louisiana Democrat Senator Russell Long exemplified the desire to help poor people, but also the determination to retain the incentive to get into work. Peter Waltraut's *The Earned Income Tax Credit: A Model for Germany?* explores the history of the EITC and shows how legislators were anxious to ensure people did not get money for nothing and that their incentive to take a job should be enhanced.

Nothing much came from the initial interest in the negative income tax idea in the 1960s, but the concept was taken up by the Nixon administration in its proposal to replace the Aid to Families with Dependent Children (AFDC) with the Family Assistance Plan in 1969. Friedman had reservations about the Plan because it was to be introduced while other means-tested benefits were retained, and Senator Long denounced the proposals as a plan 'to reward idleness'. The Family Assistance Plan was eventually rejected by Congress in 1972, but the debate that surrounded it exposed the difficult trade-offs that policymakers must face when they try to construct benefit programmes that relieve poverty but usually generate awkward incentive traps, however carefully targeted.

The EITC was introduced in 1975 as a minor amendment to President Ford's fiscal stimulus package. It was not intended to relieve poverty. Its purpose was to give some help to employees facing a rising tax burden. Social Security payroll taxes had increased to 5.85 percent and were becoming an increasingly visible tax that irked voters. The tax credit was a refundable credit for low-income families to offset their payroll Social Security tax. It phased in adding one dollar to every 10 dollars earned, phased out at 20 percent and was planned to last just one year. As payroll taxes were progressively increased, it was maintained in 1976 and 1977 and became a permanent feature of the tax system in 1978. The EITC was significantly expanded in the 1986 Tax Reform Act. The Reagan administration was seeking a method for cutting taxes and taking low-income people out of tax, and the Democrat Congress was looking for ways to relieve poverty because payroll taxes had risen further and inflation had eroded the real value of tax exemptions and the minimum wage.

Given that liberal members of Congress could not get sufficient support for targeted wage subsidies and an increase in the minimum wage as an alternative, they campaigned to expand the EITC. As a result, in 1986 its value was raised to a level slightly higher than its real value in 1975, indexed for inflation and then increased along with the personal exemptions and standard deductions in the income tax code.

In 1994 and 1996, as part of President Clinton's Work Must Pay and welfare reform, the EITC was further expanded. The minimum benefit and phase-in rates were raised and the phase-out rates was also raised. Additionally, a small tax credit for children was created. As part of the wider welfare reform that emphasised attachment to the labour market and working to receive benefit, the EITC surpassed other means-tested benefit programmes and became the federal government's principal antipoverty programme in 1996. It was further expanded with the introduction of the Child Tax Credit that refunded up to $1,000 of childcare costs per child for families with incomes above $10,500. It does not affect the marginal tax rate, because it is not reduced until income reaches $75,000.

Research into the effects that the EITC has on labour market behaviour suggests it has an influence on the labour supply of women. Nada Eissa and Hilary Hoynes's paper *The Earned Income Tax credit and the Labour Supply of Married Couples* (NBER Working Paper No 6856) found that it slightly increased the employment of married men between 1986 and 1996, but reduced employment of married women by a full percentage point. Overall labour supply and pre-tax family earnings fell among families eligible for the EITC. They judge it promoted employment among unmarried women with children eligible for the benefit, and it also 'effectively subsidies married mothers to stay at home'. Given that the benefit is means-tested and targeted on low-income families, the phase-out of the EITC combines with federal, state, and Social Security payroll taxes and lowers the incentive for secondary earners in a household to work. Eissa and Hoynes found that an apparently modest overall labour supply distortion masked substantial differences among families. Over the phase-in region of family income, the expansion of EITC resulted in higher employment of women and more hours being worked. Over the phase-out income, the employment of women was lower and fewer hours were worked.

President George W Bush modified the EITC to reduce work and marriage disincentives for couples. This raised the phasing-in and end of the phase out range of the EITC by $1,000 for married couples filing a joint tax return. By the time the changes implemented in the Bush administration took effect, the number of households receiving the EITC had increased from 6.2 million in 1975 to 19.3 million in 2003. Total real spending on it had risen from $1.25bn in 1974 to $34.4bn in 2003. The real value of the average tax credit had increased by 167 percent to $1,784 in 2003. Taking a job is a condition for receiving the EITC, so it works to increase the attachment of women to low-paying jobs, but its high net rate of withdrawal as income rises has negative implications for intensity of labour supply given the effective marginal tax rate involved.

Internal Revenue Service reported that there were $68 billion in EITC claims from 28.8 million tax filers for tax year 2013. The *Economic Report of the President* in 2016 explained the role of the EITC and showed that it has been expanded in every Administration since 1975. The American Recovery and Reinvestment Act of 2009, expanded the EITC for families with three or more children, it reduced the marriage penalty and the refundable portion of the Child Tax Credit was expanded, on a temporary basis. These changes were then made permanent by Congress last December 2015

America's complex web of means-tested transfer programmes

The EITC may be the main transfer payment relieving poverty, but it interacts with a series of other federal government means-tested transfer payments. These phase in and phase out over different parts of the earnings distribution. This system of federal transfer payments and the means-testing rules result in a complex web of cash and benefits in kind that are targeted on households by income and are withdrawn as income rises, creating high net rates of benefit withdrawal. High marginal tax rates modify labour supply incentives and create employment and poverty traps that both diminish the incentive to take a job and impede the intensity of labour supply for people in work. It is these effects that offer rhetorical opportunities for politicians such as George W Bush to provide arresting examples of how the federal tax code results in perverse disincentives for certain categories of household.

This complex web of transfer payments creating employment and poverty traps is further aggravated when the federal programmes are combined with the interaction of the different income tax and policy regimes operated by state governments and municipal authorities. The rules relating to the means-test set for access to Medicaid set by state governments are particularly important.

Does work pay?

The complex issue of 'does work pay' has been explored in an extensive literature, not least with significant contributions from the Congressional Budget Office. Asking whether work pays for a household is a difficult question given the complexity of the federal and state tax and transfer system. It is compounded by the fact that earnings in one year do not simply effect economic welfare in that year, but help to shape economic welfare over a lifetime.

A group of economists led by Laurence Kotlikoff at Boston University have tried to examine these issues over more than a decade of research, using a sophisticated software programme that has the capacity to look at the net effect of taxes on work and on inter-temporal work incentives at each stage of the life-cycle, called the *ESPlanner* and developed by Economic Security Planning Inc.

In *Does Work Pay?* published in 2002, Jagadeesh Gokhale, Laurence Kotllikoff and Alexi Sluchynsky attempted to seperate the issues involved. The paper identified five principal dynamic linkages between earnings, taxes, benefits and economic welfare over a lifetime. The first is that present earnings alter current saving and therefore future levels of capital and income taxes. Second, earning more now usually contributes to future levels of consumption and, therefore, future consumption taxes. Third, changing levels of future income and assets affect the receipt of income- and asset-based transfer payments. Fourth, the most significant transfer programme, Social Security, explicitly links future transfer payments to current earnings. And fifth, income taxes in retirement can depend on past labour earnings because Social Security benefits depend on past earnings, and these benefits can be subject to federal income tax. In assessing the different factors involved, the paper took account of all major transfer programmes such as food stamps, TAFDC, Medicaid, Medicare, housing assistance, SSL, WIC and LIHEAP.

American's tax and benefit system is progressive

The Kotlikoff paper shows that the US taxes and benefits result in several distinct features. The fiscal system is progressive. In 2002, couples working full time and earning the minimum wage would have received 32 cents in benefits net of taxes for every dollar earned. A couple earning $1m would have paid 51 percent in taxes net of benefits. Net subsidies are paid only to the very bottom of the earning distribution. Average net taxes for couples earning one and a half times the minimum wage, $32,100, were 14 percent. For working couples earning five times the minimum wage, $107,100, the net rate of tax was 38 percent. Certain low and moderate-income households face positive marginal effective tax rates that are actually higher than those faced by high-income households that would be conventionally scored as rich. Low-wage workers face very high effective marginal tax rates when they move from part-time to full-time work.

Similar high effective marginal tax rates affect secondary-earning spouses in low-income households. Marginal tax rates are high for low-earning young households. Average and marginal net effective tax rates are little influenced by the evolution of real incomes. Kotlikoff et al conclude it would appear that a major tax reform, given this framework of complex marginal and average tax rates such as a shift from income tax to consumption or expenditure taxation, could have a significant effect in raising the overall level of progression compared to the current system.

A progressive system exhibiting perverse incentive effects across the earnings distribution

In *Does it pay, at the margin to Work and Save? – Measuring Effective Marginal Taxes on Americans' Labour Supply and Saving* published in October 2006, Laurence Kotlikoff and David Rapson looked at the issues explored in Kotlikoff's 2002 paper, and found the US fiscal system continued to show similar facts to those the 2002 paper identified. It concluded that the complexity of system makes it impossible for anyone to understand their incentive to work, save and contribute to retirement investment and pension arrangements without the assistance of sophisticated advice and advanced computer software.

Figure 14.2: Federal Government Spending Received by Americans in 2004

Total Federal Spending per Household = $19,683

Note: *All others includes the following: Veteran's Health Services; Other Income Security; Police, Fire, Courts and Prisons; Other Health; Highways, Airports and Transit; Housing Assistance; Disaster Relief; Space; and Recreation and Culture.

Source: Bureau of Economic Analysis: Tax Foundation

Figure 14.3: State-Local Government Spending Received by Americans in 2004

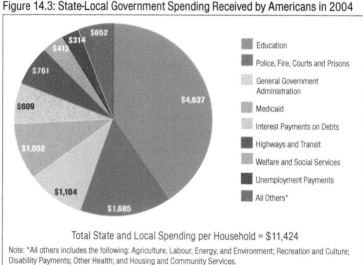

Total State and Local Spending per Household = $11,424

Note: *All others includes the following: Agriculture, Labour, Energy, and Environment; Recreation and Culture; Disability Payments; Other Health; and Housing and Community Services.

Source: Bureau of Economic Analysis: Tax Foundation

Figure 14.4: Some Households Received More Federal Government Spending Than They Paid in Federal Taxes, and Some Received Less (Calendar Year 2004)

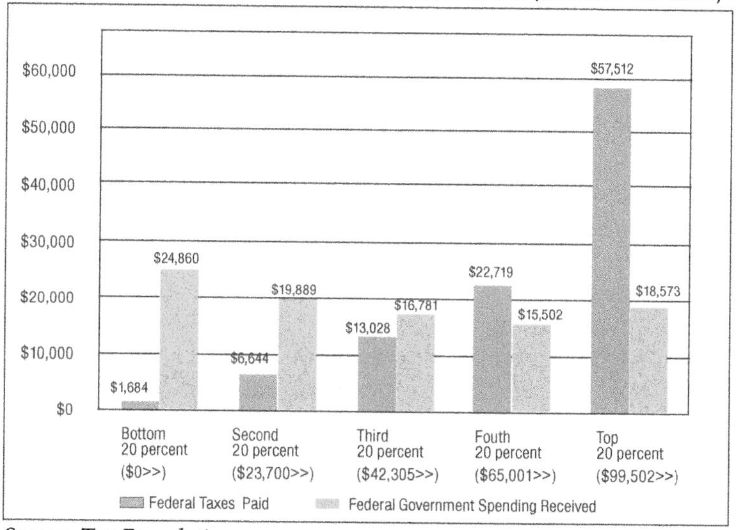

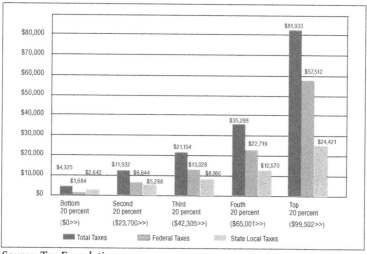

Source: Tax Foundation

Figure 14.5: Average Dollars of Taxes Paid by Households in Each Income Group in 2004

Source: Tax Foundation

The US fiscal system offers 'very strong reasons' that make it rational for households to limit their supply of labour and to curtail their saving with high marginal net rates from 24 to 45 percent on current and lifecycle labour supply. The system also offers very high-income young and middle-aged households, as well as older households, extensive opportunities to avoid taxation by contributing to tax-privileged retirement accounts. Overall, the pattern of marginal net tax rates on earnings, earnings from saving and the tax avoidance arrangements can best be described as 'bizarre'.

A distinguishing feature of the system is the way in which very young and middle-aged households across the earnings distribution can face very high marginal net tax rates. These high net rates of tax result from the interaction of different rules applied to different transfer payments that offer and withdraw benefits to households in different circumstances. The Congressional Budget Office provides detailed analysis of marginal tax rates and their effect on labour supply for some years. These, however, give an incomplete picture because they do not take account of state income taxes, sales taxes and other federal transfer programmes that would be normally scored as expenditure programmes rather than tax policies. There are at least seven major transfer programmes offering cash or in-kind benefits. These federal programmes further combine and interact with state tax and benefit programmes.

Kotlikoff and Rapson looked at a series of stylised households in different circumstances to estimate their incomes after the effects of taxes and benefits over a lifetime. They found that a single person aged 30 earning $10,000 faced a marginal net tax rate of 72 percent – partly because households that are eligible for Medicaid, TADF and other welfare benefits in the current year will not receive those benefits as their earnings rise. A 45-year-old couple with earnings of $25,000 in Massachusetts would have earned close to the minimum wage for full-time work and would have been 30 percent above the federal poverty line. Earning at that level would have been low enough in Massachusetts to make the couple eligible for Medicaid for the whole family. A couple of this age with two college-bound dependent children and a mortgage of $30,000 would have a net income of $40,000 from EITC, Medicaid and other transfer payments. If the couple earns additional income it will face a net rate of withdrawal of EITC at the rate of 21 cents per additional dollar earned and will lose eligibility for Medicare worth about $15,000. After losing its benefits, a household earning $25,000 would have to earn $50,000 in order to maintain its standard of living.

Kotlikoff and Rapson conclude that similar high net taxes apply to all low-income households regardless of age or marital status. Over the lifecycle of a 60-year-old couple, earning $55,000 a year for the duration of a working life is only marginally better off than a couple earning $10,000. The $55,000-income household will have a lifetime spending power of $480,000, compared to $473.000. And over a lifetime, all households with incomes between $10,000 and $55,000 would be worse off than households with an annual income of $10,000. The reason is that between $12-13,000, the household loses its Medicaid benefits in retirement as a result of its asset test, and with incomes between $17,000 and $18,000 a year households lose Medicaid benefits in the ages between 60 and 65. This loss of eligibility for healthcare under Medicaid amounts to hundreds of thousands of dollars when expressed in terms of net present value.

The picture that emerges from Kotlikoff's papers is that significant average and marginal tax rates limit and distort the labour supply and the saving of households across the earnings distribution, including low-income and average-income households.

This would appear to be the result of two things. The first is a public sector (federal, state and local government) that absorbs nearly two-fifths of national income. One way or another, that will impose a tax burden and incentive distortion that will travel down the earning distribution so that average households face high marginal tax rates, as do many households at quite low multiples of average earnings. The second reason is that part of that spending is targeted on helping low-income households and households that have difficulty in financing the purchase of expensive services such as university education and healthcare. This assistance is targeted and has complex conditions attached to it. It is withdrawn as incomes rise, further compounding the average and marginal tax rates needed to finance public sector expenditure of close to two fifths of national income.

This set of labour market disincentives is further aggravated by the fact that over the earnings distribution, different means-tested transfers kick in and out in an erratic way. This is because different groups of policymakers and legislators with different concerns constructed programmes that interact and conflict. This partly arises out of the interaction of federal and state programmes, but it also comes from the way different programmes are sponsored and passed into law by Congress.

Marginal tax rates across the earnings distribution: a Manhattan skyline

The present tax regime still continues to carry the imprint of the last major changes to the tax system made by President Bush in 2002, when the Economic Growth and Tax Relief Reconciliation Act (EGTRRA) was signed into law. The main purpose of this measure was to reduce marginal tax rates to improve the long-term supply performance of the economy. This was also helped by temporary tax rebates intended to act as a fiscal stimulus during the recession that followed the tech-wreck in 2000. Many supporters of the supply-side measures were sceptical of its efficacy as an immediate fiscal stimulus and the surprising thing has been how later research has indicated that it gave a temporary boost to household income and consumption when it was needed. This aspect of the Act is discussed more extensively in the chapter on fiscal policy as part of demand management. The political purpose of EGTRRA was to cut taxes and to deliver on President George W Bush's election promise to sort out the marriage penalty in the tax system.

In the *Economic Report of the President* in 2003, the Council of Economic Advisers set out the tax rates that taxpayers really face and produced as clear explanation of the issues. It explains the framework of statutory tax rates and brackets gives a misleading impression of the effective marginal rate a taxpayer will pay on their last dollar of earnings. It points out that 'even though statutory rates are relatively low at low levels of income, reflecting the progressivity of the current tax rate schedule, the effective marginal tax rates low-income taxpayers face can in some situations be unexpectedly high.'

Figure 14.6: Marginal Federal Income Tax Rates for Hypotherical Couple in 2003

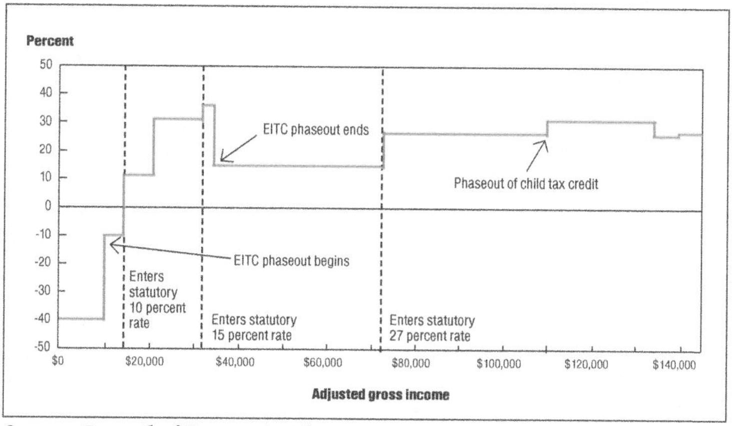

Source: Council of Economic Advisors

This shows the effective marginal tax rate for a hypothetical family of four at various income levels. The interesting feature of this is that effective tax rates do not rise consistently with income. There are 'numerous spikes and steps that reflect the phase-ins and phaseouts of various deductions, credits and other provisions'. Taxpayers may receive a benefit such as the child tax credit, but find that the tax on their last dollar of income is pushed up as the credit phases out.

Figure 14.7: Distribution of Marginal Federal Income Tax Rates for Joint Filers in 2003

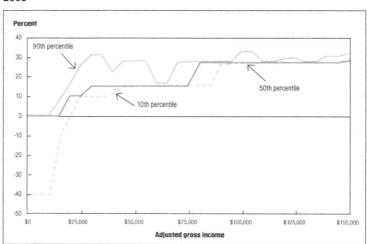

Source: Department of the Treasury

The above chart presents the distribution of effective marginal tax rates for taxpayers at given income levels and the extent to which they vary. It shows marginal tax rates for the 10th, 50th and 90th percentiles, where taxpayers are ranked at each level by their marginal tax rate. At any given income level, 50 percent of taxpayers will have marginal rates above the line indicated for the median. Ten percent of taxpayers will have marginal rates exceeding the line for the 90th percentile. Ten percent of taxpayers with $50,000 in income will have marginal tax rates that are below 15 percent, the tax rate at the 10th percentile. Some 50 percent have marginal tax rates below and half above 15.3 percent; and 10 percent have marginal tax rates above 27.8 percent. Marginal tax rates diverge considerably even among taxpayers with the same income. This is even more pronounced at lower levels of income.

Figure 14.8: Hourly Wages at Selected Percentiles for Workers Aged 16–64

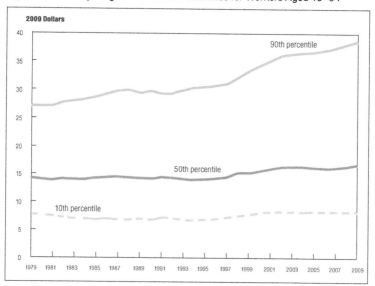

Source Congressional Budget Office using Census Bureau Data from Current Population Survey

The *Economic Report of the President* explained 'the divergence arises because of the various deductions and credits that phase in and then out at various rates, depending on a host of taxpayer characteristics and choices. Indeed, these phase-ins and phase-outs would cause considerable variation in effective marginal rates even under a flat tax rate schedule.'

The tax system is not only complex because of its rates, brackets and income-targeted transfer payments, but because of the way multiple definitions are used for the same thing in different parts of the tax system.

The *Economic Report of the President* in 2003 showed how the tax code defines a 'child' in at least five different ways for the purposes of qualifying for the child tax credit, the child and dependent care tax credit, to determine the head of household filing status, the earned income tax credit and for the exemption for dependents. Multiple definitions for taxpayers with children also apply to provisions in the tax code to assist with education expenses, household maintenance tests and earnings tests. In a paper *How Sensitive Are Taxpayers to Marginal Tax Rates? Evidence from Income Bunching in the United States* that looked at the effect of marginal tax rates generated by measures such as the Earned Income Tax Credit Child Tax Credit and temporary Making Work Pay Tax Credit between 1996 and 2014, published in February 2016 Jacob A. Mortenson and Andrew Whitten include a chart that graphically illustrates the way that the US tax system continues to present something of a Manhattan skyline inn terms of marginal tax rates for people with children:

Figure 14.9 Kinks faced by a single family with two children 2014

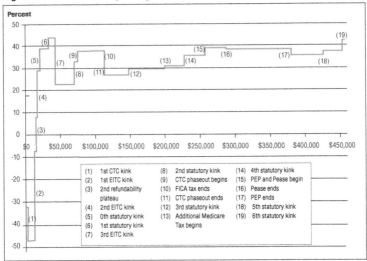

Notes: We assume that the taxpayer (i) only has wage income, (ii) pays no state income taxes, (iii) has $10,000 in itemized deductions, and (iv) claims the EITC and CTC. We ignore the Alternative Minimum Tax. To measure PEP kink sizes we take the most conservative approach, assuming the marginal increment to income is $2,500. FICA refers to the Federal Insurance Contributions Act tax, which applies to earned income up to a year-specific cap. Kinks associated with the Making Work Pay Tax Credit – applicable in 2009 and 2010 – are not pictured here.

Source: "How Sensitive Are Taxpayers to Marginal Tax Rates?" Mortenson Whiten

America's tax and benefit system is not exceptional

The US is no different from other developed countries that have tried to relieve poverty among low-income households. Governments throughout the OECD and in Europe, in particular, have found they faced a number of awkward constraints in devising acceptable and effective policy.

First, in a market society there will always be a significant proportion of people who cannot get work that ensures they will be able to have an income over their lifetime sufficient to provide them with an acceptable standard of living, as far as the wider community is concerned. This means that governments have to intervene to assist households. The question is how to do it?

Second, each of the main policy interventions has consequences for labour market and saving incentives. Minimum wages either put people out of work or create segmented labour markets where people with low marginal revenue products are excluded, or they are set at a level where there is little adverse impact on employment but the level of pay does little to reduce household poverty, particularly where there are large numbers of children involved. Generous benefits for non-working households financed through general taxation and payroll social security taxes create a tax wedge that damages the incentive to work.

The targeted benefits paid to people with jobs result in very high net rates of withdrawal similar to high marginal taxes as incomes rise and the means test withdraws benefit. The US, like the UK with its complex system of working families tax credits partly modelled on the EITC, exhibits limitations to labour supply created by high marginal rates of withdrawal for many households. In contrast, continental European countries affect labour supply through a combination of high tax rates, high minimum wages and other employment measures. What is interesting is that although the policy rationales and chosen institutional arrangements may be different, the outcomes are similar in terms of labour supply. America is not so very different from other advanced OECD economies and it appears to suffer from labour market distortion of the sort exhibited by European economies.

Latent structural problems in a labour market can be masked for many years by a generally good macroeconomic performance, such as the one that followed the recovery in American economic activity after the recession in the early 1990s. But structural rigidities are exposed when an economy suffers an adverse shock of the magnitude of the Great Recession. The way jobs were lost and the slowness in the fall in unemployment as output stabilised and recovered appear to suggest something structural is wrong. Initially, the reaction of many economists and policymakers was to regard the sharp deterioration in labour market conditions as evidence of impressive gains in productivity. The fact there was such a large quantity adjustment for the fall in output, however, suggests the deterioration in the labour market was not simply another iteration of American jobs flexibility, but rather specific evidence of structural labour market problems in the US economy. American public policy has worked cumulatively to raise employment costs, reducing demand for labour and constraining the supply of labour through the perverse and distorting effects of the tax and benefit system.

Brett Fawley and Lucinda Juvenal, two economists at the Federal Reserve Bank of St Louis, in a research note *Unemployment and the Role of Monetary Policy* published in December 2010 look at duration of unemployment for all months since 1948, and find that in the last three economic cycles since the trough in output in 1991, duration of unemployment has risen. They conclude that 'on balance, structural unemployment during economic downturns has increased since 1991'. They potentially attribute the cause of this change to 'an increasingly rapid pace of technological change', which 'erodes worker skills more rapidly than in the past, and that the erosion becomes evident primarily through downturns when separated workers seek jobs with new employers'.

Increased duration of unemployment makes future attachment to it more difficult. Part of such an explanation will turn the relative cost of labour, and that will be influenced by the wider institutional background.

These increasingly evident structural labour market problems will aggravate the perception that the US economy cannot deliver rising living standards as easily as it once did. The belief that life gets better for everyone in America – and especially for lower- and middle-income earners – is an important part of the self-perception of Americans that is vividly expressed in the rhetoric of US politicians and business people. Protracted stagnation of middle-income wages combined with rising household costs over the lifecycle would be compounded if getting a job at all is made more difficult for marginal participants in the labour market. In terms of the contribution they make to overall household income, these so-called marginal labour market participants make an important contribution to household welfare.

Chapter 15

Distribution of income in the US

A dvanced market economies normally exhibit a wide range of income and earnings in the labour market. This means many people and households are not able to afford the goods and services considered necessary for an acceptable life by the political communities they live in. Low incomes and the unevenness of earnings mean that many households find it difficult to smooth their spending and consumption over their lifetime through saving, borrowing and the orderly spending of savings. The combination of imperfect information of a fundamental character – such as how long a person will live – and imperfect credit and investment markets mean households cannot easily match lifetime income, savings and spending. In addition, certain households will never have sufficient lifetime income to meet their spending requirements. A good example of that would be a person whose period of labour market earnings is limited by disability, who lives for a long period and has complex chronic care and health expenses. The dispersion of earnings is at the heart of the reason why extensive public intervention is needed in market economies.

Information about the dispersion of earnings and distribution of income is important as a background to understanding public expenditure and how efficiently private markets and public policy works. There may be cases where private markets do not work competitively and result in economic rents that public policy seeks to correct. This is the central proposition that informs competition policy, and the anti-trust Sherman and Clayton Acts passed at the end of the 19th and early 20th centuries. Maladroit public intervention itself may establish opportunities for economic renting seeking by different lobby group interests. There has also been increasing concern over the last 20 years about the problems of agency and the framework of corporate governance in the US and in other advanced market economies.

It is therefore useful to take the time to understand available evidence around the evolution of incomes and their distribution. Average household real income growth has been constrained over the past 30 years and there has been a pronounced polarisation of income, with a widening gap in income between the top and the bottom of the distribution. This has happened during a time when household costs for things such as healthcare and university tuition fees have become more expensive. There is an extensive literature on recent trends in the distribution of wages and income in the US and its causes and this chapter focuses on identifying the main trends.

During the Great Recession household incomes fell and only recovered slowly in the seven years that followed its start. The US Census Bureau in *Income Poverty 2014* published in September 2015, provides a clear picture of the dispersion of household income and some indication of its longer term evolution. It reports that median household income was $53,657 in 2014, not statistically different in real terms from the 2013 median of $54,462. This is the third consecutive year that the annual change was not statistically significant, following two consecutive years of annual declines in median household income. In 2014, real median household income was 6.5 percent lower than in 2007, the year before the Great Recession. The Census Bureau reports two measures of income inequality: the shares of aggregate household income received by quintiles and the Gini index. In addition to these measures, the Census Bureau also produces estimates of the ratio of income percentiles; the Theil index, which is similar to the Gini index in that it is a single statistic that summarizes the dispersion of income across the entire income distribution. Changes in income inequality between 2013 and

2014 were not statistically significant as measured by the shares of aggregate household income by quintiles, the Gini index, the MLD, the Theil index, and the Atkinson measures. Households in the lowest quintile had incomes of $21,432 or less in 2014. Households in the second quintile had incomes between $21,433 and $41,186, those in the third quintile had incomes between $41,187 and $68,212, and those in the fourth quintile had incomes between $68,213 and $112,262. Households in the highest quintile had incomes of $112,263 or more. The top 5 percent had incomes of $206,568 or more. The Gini index was 0.480 in 2014, not statistically different from 2013. Since 1993, the earliest year available for comparable measures of income inequality, the Gini index was up 5.9 percent. Since 1993, the earliest year available for comparable measures of income inequality, the Gini index was up 5.9 percent Comparing changes in household income at selected percentiles shows that income inequality has increased between 1999 (the year that household income peaked before the 2001 recession) and 2014. Incomes at the 50th and 10th percentiles declined 7.2 percent and 16.5 percent, respectively, while income at the 90th percentile increased 2.8 percent between 1999 and 2014. In 2014, the 90th to 10th percentile income ratio was 12.83, not statistically different from the ration in 2013. From 1999, the 90th to 10th percentile income ratio increased by 23.1 percent.

Another measure of income inequality the Census Bureau presents is an equivalence adjusted income estimate that takes into account the number of people living in the household and how those people share resources and take advantage of economies of scale. For example, the money-income based distribution treats an income of $30,000 for a single-person household and a family household similarly, while the equivalence-adjusted income of $30,000 for a single-person household would be more than twice the equivalence-adjusted income of $30,000 for a family household with two adults and two children. The equivalence adjustment used by the Census Bureau takes account of an average, child consume less than an adult; that as family size increases, expenses do not increase at the same rate; and that the increase in expenses is greater for a the first child of a single-parent family than the first child of a two-adult family. In both 2013 and 2014, the Gini index was lower when based on an equivalence-adjusted income estimate than on the traditional money-income estimate, suggesting in the judgement of the Census Bureau, a more equal income distribution. The income shares in the lower quintiles are higher with equivalence-adjusted income than money income while the reverse is true for the higher quintiles. This redistribution would be expected because the lower end of the income distribution has a higher concentration of single-person households and smaller family sizes than those at the upper end of the distribution. Equivalence adjusting therefore increases the relative income of people living in lower-income groups. Based on equivalence-adjusted income, changes in inequality between 2013 and 2014 were not statistically significant as measured by the shares of aggregate income, the Gini index, the MLD, the Theil index, and the Atkinson measures.

Real earnings growth

One of the most comprehensive studies on the distribution of wages, is by the Congressional Budget Office titled *Changes in the Distribution of Workers' Hourly Wages Between 1970 and 2009* published in February 2011. It shows that during the 30 years to 2009, median average wages rose by 20 percent in real terms and reached $17 an hour. For long-term comparisons, it is better to look at earnings for men because they have been less affected by changes in labour market participation than wages for women. Male median wages rose to $18.50 an hour – around $37,000 annually for a fulltime employee over a year. Between 1979 and 2009, median male wage rates rose by around 8 percent. At the top end of the earnings distribution, 90th percentile wage rate increased by 40 percent to $43 – or $86,000 annually. Towards the bottom end of the distribution, real wages increased by 5 percent in the 10th percentile to $8.90 an hour, or $17,000 annually. These numbers offer two important pieces of information.

The first is the slow growth in average real wages and the very slow growth of low wage earners, and secondly a sharply wider distribution of income from hourly wages.

Table 15.1: Hourly Wages at Selected Percentiles and in Selected Years for Men and Women Aged 16–64

(2009 dollars)	Percentile			Percentage Difference	
	10th	50th	90th	10th vs. 50th	90th vs. 50th
Men					
1979	8.50	17.10	30.70	-50	80
1986	7.60	17.20	33.60	-56	95
1989	7.80	16.10	32.30	-52	101
1999	8.50	17.30	37.00	-51	114
2007	8.70	17.80	40.50	-51	128
2009	8.90	18.50	43.00	-52	132
Women					
1979	7.40	11.00	19.70	-33	79
1986	6.30	11.90	22.50	-47	89
1989	6.30	12.00	23.80	-48	98
1999	7.50	13.50	28.60	-44	112
2007	7.80	14.70	32.60	-47	122
2009	8.00	15.10	33.50	-47	122

Note: Wages are converted to 2009 dollars using the personal consumption expenditure price index and rounded to the nearest 10 cents and a worker's wage is weighted by his or her hours worked. Data are shown for 1979, 1989, 1999, and 2007 because those years are all close to business-cycle peaks. Data for 1986 are shown to highlight trends that shifted in the mid-980s, and data for 2009 are shown because they are the most recent available.

Source: Congressional Budget Office based on monthly data from Census Bureau, Current Population Survey, Outgoing Rotation Groups, 1979 to 2009.

Figure 15.1: Hourly Wages at Selected Percentiles for Men and Women Ages 16–64

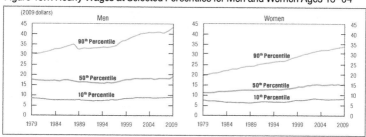

Note: Wages are converted to 2009 dollars using the personal consumption expenditure price index and rounded to the nearest 10 cents and a worker's wage is weighted by his or her hours worked.
Source: Congressional Budget Office based on monthly data from Census Bureau, Current Population Survey, Outgoing Rotation Groups, 1979 to 2009.

Price deflator chosen

The price deflator used by the Congressional Budget Office in this study is the personal consumption expenditure price index (PCEPI) rather than the consumer price index (CPI). In the 1990s, there was an extensive debate about whether the CPI over-stated inflation. This debate focuses around the construction of the index and the weights it employed, and the extent that it factored in improvements in quality.

Table 15.2: Median Hourly Wages of Men and Women Aged 16–64, by Educational Attainment

	Less than High School	High School Diploma or GED	Some College or Associate's Degree	Bachelor's Degree	Graduate Courses or Degree
Median Hourly Wage (2009 dollars)					
Men					
1979	13.30	16.80	17.70	21.40	23.70
1989	11.10	14.90	16.20	22.50	27.00
1999	10.10	15.00	17.20	24.70	31.20
2009	11.10	15.20	17.50	26.20	34.30
Women					
1979	8.60	10.60	11.60	14.40	17.60
1989	7.90	10.80	12.60	16.80	20.90
1999	8.20	11.40	13.20	19.20	24.90
2009	9.00	12.10	14.00	20.30	26.60
Percentage Difference in Hourly Wage Relative to that of High School Graduates					
Men					
1979	-21	n.a.	5	27	41
1989	-26	n.a.	9	51	81
1999	-33	n.a.	15	65	108
2009	-27	n.a.	15	72	126
Women					
1979	-19	n.a.	9	36	66
1989	-27	n.a.	17	56	94
1999	-28	n.a.	16	68	118
2009	-26	n.a.	16	68	120

Note: The survey question on educational attainment changed in 1992 to put more emphasis on credentials obtained rather than years completed. Wages are converted to 2009 dollars using the personal consumption expenditure price index and rounded to the nearest 10 cents, and a worker's wage is weighted by his or her hours worked.

Source: Congressional Budget Office based on monthly data from Census Bureau, Current Population Survey, Outgoing Rotation Groups, 1979 to 2009.

The argument made was that inflation was over-stated and if it were more accurately measured real income would be higher than those that had been reported in official statistics. The PCEPI is a more broadly based measure of price change constructed by the Bureau of Economic Analysis as part of its national income accounts. It accounts for changes in behaviour when consumers adjust their spending pattern in response to changes in relative prices. The average annual PCEPI inflation rate between 1979 and 2009 was 3.2 percent. In contrast, the average rate of annual inflation measured by the CPI was 3.4 percent.

Arguments about real earnings growth and the standard of living of households at the lower end of the earnings distribution have often been based on whether the deflator used understates the real level of earnings. The merit of using the PCEPI is that it enables economists to step aside from the debate surrounding the accuracy of the CPI.

Slow real wage growth

Real earnings growth in the US has been slow for most households over the past 30 years. Real growth in output per worker rose by 59 percent between 1979 and 2009 – during this time, median wages only rose by 20 percent. The share of national income taken by workers' compensation fell by 3 percentage points over that period, falling from 67 to 64 percent. This represents a modest and significant shift in factor shares away from labour to capital. Factor shares historically are stable with very little movement, so a shift of 3 percentage points is a significant, albeit modest, movement.

Dispersion of wages increases

The dispersion of wages widened significantly. In the upper half of the wage distribution, the difference between wages in the 90th percentile and the 50th percentile widened throughout the period from 1979 to 2009. In 1979, the difference was 80 percent. By 2009, the difference had increased to 132 percent for men.

The dispersion in the lower half of the earnings distribution also increased. The 10th percentile male wage rate was 50 percent lower than the 50th percentile in 1979. In 2009, the difference was 52 percent. Overall the principal driver widening the dispersion of wages was growth in wage rates at the top end of the earnings distribution.

Wages are only part of the story: the employment cost index

Wages are only part of many employees' compensation. There are often additional non-wage benefits such as paid leave, pensions and health insurance. In 2007, non-wage benefits represented 27 percent of total compensation – 8 percent went towards healthcare, 6 percent paid leave, 3 percent retirement benefits and a further 9 percent went on legally required benefits. Average employee benefit costs to employers have risen as a ratio of total compensation from 25 percent in 1987 to 27 percent 2007. In 2007 a smaller proportion of jobs carried health insurance than in 1987, but the average cost of those benefits increased from 5 percent to 8 percent of compensation.

Variation in compensation is greater than that for wage rates, particularly in the bottom half of the earnings distribution. The 10th percentile of wages was 50 percent lower than the median average wage, while its non-wage compensation was 56 percent lower than median compensation. The principal difference arises not from differences in costs of benefits, but from provision or non-provision of benefits. Employees with wages closer to the average wage were more likely to receive health insurance and paid leave than employees closer to the bottom of the earnings distribution. The difference in compensation and wages in the upper half of the distribution was less. The 90th percentile of wages was 129 percent higher than the median wage, but of its non-wage compensation was 133 percent higher than the average.

Rising employer health insurance costs

The cost of health insurance has risen, but it is not clear how this has affected either employment or employee welfare or incomes. A study published in the US Monthly Labour Review in June 2008, *Employer's health insurance cost burden, 1996-2005,* by Christine Eibner and Susan Marquis shows that while the health insurance component of the employment cost index has risen sharply, benefits packages for employees became less generous – particularly for those at the lower end of the earning distribution. Between 1996 and 2005 the cost of health insurance rose relative to payroll by 34 percent. The average employer offering health insurance by 2005 was paying in excess of 10 percent of its payroll cost to provide it. The increase in health costs was highest for businesses paying low wages, where the cost rose by 56 percent. The article shows that annual wage earnings in the lowest quartile of the earnings distribution fell in real terms from $15,437 to $12,975 (2005).

Eibner and Marquis make an interesting observation that this is consistent with the large body of economic literature exploring the widening gap in wages between skilled and unskilled workers since the late 1980s, suggesting that increasing health insurance costs relative to payroll at a business employing lower-skilled workers 'could be associated, at least in part, with growing wage inequality'. The implication is that higher employment benefit costs arising out of higher health insurance are partly offset by lower wages.

The general assumption of most economic analysis is that in the long term, healthcare costs simply replace cash earnings within the compensation package. Employers have also responded to higher health insurance costs by increasing employee contribution requirements, reducing the generosity of insurance plans and increasing co-payments and co-insurance. They find that the 'most disadvantaged workers may be the most adversely affected by rising healthcare costs'. Despite the rise in costs between 1996 and 2006, there was an increase in the proportion of employers that offered health insurance cover. Coverage actually rose by 11 percent, according to Eibner and Marquis.

The employer offer of health insurance has been maintained even in those establishments that have experienced some of the greatest costs – small businesses and non-unionised establishments. This may reflect the passing of the Health Insurance Portability and Accountability Act in 1996, which offered opportunities for greater pooling of risk with the result that average health costs have increased without individual employers experiencing a pronounced cost increase. In addition, low-income employees may have become more interested in being offered health insurance from their employer, as pressures on state finances in the Noughties resulted in restrictions on Medicaid.

During the same period access to Medicaid was expanded, but at the expense of its coverage. Eibner and Marquis point out that while the employee offer of health insurance remained a benefit, the take-up of it declined among employees as their contribution rates went gone up. The proportion of non-elderly Americans covered by an employer-sponsored health insurance fell by 4.6 percent between 2000 and 2004. Employee contributions were maintained over the period as costs to workers increased in proportion to overall cost growth, while overall employee coverage fell.

Why has the wage gap widened?

The causes of the widening wage gap in US over the past 30 years are complex and a full analysis is beyond what can be covered here. However, there are some obvious influences

Market forces appear to have been the main drivers of change in widening the wage gap. David Auter, Lawrence Katz and Melissa Kearney, in their paper *The Polarization of the US Labor Market* (NBER 2006), explored the issues involved and concluded that the main cause was a shift in demand for certain job tasks 'spurred by advancing information technology and indirectly by its impact on international outsourcing' went some way towards explaining the polarisation of wages in the US.

The other factors are changes in the demand for different types of labour relative to their supply. Where the demand for more highly skilled labour has risen and that for lower-skilled labour fallen, the relative supply of lower skilled labour has increased. There has been a reduction in the demand for labour in the middle of the earnings distribution, with the number of jobs falling relative to the lower and higher part of the earnings distribution. This has resulted in labour market polarisation at both ends of the earnings spectrum. This is the so-called U-shaped effect, where jobs and earnings in the middle diminish and those at either end rise. This has been driven, in part, by the technology that has replaced many routine tasks yet demands greater education and skills to manage. Increased international trade has exposed domestic US markets to greater competition, which works to reduce wages in America relative to those in lower wage economies through the operation of competition and comparative advantage. This then results in the manufacturing sector contracting, and with it a reduction in many jobs paying incomes bunched around the average of the earning distribution that would traditionally have been regarded as 'good jobs' by many people.

Technology, education and the demand for skilled labour

Through out most of the second half of the 20th century, there was an increase in demand for workers with more, rather than less education, as part of skill-biased technological change. In the late 1980s, this change was further embodied in production and business processing methods as a result of advances in microchip technology and other computer-related technical progress. This reduced demand for employees doing routine cognitive work, typical of many middle-skilled jobs concentrated in the middle of the earning distribution. It increased demand for employees doing more complex work involving analysis, evaluation and making decisions. Increased international trade also changed the demand for different levels of skills as the pattern of goods and services produced domestically in the US changed through increased globalisation and increasingly contested domestic markets. The result has been both higher wages for more skilled and educated workers relative to those of less well educated and trained workers and an increase in employment in occupations demanding higher levels of education.

Figure 15.2: Mean Years of Schooling by Birth Cohort

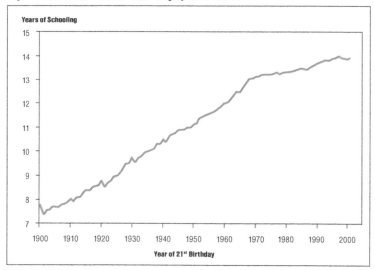

Note: Years of schooling at 30 years of age, Methodology described in Goldin and Katz (2007). Graph shows estimates of the average years of schooling at 30 years of age for each birth cohort, obtained from regression of the log of mean years of schooling by birth cohort-year cell on a full set of birth cohort dummies and a quartic age. Sample includes all native born residents ages 25 to 64 in the 1940–2000 decennial census IPUMS samples and the 2005 CPS MORG.

Source: Department of Commerce (Bureau of the Census), 1940–2000 Census IPUMS, 2005 CPS MORG; Goldin and Katz (2007).

In the 1980s, before the surge in information technologies the share of total employment in occupations requiring low levels of education fell. The increase in demand for education was widening the wage gap between workers in the 10th percentile of the earning spectrum and the average, as well as between average income workers and those in the 90th percentile. In contrast in the 1990s, technological change increased demand for non-routine cognitive work relative to routine cognitive work, with the demand for manual work appearing to be unchanged. The total share of employment in occupations needing higher education levels has increased relative to the share of employment accounted for by average-education occupations. The demand for low-education or manual occupations rose relative to the share in total employment of average-education occupations. The demand for routine manual work that must be done at specific times and locations or involves interacting with people – such as janitors, waiters and home healthcare workers – also rose.

This has resulted in the US labour market exhibiting increased polarisation, with employment and wages being concentrated more towards the bottom and the top of the wage distribution. Variation of wages in the bottom half of the distribution since 1990 appears to have arisen out of slower growth in demand for routine cognitive workers relative to that of manual work. As a result, wages in the 10th percentile of the earning spectrum have stopped falling relative to the average wage rate. The continued rise in wages at the 90th percentile reflects the widening gap between the top of the wages scale and the both the average and 10th percentile.

Supply of skilled and educated workers

While the demand for more educated and skilled workers rose in the 1980s and 1990s, the supply of educated workers entering the labour market relative to the existing stock of educated workers slowed significantly compared with the 1940s, 1950s and 1960s. This combination of higher demand and slower improvements in the relative level of education worked to raise wages over the past 30 years.

Figure 15.3: Median Hourly Wage, by Educational Attainment, for Men and Women, Ages 18–64

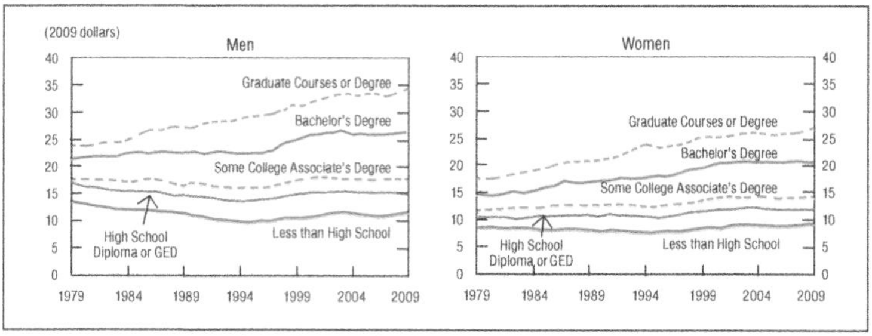

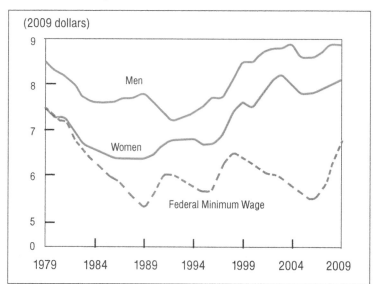

Source: Congressional Budget Office based on monthly data from Census Bureau, Current Population Survey, Outgoing Rotation Groups, 1979 to 2009.

Figure 15.4: Hourly Wages at the 10th Percentile for Men and Women and the Federal Minimum Wage

Source: Congressional Budget Office based on monthly data from Census Bureau, Current Population Survey, Outgoing Rotation Groups, 1979 to 2009; and the US Department of Labor.

The Education of birth cohorts entering the labor market rose sharply until the cohort born around 1950. At that point, education stopped improving for men and increased much more for women. The educational attainment of young people entering the labour market increased much more slowly after 1970. The average stock of human capital continued to increase despite this slowdown, because the new workers entering the workforce had more education than those leaving through retirement. The average number of years of education completed by workers between 1969 and 1979 increased by one year from 11.5 years to 12.5 years. Between 1979 and 1989 it only increased by 0.5 years and in the 20 years between 1989 and 2009 it increased by 0.4 years.

The slowdown in improvements in educational attainment during a period of rapid growth in demand for more educated workers increased the wage premium for university graduates, one of the main reasons for the increase in wage dispersion in the top half of the wage distribution.

Federal minimum wage

Public policy has also changed. The federal minimum wage for many years was left unchanged and lost around 30 percent of its real value. Since the Clinton administration in the 1990s, it has only been partially and erratically indexed. Minimum wage legislation tends to be a highly contentious issue. The balance of economic judgment currently is that a higher minimum wage can help some workers on low wages living in poverty, but it comes potentially at the expense of fewer jobs being available to those workers. As a public policy instrument it is not necessarily well targeted, because poverty relates to household income and the number of people in a household and their needs. Some workers on the minimum wage will be part of households that are not in poverty, and in that sense it can be a poorly aimed instrument. Whether it does actual damage to employment depends on how high it is set and how it interacts with other terms and conditions, such as discretionary employee benefits.

Declining power of trade unions in the private sector

Trade union membership and union power have diminished in the private sector in the US over the last 35 years. This reflected structural shifts in the composition of output and employment. Traditionally, unions have found it easier to organise and recruit in manufacturing plants. As employment has shifted out of manufacturing, unions have found it hard to recruit and organise in the services that have developed. Unions can only be effective in the long-term where they are dealing with an employer that enjoys monopoly or at least some persistent market power in less than fully competitive markets, enabling them to negotiate to share the economic rent with the employer.

Where such monopoly or quasi-monopolistic power diminishes, there will be less scope for unions to extract a pay premium or wage mark-up. Over the past 30 years, US markets have been exposed to greater competition through domestic deregulation and international competition. Against such a background, unions have found it harder to be effective. Some labour market analysts would attribute part of the widening in the wage gap to the reduction in trade union power. Whether this is part of the cause or simply the manifestation of more fundamental shifts in the demand for labour and the changing character of market structures is less clear. In a strict neo-classical analytical framework, trade unions cannot in aggregate raise wages for all workers. They may succeed in raising the wages of some individual workers, but in the long-term they will not raise wages within national income, because higher wages will displace employment.

Migration and the impact of immigrants

There has been a contentious public debate about the impact immigrants have on the US labour market in terms of unemployment, lowering wages and raising the overall performance of the economy. The research evidence is very mixed, and a clear picture does not emerge from it. There is general agreement that the American economy benefits from highly skilled migrants. The impact of less-skilled migrants on native-born Americans is less clear. Harry Holzer, formerly chief economist at the Department of Labor, in a paper titled *Immigration and Less-Skilled Workers in the US* (Urban Institute January 2011) looks at the research literature and concludes that there is little identifiable impact on the employment and incomes of native born Americans. He says 'even the most negative estimates of the impact on similar US workers suggest that in the long run, immigration accounts for only a small share of the deterioration we have observed in less-skilled Americans' labour market employment and earnings'.

There is some effect in lowering the wages of other immigrants competing at the very bottom end of the labour market, and migration may have contributed to some young people dropping out of secondary school and the labour market – these effects may be found mainly among black and other minority communities. The two main bodies of research on the impact of recent immigration have been done by David Card of the University of California at Berkeley and George Borjas of Harvard.

In *'Is the New Immigration Really So Bad?'* published in the Economic Journal in 2005 and 'Immigration and Inequality' published in the *American Economic Review* in 2009, Card finds that less-educated immigrants have very little impact on less-educated, native-born Americans. Borjas, in 'Immigration Policy and Human Capital' published in *Reshaping the American Workforce in a Changing Economy* in 2007, identifies a more substantial and negative impact on native-born American workers.

Holzer points out that their research methods differ. Card's work looks at differences between US metropolitan statistical areas, while Borjas argues these 'cross-sectional' estimates understate the likely negative impact of migration, because immigrants are attracted to strong labour markets where they might be easily absorbed and native-born workers move out of these labour markets. Holzer concludes migration has had little long-term impact on labour market earnings, which is similar to the conclusion of the Congressional Budget Office study looking at long-term trends in wages.

Market household income

The Congressional Budget Office in October 2011 published *Trends in the Distribution of Household Income Between 1979 and 2007*. This study looked at the trend in household income over the same period as the study on real hourly wages, from 1979 to 2007. The beginning and end points are convenient, because each year is similar in terms of overall economic performance and the level of economic activity. Both years represent economic peaks shortly before a recession in output. The study used data from the Internal Revenue Service and the US Census Bureau to look at the growth in household income and its dispersion. Real mean average market household income grew by 58 percent between 1979 and 2007, and real median market household income grew by 19 percent.

Figure 15.5: Concentration of Major Sources of Market Income, 1979 and 2009

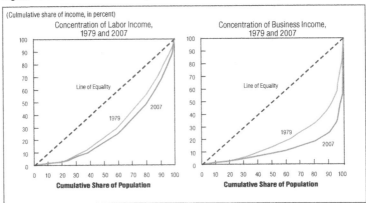

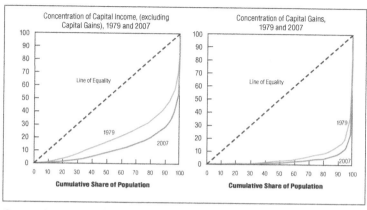

Source: Congressional Budget Office

During this period, market household income became much more dispersed. The Gini index for household market income rose from 0.479 in 1979 to 0.590 by 2007, a 23 percent increase in dispersion of household income. Between 1979 and 1988 the Gini Index increased by about 1.25 percent a year. From 1991 to 2000 it increased by 1 percent a year and at an annual rate of 2 percent from 2002 through 2005, then changed little between 2005 and 2007. All sources of market household income became more dispersed. Labour income was the biggest contributor, because it is the largest source of income, even though the increase in concentration was smaller than in the increased concentration of other sources of income. The fall of wages and employee compensation within national income, and the increased share of profits within income, along with higher capital gains contributed to the increase in inequality of market income for households.

Household income after taxes and benefits

Taxes and benefits significantly affect household income in the US. The Congressional Budget Office study confirms their effect on household income is progressive. The distribution of after-transfer and after federal tax household income is more equal than the distribution of market household income. In 2007, the dispersion of after-tax income was about four-fifths as large as the dispersion of market income. The study estimates roughly 60 percent of this change was attributable to transfers and 40 percent to the effect of federal taxes.

Real mean average household income after federal taxes and transfers grew by 62 percent between 1979 and 2007. In the same period, real median after-tax income grew by 35 percent. Federal transfers and taxes reduce the Gini index by 10 percentage points, by 17 percent from 0.590 to 0.489. Changes to federal taxes and benefits between 1979 and 2007 have reduced the influence of taxes and transfers in mitigating income inequality. If transfers and taxes had the same impact they had in 1979, by 2007 the Gini index would have been 0.452 instead of its actual value of 0.489. As a result of the diminishing effect of transfers and federal taxes, the Gini index increased by 33 percent between 1979 and 2007.

This appears to have been the result of changes in the distribution of transfer payments, the rate of taxation and the composition of tax receipts. Although the scale of the transfer payments rose slightly, their distribution among households shifted. Transfer payments to the lower part of the income distribution were reduced. In 1979, the bottom 20 percent of households received more than 50 percent of transfer payments. In 2007, the bottom 20 percent of households received 35 percent of transfer payments. This shift reflects the growth in spending on programmes principally directed at assisting older households in retirement, such as Medicare. As a result, government transfer payments reduced the dispersion of household income less in 2007 than they did in 1979. The equalising effect of federal taxes also fell. The overall average federal tax rate fell slightly and the composition of revenue shifted from taxes that are progressive in their effect to less progressive payroll taxes. These offset the slightly greater concentration of income tax receipts from the higher end of the income distribution.

Importance of household income for economic welfare

A clear picture has emerged of relatively slow real growth in average wage and salary incomes and a wider dispersion of wages and salaries earned in the labour market. Wages and incomes are just part of the picture in terms of income distribution. Real median household income both before and after tax and benefits has grown modestly over the last three decades. The surprising suggestion from the two Congressional Budget Office studies of wages and household incomes is that real household incomes, before the effects of taxation and transfers, have not grown faster in relation to male wages. The study of household income trends used the CPIU-RS, the consumer price index for all urban consumers. It is likely that the CPI measure of inflation used in the study of household income may have exaggerated the effect of price change, resulting in an understatement of real household income. Over 30 years the scale of the effect is perhaps 5 or 6 percentage points.

In terms of economic welfare, overall income for a household is more important than simply looking at the evolution of wages. And income is also made up of pension and investment incomes and transfer payments made collectively through the public sector. Jonathan Heathcote, Fabrizo Perri and Giovanni Violante have explored these wider considerations in a research paper published by the Federal Reserve Bank of Minneapolis in October 2009 – *Unequal We Stand: An Empirical Analysis of Economic Inequality in the US, 1967 to 2006*. It provides an analysis of the key drivers of inequality, wages, income consumption, and wealth. It argues that changes in the structure of wages offers 'the most primitive measure of inequality' and that it is necessary to look at individuals earnings, household earnings, pre-government income, disposable income and, ultimately, consumption and wealth, as well as wages.

They confirm the widening differences in hourly wages since the early 1970s. They found the Gini coefficient for hourly male wages rose substantially by 11 points between 1976 and 2006. The increase in wage dispersion was concentrated at the bottom end of the distribution in the 1970s, across the distribution of wages in the 1980s and at the top from 1990. In terms of earnings, the number of hours worked is very important. From the 1970s until the mid1980s, the number of hours worked by low-skilled men declined as unemployment rose. Higher unemployment exacerbated inequality in earnings at the bottom of the wage distribution. When earnings are looked at in the context of households, household earnings inequality increases less than earnings inequality for the main earner.

Changing gender roles in household income

Average real male wages between 1967 and 2006 only rose 14 percent, and actually declined in the 1970s and 1980s. In contrast, real wages for women rose by 36 percent. The average number of hours worked each year by men fell from just under 2,200 hours to around 1,900 hours in the 1980s and have since remained at that level. The number of hours worked by women increased dramatically in the 1970s, rising from around 800 hours a year to almost 1,400 in the late 1990s. The increasing role of women in the labour market is central to understanding the relation between stagnant real hourly wages and hours worked for male workers with the rise in per capita labour income. Between 1967 and 2006, two-thirds of the growth of labour per capita income is attributable to growth in female income. Higher female income largely arises out of a 92 percent increase in the number of hours worked by women.

Taxes and benefits significantly narrow inequality of income

Disposable income, as opposed to earnings, after taxes and public sector transfer payments helps reduce inequality in the US. Public sector intervention has operated as a significant restraint that mitigates the consequences of increased earnings inequality since the 1970s. For people of working age, public transfer payments such as unemployment insurance and the welfare system along with taxes reduces dispersion of income.

Table 15.3: Sources of Change in the Gini Index for Market Income

	1979 to 1988	1988 to 1991	1991 to 2000	2000 to 2002	2002 to 2007	Total, 1979 to 2007
Change in Gini Index (percentage points)	5.7	-1.2	4.8	-1.8	3.6	11.1
Source of change (percentage points)						
Shift to more or less concentrated income sources	0.4	-0.8	2.2	-2.3	3.1	2.3
Change in concentration within each income source	5.3	-0.3	2.6	0.4	0.5	8.8
Share of change from each Source (percent)						
Shift to more or less concentrated income sources	8	70	45	124	85	21
Change in concentration within each income source	92	30	55	-24	15	79

Source: Congressional Budget Office

As a result of policy changes in the 1980s and in the 1990s the dampening effect of progressive income taxes and welfare benefits was reduced. Taxes became less progressive under President Reagan and then slightly more progressive under President Clinton. Transfer benefits changed in the mid-1990s and their role through traditional federal welfare was dramatically reduced as a result of the PROWORA Act 1996, which reduced cash assistance to poor households. At the same time, there was a big expansion of assistance through tax credits. The earned income tax credit more than tripled. Heathcote, Perri and Violante estimate that public policy reduces income inequality by up to about 30 percent.

Employment – but at the price of constrained real incomes

One of the interesting features exhibited by the US economy from the late 1970s, was how well it performed in producing new jobs. Despite the fall in demand involved in lowering inflation between 1979 and 1982 as a result of Paul Volcker's intense monetary squeeze, increased international trade and competition and big changes in manufacturing, US employment performance was noticeably better than that of other advanced economies experiencing similar challenges. Until the Great Recession started in 2007, the US labour market appeared to perform well in terms of price flexibility, meaning that the quantity adjustment in terms of employment growth and structural unemployment was relatively good.

The consequence was a sharp widening in the earnings distribution, which means for many households with earnings around the average, the evolution of their welfare has been lower than the expectations they were encouraged to have as a result of the wider public and economic debate. And it was certainly less than the promise implied by most presidential platforms since President Reagan in 1980.

Constrained growth of wage and salary income over the longer term is part of the story, but so are the higher costs for health and further and higher education – which have risen sharply in relative terms. International trade has helped to raise real living standards for most households and has also lowered the price of some household purchases, particularly helping low-income households. Some economists argue as a result that official measures of inflation such as the CPI do not properly take account of such factors in raising real household income over time. Yet it is not clear whether conventional price deflators in the national accounts properly or fully capture all healthcare and university costs that have been increased by imperfectly operating markets, often made worse by clumsy public policy intervention.

Public policy should improve, not weaken, the working of market economy

A market economy will have an uneven distribution of income, and this will present challenges for a community that benefits from the dynamism of its wealth creation in the long run. Robust supporters of the efficiency of markets also have to recognise their limits, defects and the fact that many people will need public policy assistance as they are simply not in a position to help themselves. If such intervention is properly framed, it should contribute to markets working better in the medium and long term. In contrast, awkward, poorly constructed and badly targeted public policy can hamper the efficient operation of markets. The dispersion of income in a free economy, however, means that people who support markets have to recognise the case for what, in historical terms, would be regarded as extensive public intervention.

In the US, government action through taxation and transfer payments significantly affects income inequality. The US federal government reduces the inequality in household income significantly through the operation of taxes and benefits. Yet the way the transfer payments are funded through taxation and cash benefits are provided and withdrawn aggravates the disincentive effects of high marginal net rates of withdrawal, add to the complexity of the tax and benefits system.

Table 15.4: Share of Money Income by Quintile During Selected Years, 1950–2009

	Lowest 20 percent of recipients	Second Quintile	Third Quintile	Fourth Quintile	Top 20 percent of recipients
Family income before taxes					
1950	4.5	12.0	17.4	23.4	42.7
1960	4.8	12.2	17.8	24.0	41.3
1970	5.4	12.2	17.6	23.8	40.9
1980	5.1	11.6	17.5	24.3	41.6
1990	4.6	10.8	16.6	23.8	44.3
2000	4.3	9.8	15.4	22.7	47.7
2009	3.9	9.4	15.3	23.2	48.2
Impact of taxes and transfers on household incomes, 2009					
Before	3.5	8.6	14.5	23.9	49.5
After	4.6	10.8	16.3	23.9	44.5

Source: Bureau of the Census, Current Population Survey, Series P-60; Statiistical Abstract of the United States, 1995 table 733; Congressional Budget Office; 1994, Green Book; Bureau of the Census "The Effects of Taxes and Transfers on Income and Poverty in the United States", 2009; and Bureau of the Census, "Income, Poverty and Health Insurance Coverage in the United States", 2009.

Distorted markets, rent seeking and the very rich

The widening of the earnings distribution has been part of a widening in the distribution of total incomes over the past three decades.

Emmanuel Saez, an economist at the University of California Berkeley, studied the evolution of incomes and incomes at the top end of the earning spectrum. In a series of papers – such as *Striking it Richer: The Evolution of Top Incomes in the US* published in August 2009 – he looked at US federal income tax data and examined the distribution of income and the evolution of real incomes over the last century. A feature of this work is that it looks at income in the widest and fullest sense, including wages, salaries, pensions, profits from businesses and income from capital such as dividends, interest, rents and realised capital gains. This is fairly close to a comprehensive estimate of the change in a person's economic power from one year to another, the classic test for a comprehensive income tax. Although it does not quite strictly match that test, as it does not take account of unrealised capital gains that are an additional increment to economic power. It is all market income before individual income taxes.

The top decile in the earning spectrum accounted for 45 percent of total income from the mid-1920s to 1940. It then declined to 32.5 percent during World War II, and was fairly stable at around 33 percent between 1945 and the 1970s. It then started to rise sharply. In 2007, the top decile accounted for 49.7 percent of all income, its highest share of income since 1917 and even surpassing the ratio the top decile enjoyed in 1928 the peak year before the stock market bubble burst at the end of the roaring 1920s.

When the top decile of the income distribution is broken down by percentiles, it appears changes in income at the very top play a central role in the evaluation of the distribution of income during the 20th century. The share of the top percentile – the richest 1 percent – has fluctuated enormously. In 1917 it was about 18 percent of all income, in the late 1920s almost 24 percent, In the 1960s and 1970s it fell to 9 percent and rose to 23.5 percent in 2007. The central role of incomes at the very top in shaping the distribution is also illustrated by Saez when changes in real incomes per family are examined. Real income per family rose 1.3 percent between 1993 and 2008, an increase of 21 percent over 15 years. If the top 1 percent of the income distribution is excluded, real average income growth falls to 0.75 percent a year, an increase of 12 percent. The top 1 percent enjoyed real income growth of 3.9 percent a year, a cumulative increase of 79 percent. Saez points out that this implies that the top 1 percent of incomes captured slightly more than half the economic growth over the period between 1993 and 2008.

This pattern of rapid increase of incomes at the top end of the income distribution has been repeated over the two most recent economic cycles. During the economic expansion between 1993 and 2000, the top 1 percent of the distribution enjoyed real annual income growth of 10.3 percent. In the economic expansion between 2002 and 2007, the top 1 percent exhibited annual real growth in income of 10.1 percent. The bottom 99 percent of the income distribution enjoyed annual real income growth of 2.7 percent and 1.3 percent in the periods 1993-2000 and 2002-2007 respectively. During the latest cycle of economic expansion, the top 1 percent of the income distribution accounted for two-thirds of the total growth in income.

The composition of the incomes of the top percentile of the distribution has changed significantly over the last century. The share of income from wages and salaries has increased sharply since the 1920s, and particularly since the 1970s. The total share of wages and salaries earned by the top 1 percent of incomes has more than doubled since 1970 from 5.1 percent to 12.4 percent in 2007. The evidence from recent tax returns suggests that people in receipt of the very highest incomes are not principally rentiers deriving income from past or inherited accumulations of wealth, but people engaged and participating in the labour market. They are highly paid business executives and new entrepreneurs, who have not yet had the opportunity to accumulate fortunes of the sort associated with the scions of the 'robber barons' and the gilded age of the Great Gatsby.

The *Economic Report of the President* in 2016 drew attention to the issue of economic rents in contributing to inequality. This is an explanation of inequality that has been explored by economists in recent years. The suggestion is that investors or highly paid workers receive more income than they would require to undertake their production or work. The classic examples of such a rent would include the monopoly profits and the unearned benefits that arise from preferential government regulation. Rents can result from abuses of market power that tend to encourage "rent-seeking behaviour," the unproductive use of resources to capture such rewards. The unequal distribution of these rents, may explain increased inequality rather than the conventional explanation that inequality arises from differences in worker productivity or the allocation of capital.

It ought to be possible to reduce inequality without hurting efficiency by modifying the distribution of such rents or better still by increasing economic efficiency as a result of removing or restricting these rents. There is relatively little academic literature examining these issues. Data are scarce given that rents cannot be directly observed, yet considerable evidence appears to support the suggestion that rents are aggravating inequality. Not all economic rents are undesirable. In a perfectly competitive market, where the prices settle at a level below that which some buyers would be willing to pay and above that which some sellers would be willing to accept. The rents collected by these buyers and seller, consumer and producer surplus, would be considered one of the principal benefits yielded by market competition. Temporary monopoly power that generates rents for a firm can be act incentive for additional innovation. That is the rationale for having a patent system.

An economy that exhibits accumulating evidence of rents, where there is an increasingly uneven division of rents between workers and firms, and where rent-seeking behaviour arises from inefficiency and losses of economic welfare, represents an economic problem. The structure of the modern American economy appears to generate greater rents and distributes them as part of profits. The evidence that rents have increased is implied by the divergence between rising corporate profits and declining real interest rates. Without the presence of economic rents, corporate profits should roughly follow the path of interest rates that reflect the return on capital in the economy. Over the last thirty years, corporate profits in the US have risen as interest rates have fallen. The implication is that some corporate profits reflect an increase in the economic rents collected by corporations, not a "pure" return to capital. This divergence between them can be explained by things like credit risk, but such factors are unlikely to count for the full gap.

Another piece of evidence identified by the *Economic Report of the President* that may explain the increasing significance of rents is increased market concentration across a number of industries. The share of revenue earned by the largest firms increased in most industries between 1997 and 2007. This observation complements a range of studies that have found increasing concentration in air travel, telecommunications, banking, food-processing, and other sectors of the economy. Increased concentration may play a role in explaining increased dispersion in returns on capital among major corporations in different sectors of the economy. The returns earned by firms at the 90th percentile are now more than six times larger than those of the median firm, up from less than three times larger in 1990.

Occupational Licensing is another source of rents highlighted by the report. Economic rents arise from increasingly evident requirement of a government-issued license to be employed in certain professions ("occupational licensing"). The share of the U.S. workforce covered by state licensing laws grew five-fold in the second half of the 20th century, from less than 5 percent in the early 1950s to 25 percent by 2008. State licenses account for the bulk of licensing, the addition of locally and federally licensed occupations increases the share of the workforce that is licensed to 29 percent. These licensing requirements create economic rents for licensed practitioners at the expense of excluded workers and consumers. This restrains trade and reduces efficiency and potentially also increasing inequality. They create barriers to employment. Licensing raises wages for people who have acquired a licensed occupation, by restricting employment in the licensed profession and lowering wages for excluded workers. *The Economic Report of the President* suggested that unlicensed workers' wages are between 10 and 15 percent lower than licensed workers with similar levels of education, training, and experience. The more restrictive licensing laws lead to higher prices for goods and services, used in many instances by lower-income households, while the quality, health and safety benefits often asserted as the policy rationale to justify them are not always clearly apparent. State-specific licensing requirements, moreover, create unnecessary barriers to entry for out-of-state licensed practitioners, reducing mobility across state borders.

Another dimension of rent seeking arises from land use and planning regulations. Land-use regulation in the housing market can operate to improve economic welfare. These restrictions would for example prohibit industrial activities generating damaging externalities from being near or within residential neighbourhoods or limitations on the size of a dwelling due to a constrained sewerage or local water supplies. Excessive or poorly constructed planning restrictions that result in protecting the interests of current landowners and maintaining property values, make housing more expensive and reduce productivity and economic growth. The presence of rents in the housing market, also constrain labour mobility and increase in inequality. The principal indication that US land-use regulations are generating economic rents is evidence from rises in real house prices which are greater higher than real construction costs. This differential has continued to increase since the early 1980s. Strict land-use regulation appears to have increased house prices faster than construction costs since 1970. Before the 1970s in America quality improvements had driven much of the increases in house prices. In many American cities, including major population centres, such as New York and Los Angeles and that exhibit high productivity and economic dynamism high-productivity, such as cities like San Francisco, house prices are more than 40 percent higher than construction costs. And the *Economic Report of the President* added that rents paid by households to occupy property have risen faster than wages, which reinforces the implication that there is a significant and growing presence of economic rents in US property markets.

US exhibits problems of agency and corporate governance

The implication of this is that problems in corporate governance – highlighted by Enron, Lehman Bros and other episodes – have led to agency problems on such a scale that in recent decades it has effected the pattern of aggregate earnings, in the same way that shifts in the demand for labour arising out of changes in technology, trade and other factors can be identified. Part of the rise in wages at the very top is an artefact of unusual innovation associated with creative thinkers such as the founders of Google, Apple and Facebook. Plainly, such innovation is deserving of a significant Ricardian economic rent that reflects the scale of their achievement, the value they have added and the economic welfare they have created. This has transformed people's everyday lives. However, this nuance or coda to a broader picture of rent-seeking and agency problems should not distract attention from a serious problem. The implication of sustained rent-seeking is that private markets are malfunctioning and working in a distorted manner that damages both economic efficiency and a proper sense of economic welfare.

This would help to explain why average labour market incomes have grown so slowly relative to the increase in GDP as a whole. It is also consistent with the modest shift in factor shares from labour to capital reported in the national accounts, the long-term returns to capital and savings exhibited by pension fund performance and that of private investment portfolios. These are, at best, tepid in real terms. The blunt inference is that senior managers of capital have been able to allocate a greater share of the income yielded from it to themselves at the expense of the owners of capital (private shareholders and institutional shareholder such as pension funds and insurance companies, and collective investment funds such as mutual funds that invest the savings of the general public). Senior executives have arranged to take increased amounts of money out of companies in terms of wages and salaries. In addition, they have structured company balance sheets in a manner that maximises their returns in terms of capital gains and stock options, with companies pursuing the repurchase of their own shares. Saez has identified what in effect is an economic rent of about 3 percentage points of GDP extracted by senior company directors from the economy.

Public policy has a role to play in ensuring competitive markets and proper corporate governance law protects shareholders in complex corporations. This is clearly a challenge where the ownership, control and management of capital are divorced. It is a contemporary problem as important as that of ensuring there are proper market structures consistent with competition. Historically, the US has recognised the need to promote competition and break up private monopolies. American jurisprudence has played an important part in developing the modern law of fiduciary duty. And American economists have played a central part in developing the analysis of market failure and the proper criteria for judging their performance and operation. There is nothing inconsistent between either commitment to a market economy or an American public policy tradition about developing public policies to address important and difficult problems.

Conclusion

This chapter establishes that the US economy is a market economy with a wide dispersion of earnings and income – precisely the manner of income dispersion that justifies public intervention through taxation and the provision of cash benefits and benefits in kind that help to improve economic welfare and the functioning of the economy. Over the last 35 years, the dispersion of income has widened. It is that wide dispersion of income that is one of the main rationales for public intervention to finance pensions, schools and medical care for households that would have difficulty in paying for such things, especially given the lumpiness of income over a person's lifetime. How such services should be organised, how much should be spent on them and what is affordable in terms of an economy's taxable capacity and the evolution of its trend rate of growth are separate questions.

In contemporary market economies there are increasingly evident agency problems and problems that arise from unearned and unmerited economic rents that go to the heart of corporate governance in the modern firm, and in the wider economy. While profits in national income have increased, it is not clear that they have been distributed appropriately to corporate shareholders and their ultimate owners, the people who regularly save through pension plans and insurance companies.

Chapter 16

The economic welfare of ethnic minorities and public policy

In most advanced economies, the combination of mass migration and the legacy of colonialism has created substantial ethnic minority communities. These often exhibit low levels of economic welfare, weak attachment to the labour market and low levels of marginal revenue product. This reflects a combination of relatively low levels of human capital in terms of education, training and work experience. Such labour market characteristics then adversely interact with the long-term incentive effects of welfare states and raise complex challenges for public policy. Discrimination on the basis of race, culture and religion also provides a public policy imperative in many advanced OECD economies for measures to remedy it.

In the US these issues are present, but show themselves in a particular and distinctive manner. In terms employment and income there is a wide dispersion between different ethnicities with Asian household being very successful. The country has experienced significant recent economic migration, which has extended its range of ethnic minority communities – but it also has a separate and wholly distinctive legacy of ethnic minority discrimination. The legacy of slavery and segregation means that the US has a set of economic, social and political challenges that are wholly unique. This chapter focuses on black economic welfare, because it has a distinctive American dimension to it.

Black employment, education and income

The US census bureau's report, *Income and Poverty 2015*, published in September 2016 shows that in 2015 24.1 percent of black people in the US were living below the official federal indicator of poverty, compared to 11.6 percent of white people. Black household income in 2015 was $36,898. Whereas non-Hispanic white household income was $62,950. A comparison of the 2015 income of non-Hispanic white households with that of black households shows the ratio of black to non-Hispanic white income was 59 percent, a ratio broadly unchanged from 1972.

While the real median income of Asian households in 2014 was not statistically different from the pre-2001- recession peak. Household income in 2014 was 4.0 percent lower for non-Hispanic whites, down from $62,762 in 1999, 13.2 percent lower for blacks down from $40,783 in 2000. *Income Poverty and Health Insurance Coverage in the US* published in 2009 found that median black household income in 2009 was $32,584, about 60 percent of white non-Hispanic median household income.

Labor Force Characteristics by Race and Ethnicity 2015, published by the Bureau of Labor Statistics in September 2016, showed that median weekly and salary earnings for black workers were $641, compared with $835 for whites and $993 for Asians. Black earnings were 76.7 percent of white earnings. Black men earned $680, compared with white men who earned $920. In 1967, black per capita money income was 53 percent of white per capita income. In 2009 it was 65.7 percent of white per capita income.

Table 16.1: Educational Attainment by Race, Ethnicity, and Gender, 2004

	Share with high school degree or higher	Share with bachelor's degree or higher
Total	87	29
Non-Hispanic White	93	35
Black	88	17
Hispanic	62	11
Asian	96	61
Men	85	26
Women	88	31

Note: Data refers to noninstitutionalized population aged 25–29. Since data excludes incarcerated population, they likely overstate educational attainment of US residents.

Sources: Department of Commerce (Bureau of the Census)

Table 16.2: Average Annual Earnings By Education (2004 dollars)

	1975	1990	2000	2004
Bachelor's degree only	39,065	43,591	54,396	51,568
High School degree only	24,845	24,968	28,179	28,631
$ Difference	14,220	18,623	26,217	22,937
% Difference	57%	75%	93%	80%

Note: Data refers to all workers aged 18 and over.

Source: Department of Commerce (Bureau of the Census)

There is a consistent pattern of black disadvantage in the labour market and in terms of wider life chances and mobility. Black attachment to the labour market is generally weaker. Workforce participation by blacks in 2015 was 61.5 percent, compared with 62.8 percent for whites, and the lowest participation rates among ethnic groups, apart from Native Americans Indians. The employment rate of Blacks was 54.7 percent compared to 59.9 percent for Whites. The unemployment rate was 9.6 percent for Blacks compared with 4.6 percent for Whites.

Teenagers are particularly vulnerable to unemployment as new entrants to the labour market with less skills and work experience. Among 16- to 19-year-olds, black teenagers had the highest unemployment rate – 28.4 percent – compared with 14.8 percent for whites. Unemployed blacks tend to be without work longer than other groups. In 2015, the median duration of black unemployment was 15.5 weeks compared with 10.5 weeks for whites, and black men are more likely to be out of the labour force. The proportion of black men who did not participate in the workforce among 25 to 54-year-olds was greater than that of white, Asian and Hispanic men. Blacks made up 12 percent of the civilian labour force in 2015, but accounted for 23 percent of the people marginally attached to the labour force – in other words, people who wanted work and had looked for a job during the previous 12 months, but not in the previous four weeks. In contrast whites were underrepresented among the marginally attached relative to their share of the labour force—79 percent of the labour force versus 66 percent of the marginally attached. Blacks accounted for 28 percent of all discouraged workers, the subset of marginally attached people who are not currently looking for work because they believe no jobs are available.

In terms of education and occupation, blacks are less well placed than whites and Asians. In 2015, 90 percent of blacks, whites and Asians had a high school diploma. Asians are the group most likely to have a bachelor's degree – 61 percent of Asians have a degree, compared with 39 percent of whites, 28 percent of blacks and 19 percent of Hispanics. Higher education is associated with higher employment and incomes across all groups. Yet at every level of education, blacks and Hispanics were more likely to be unemployed than Asians and whites, and they were also less likely to occupy professional and management positions. Some 51 percent of Asians were in managerial, professional and related occupations compared with 40 percent of whites, 30 percent of Blacks and 17 percent of Hispanics.

The picture is clear – and it is one of black disadvantage. Within the overall setting is a further bleak story. Blacks do not only exhibit lower employment and earnings, but there is a wide dispersion in employment and earnings, particularly among black men. The *OECD Economic Surveys United States 2016* notes that 'in part, differences in educational attainment may account for these differences, though improvement in test scores by minority students over time has not translated into the wage gap narrowing over the last few decades'. And that 'Black and Hispanic workers tend to work in lower-paying jobs and their returns to experience have tended to be lower.' The position of black men without families and children who are either unemployed or are low earners is worse, as they also receive little support in terms of Social Security transfer payments or social benefits in kind such as access to Medicaid.

A legacy of slavery and segregation

The economic position and welfare of black people cannot be avoided in any real discussion of the role of the state and public policy in the US, not least because public policy played a large part in determining the present social and economic institutions that account for the welfare of black people, compared with that of the white majority and other ethnic minorities that have chosen to migrate to the US over the last century or more. The combination of slavery for more than two centuries followed by systematic legal discrimination and segregation during the century that followed the abolition of slavery still shapes the welfare and destiny of America's black citizens.

This history not only helps to explain the economic and social condition of around 13 percent of the population, it also provides an opportunity. A large proportion of America's population could be attached to the labour market to a significantly greater extent than they currently are, and this has the potential to increase the labour supply and economic welfare of society as a whole.

Slavery ended in 1865, but its legacy in terms of economic and social endowment are still present in the 21st century. Black education, employment, income and wealth remain lower than that of the white majority. The segregation and Jim Crow laws entrenched black disadvantage for a further century after the ending of slavery. Black people were discriminated against in terms of education, employment, provision of public and private services and ownership of property. Segregation was not limited to the states of the former Confederate South, but was also applied in the 20th century in the federal government and in its institutions, such as the armed services.

In some instances, the effect of segregation was to enable the development of black businesses and professions, because the process of segregation created segmented markets where specifically black businesses could develop. While this may have helped certain black individuals to flourish in markets and professions sheltered from full competition, this should not be mistaken as a kind of accidental service that helped black communities. It was simply an artefact of economic institutions where black people did not have full access to the division of labour and the provision of goods and services provided in a free economy with competitive markets, and represented a reduction in their overall level of welfare.

Progressives, the New Deal and the Post-War Welfare State

There is a peculiar paradox in American public policy: far from helping the black minority, the progressive tradition and the development of welfare institutions in the US have often worked against the interests of the economic welfare of black households. This was partly as a result of deliberate public policy choice and partly because of the structural consequences that some welfare measures have on labour market incentives for people who are vulnerable to unemployment and exclusion from the labour market.

When the welfare state was initially constructed in the US, progressives in both the Republican and Democrat parties – along with a wider range of policy experts and religious campaigners – were in the vanguard of its creation. They reflected the state of opinion of their time. It was in a period when the Ku Klux Klan (up to the 1920s) was part of the political mainstream rather than an aberration in the South. In the North, progressives such as Oliver Wendell Holmes may have regarded blacks as equal before the law, but they did not regard them as socially or economically equal.

In the same way that many progressives had views on eugenics that would now be regarded as repugnant, they also had similar views on race. The Progressive movement was, for example, divided on the issues of whether the US should enter World War I. Some thought it should join the Allied democracies against the autocratic central powers, while others opposed the war because of the bloodshed it would involve and the people who would be killed. These opponents of war should not be viewed as benign pacifists – part of their opposition was the concern that the 'wrong people' would get killed. Holmes argued the problem with war was not loss of life, but that the wrong people got killed.

The President who took America to war in 1917 was Woodrow Wilson. No one exemplified progressive liberalism either at home or abroad more than Wilson. The Federal Reserve System was created and a federal income tax introduced in his first term. His liberal internationalist idealism was codified in his Fourteen-Point Plan for Peace, with its emphasis on the right to self-determination for small nations. His second term eventually foundered because of domestic political opposition to his support for the League of Nations. To the world then, and still today for much of traditionally educated opinion, Woodrow Wilson exemplifies the high-minded American liberal.

Yet he was also a true son of the South. He may have been Governor of New Jersey and president of Princeton, but he was born in Staunton, Virginia, and grew up in Augusta, Georgia, where his father – a distinguished Presbyterian minister – was a strong supporter of the Confederacy. As segregation laws were placed on the statute book in former slave-owning states that effectively removed normal political and civil rights from black citizens, the Wilson administration was not so much indifferent as complicit. It was Wilson, who as president allowed federal government departments, including the US Treasury Department and the US Post Office, to introduce segregation. At Princeton University institutions and buildings that commemorate Wilson's life have become a source of contemporary acrimony.

The New Deal

Nothing exemplifies America's progressive liberal tradition more than President Roosevelt's New Deal polices in the 1930s. Yet the policies and institutions established by the New Deal often amounted to affirmative action for the white majority. Ira Katznelson's book *When Affirmative Action was White: An Untold History of Racial Inequality in Twentieth-Century America* explains why and how the principal institutions of the New Deal directly discriminated against blacks and helped whites. Even the non-discriminatory programmes to help demobilised World War II veterans in the 1940s were effectively affirmative action for whites, given the context of systematic and legally sanctioned institutions of segregation. Federal government assistance in paying for a university education, starting a business or buying a home were of little help if there are no good universities that would admit you, and if no banks or thrift institutions would lend to you because of the colour of your skin.

Professor Katznelson explains that President Roosevelt was dependent on the votes of Southern Democrats in Congress to get his legislation passed. In the main they were happy to have social spending programmes directed at mitigating the hardship of the Depression years – with one significant caveat. These programmes were welcome, provided they could be administered by state governments and did not upset local labour market practices set by a toxic combination of custom, law and intimidation ultimately enforced by beating and lynching.

The Southern Democrat 'oligarchy' – as WEB Du Bois called it – welcomed federal money, because white or black the agricultural South was dirt poor. In 1937, per capita income in the South was $314 compared with a national average of $604. A measure of the poverty in the South is provided by the fact that on average, New Deal programmes involved shared expenditure divided on a ratio of 70 percent federal funding, 30 percent state funding – in the South, the ratio was 90:10. Southern members of Congress campaigned for federal assistance, not least because they wanted to head off a potential left-wing response from the unions.

As Katzneslon puts it, Southern Congressman were impelled to pursue federal assistance through poverty, but had to try to ensure that federal assistance could be in the form of low payments that were racially differentiated so that the institutions of a low-wage economy and racist segregation were not disturbed. The key was obtaining agreement that payments made by the Federal Relief Emergency Administration should not be higher than the local prevailing condition and ensuring that the administration of New Deal programmes was devolved to state governors and legislators so that the institutions of segregation were not undermined, but – if anything – were maintained and further entrenched.

The success of this strategy was reflected in the resignation of the FREA's black Director for Negro Affairs in Atlanta in 1934, who said 'the way coloured people have suffered under the New Deal … is a disgrace that stinks to heaven'.

The Social Security Act passed in 1935 is the most enduring New Deal institution. It established old age-pensions, unemployment benefits and assistance to low-income families with children. Southern senators and committee chairmen in Congress supported the bill because they wanted the financial assistance it offered their communities, but they were equally determined the legislation should be shaped to exclude black people and to ensure the Jim Crow regime of segregation – or as they quaintly expressed it, their 'way of life' – was not compromised.

During hearings on the bill, Senator Harry Byrd explained how Social Security should not become an instrument the federal government could use to interfere in the way the white South dealt with what he called 'the Negro question'. This was achieved through a combination of exclusion of black people from the likelihood of being covered by the terms of the act and through local administration of it at the state level. Farm workers, domestic servants and people doing 'home work' were excluded from the pension and unemployment insurance part of the Act. These provisions were nationally administered, but were made acceptable to the Southern Democrat oligarchy because over two-thirds of black people were outside its social insurance provisions.

The part of the Act that offered relief from poverty to families with dependent children and help for elderly people living in poverty was made acceptable to them because it was decided it should be locally administered. The states were given a great deal of discretion over both administration and the level of benefits, and the cost of the legislation was shared between the states and the federal government. Much of the complexity that arises out of the interaction of federal government programmes and local state administration – such as different rules, levels of benefit and different employment and poverty traps – can be traced from the way New Deal programmes were set up in the 1930s.

The Social Security Act was a piece of legislation designed to discriminate. Robert Lieberman, a political scientist, described it in his book *Shifting the Colour Line* as 'discrimination by design'. He describes the exclusion of certain categories of work mainly done by black people as dividing the 'population along racial lines without saying so in so many words'. The effect of devolution and cost-sharing in the poverty relief parts of the Act was decisive.

As Katznelson describes, Aid to Dependent Children's 'key contours, organisation and supervision' was 'in the hands of state governors, legislators, and bureaucrats. Though they failed to get Congress to pick up the whole bill for the poorest states, the bulk of which were southern, they did manage to pass a programme of assistance to poor families that left all its key elements in local hands'. Aid to Dependent Children offered grants to families with young children where a parent – usually the father – was absent from home. From the beginning of the programme, these families were disproportionately black. Nationally, 14 percent of children in the US were black.

In southern states it was a different story. State authorities used their discretion to exclude large number of black households from the benefit. Katznelson uses data from Richard Sterner's *The Negro's Share A Study of Income Consumption Housing and Public Assistance* published in 1943 to show that in Louisiana, 37 percent of the children were black – yet only 26 percent of the recipients of help through Aid to Dependent Children were black. This pattern was repeated throughout the South, except in those states such as Mississippi that did not participate in the programme. Richard Sterner, a Swedish demographer, found that in the state of Georgia only 1.5 percent of eligible black families were funded under the programme, compared with 14.4 percent of white families.

Table 16.3: Proportion of Black Children receiving help from the federal 'Aid to Dependent Children' program (percentages)

	Black Children as a proportion of population cohort	Black Children as a proportion of ADC Clients
Louisiana	37	26
North Carolina	30	22
South Carolina	49	29
Alabama	39	24
Arkansas	24	15

Source: Ira Katz Nelson 'When Affirmative Action Was White/The Negro's Share, A Study of Income Consumption and Public Assistance 1943'

The New Deal had a big impact on labour relations law. Trade union collective bargaining was significantly enhanced as a result the National Labor Relations Act and the creation of the National Labor Relations Board. This legislation had less impact on labour relations in the South, given the lack of union organisation and its dependence on agriculture at the time, but the legislation had a lasting impact on manufacturing industries concentrated in the

North – particularly sectors such as the motor industry in Detroit – that had significant implications for future black earnings and employment, and later for de-industrialisation that has significantly shaped contemporary black labour market outcomes. The New Deal also changed conditions at work. The Fair Labor Standards Act, passed in 1938, established a national minimum wage and regulated conditions at work – for example, banning child labour. The Southern Democrat oligarchy supported this legislation, but ensured that farm workers and domestic servants were excluded from it in order to exclude blacks.

As Katznelson explains the result was that 'these new arrangements were friendly to labour, but unfriendly to the majority of African-Americans who lived below the Mason-Dixon line'.

The National Industrial Recovery Act (NIRA) passed in 1933 as part of President Roosevelt's landmark first 100 days of legislation aimed to raise economic activity by allowing cartels to organise and share their profits with workers through codes of minimum wages intended to raise the wage level. It provides a fascinating example of the extent of government interference in the economy during the Depression. It also illustrates the perverse and damaging economic character of much of the New Deal programme in terms of its micro impact. Southern Senators, like the notorious Huey Long of Louisiana, complained the Act failed to properly define industry so as to exclude agriculture. In response, the Democrat Senator for New York piloting the legislation through the Senate lamely reassured Long that the bill excluded agriculture. This meant that once it was passed, the National Recovery Administration judged that farming was excluded from the intent of the Act – and not just farming, but many of its related industries and processes. In the 1930s the Southern oligarchy took great care to ensure legislation such as the National Labor Relations Act and the Fair Labor Standards Act also excluded agricultural workers and domestic servants. Congressman Martin Dies of Texas set out their position clearly: 'What is prescribed for one race must be prescribed for the others, and you cannot prescribe the same wages for the black man as for the white man.'

It was not until there was a Republican majority in both houses of Congress that the discrimination against black people arising from the exclusion of agricultural workers and domestic workers was ended and the principal unemployment insurance and pension provisions of Social Security were effectively extended to black people in the 1950s.

The economic position of blacks after the Civil Rights Act 1964

The ending of Jim Crow and segregation in the 1960s might have been thought to have brought about a transformation in the relative economic position of black people. The picture offered by data on income and wealth is a much more ambiguous one. The difference between white and black earnings has narrowed since the 1940s, yet much of that narrowing took place between the 1940s and the 1970s. Indeed, the gap in black earnings and white earnings appears to have widened since the 1970s. The gap in household wealth between white and black households is wider than that in wages and earnings and has persisted.

In the 1960s and early 1970s there was a rapid narrowing in the difference between black and white wages. Finis Welch sets this out in his article 'Catching up: wages of black men' published in the *American Economic Review* in 2003. Although relative wages were rising, there was little evidence of improvement within the cohort. The gains were observed among new arrivals that did better than previous entrants into the labour market. There was evidence employment had shifted to industries and sectors more likely to respond to affirmative action programmes, such as industries in receipt of federal government subsidies and larger firms that had to report to the US Equal Employment Opportunity Commission (EEOC).

These wage gains were not restricted to such sectors and it appeared that the quantity and quality of schooling was having an impact on the labour market. From the late 1970s, the ratio of black to white wages stabilises and, if anything, appears to widen slightly. Although some labour market commentators suggested this resulted from waning support for affirmative action – and specifically during the Reagan Administration to reduced funding for the EEOC – the decline in the ratio appears to have started in the mid-1970s during the Ford and Carter administrations.

The fall in the relative level of black wages coincided with the start of the 1974-75 recession, and it was accentuated by the Carter-Reagan recession between 1979 and 1983. Welch's conclusion is that black workers suffer disproportionately during contractions in output. In the 1980s, part of the decline in the ratio of average wages was an artefact of an increase in wage dispersion in the economy as a whole. Inequality increased among cohorts that otherwise matched in terms of age, schooling, gender and race.

Economists at the Federal Reserve Bank of St Louis looked at the economic progress black men have made since desegregation, when discrimination in the workplace was made illegal. Natalia Kolesnikova and Yang Liu in 'A Bleak 30 Years for Black Men', published in The Regional Economist in July 2010, looked at wages and labour force participation of black men in labour markets across 14 large metropolitan areas of the US. Labour markets vary and black people have had very different experiences in different regions in the US, which means geographical location is important when looking at differences in income and employment by race. The average weekly wages of black men rose between 1970 and 2000 in all but three of the 14 cites studied. The greatest progress was in Atlanta, where the ratio of black to white weekly wages rose from 62 percent to 78 percent. In Philadelphia, Chicago and Detroit, the ratio fell from 79 to 77, 75 to 74 and 81 to 78 respectively. Most of the convergence that took place happened between 1970 and 1980. In four cities – Houston, Cleveland, Chicago and Detroit – weekly wages as a percent of white male wages fell between 1980 and 2000. In five cities – San Francisco, Los Angeles, Detroit, Cleveland, and Houston – wages fell between 1990 and 2000.

Many studies concentrate on wage rates as a measure of earnings, because 'the wage is the price that labour markets put on a unit of skilled labour'. This means a narrowing in the 'labour market's valuations of black and white labour were converging. It would also indicate the convergence of skill levels of black and white workers'. Wage rates that reflect differences such as skill, education, and sector of employment are one source of racial economic disparity. An equally important factor is labour market participation – simply put, does a person of working age have a job? Different levels of attachment to the labour market, employment and unemployment annual earnings provide a fuller guide to the labour market position of different categories of people than simply looking at wage rates.

Annual earnings ratios suggest much less progress have been made in improving the labour market position of black men relative to that of white men. Relative annual earnings fell in most of the 14 cities studied between 1970 and 2000. The fall was greatest in Chicago, where the ratio of black male annual earning to white male annual earnings fell by 14 percentage points, from 69 percent to 55 percent. Most of the Midwestern and Eastern cities experienced a similar fall in relative black annual earnings. In the South, the ratio of annual black male earnings rose in each of the five cities studied apart from Houston, where it was unchanged. In 1970, black wages were 65 percent of white weekly wages in Southern cities and annual earnings were about 57 percent of whites. In the cities of the non-segregated southern parts of the US, the weekly wage ratio was about 76 percent and the annual earnings ratio was about 68.5 percent. By 2000, in the Southern cities studied the ratio of black weekly wages had risen to 77 percent of white male wages and the ratio of annual earnings had increased to around 65.5 percent of white male annual earnings. In cities outside the south, in contrast the ratio of black weekly male wages relative to white male wages fell to 69 percent and annual black male earnings to around 61.5 percent.

It would appear that in the South there was a noticeable narrowing of the difference in wage rates and this was also reflected in an improvement in annual earnings, but the improvement in annual earnings did not match improved wage rates. Outside of the segregated Southern cities, there was a slight fall in wages rates and a sharp fall in the ratio of annual black male earnings relative to white males.

The main explanation appears to lay in changes in labour market participation rates. Between 1970 and 2000, the average number of weeks black men worked fell in each of the cities studied, in some cases by as much as 25 percent. During this period there was a fall in the proportion of black men who had a job and an increase in the proportion of black men who reported themselves to be out of the labour market. In most of the cities studied, the rate of black unemployment increased by over two-fifths, from 4.6 percent and 6.5 percent, and the proportion of black men not in the labour force more than doubled, from 9.2 percent to 20 percent.

The fall in the proportion of black men with a job has been consistent in each of the cities in the study, but it was more pronounced in industrial cities outside the South. In Chicago, the rate of employment for black men fell from 88 percent in 1970 to 69 percent in 2000. In Detroit, the pattern was repeated as the rate of black male employment fell from 86 percent to 69 percent. The same pattern prevails in the cities of the South. In 2000, in 10 out of the 14 cities studied 20 percent of black men were out of work. Even in cities where the unemployment rate was relatively stable – around 1-9 percent – such as Los Angeles and San Francisco, there was a high ratio of discouraged workers, at 21 percent and 22 percent respectively. The only city in the study where black employment did not fall between 1970 and 2000 was Atlanta. The result was that overall black labour market participation fell dramatically in the 30 years following desegregation.

De-industrialisation appears to be the explanation for the fall in black labour market participation and in the ratio of black wages relative to white male wages outside of the South. Manufacturing employment has fallen and there has been an increase in service sector jobs. Employment of men in manufacturing in cites fell by 8 percentage points. In industrial cities such as St Louis, Cleveland, Chicago, Detroit and Baltimore, manufacturing employment fell by between 17 and 19 percentage points in the 30 years to 2000.

The process of de-industrialisation damaged the labour market positions of both black and white households, but has had a disproportionate effect on black households. A greater proportion of black men were employed in manufacturing then white men. In Detroit, the proportion of black men working in manufacturing fell from 56 percent to 26 percent. On average, black men had a lower level of educational attainment than white men. This made it more difficult for them to adapt to a changing labour market with a greater emphasis on services. Black people were geographically concentrated in cities with high levels of manufacturing, because they had originally been drawn by the employment opportunities these cities offered. So when labour market conditions deteriorated in cities disproportionately affected by de-industrialisation, black households suffered to a greater degree. In cites with a wider economic base such as Atlanta and Washington DC, the labour force participation of black men did not drop as dramatically. The overall result is that 2000 black household income has fallen in real terms by around 15 percent over two economic cycles.

Figure 16.1: Black Medium Household Income from Nixon to Obama, 1968 – 2012 (in 2012 dollars)

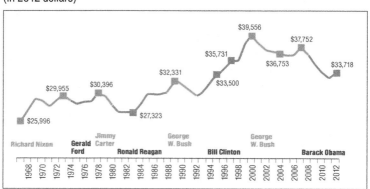

Retrieved from Blackdemographics.com
Source: US Census Bureau, Current Population Survey, Annual Social Economic Supplements.

Former chief economist at the Department of Labor Williams Rogers regards the labour market position of black people as largely shaped by wider trends in the economy. Black people are simply more vulnerable to these trends on average than other groups. But as trends become more pervasive, increasingly the majority of workers are getting caught up in a complex experience of slow earnings growth, widening inequality and higher unemployment. Rogers identifies these factors as weaker jobs growth during periods of expansion, diminished trade union power, the shift from the manufacturing to the services industries and increased employment turnover with more regular displacement and shorter job tenure.

A large part of the narrowing of the gap in white and black earnings took place in the three middle decades of the 20th century. It resulted from mass black migration from the South, largely because of the job opportunities offered in manufacturing industries in the North. The potential earnings for black workers in the manufacturing sector were further enhanced by the confluence of three things: shortages of workers in wartime, peacetime full employment and trade union power in the private sector in the 1950s.

Market forces appear to be more powerful than either discrimination or public policy. Acute discrimination in the 1930s and 1950s could not prevent a narrowing of the gap between black and white earnings, nor could public policy making discrimination in the workplace unlawful – buttressed by a variety of affirmative action programmes – overcome a combination of market forces and differences in education and other cultural positioning matters that influence labour market outcomes.

Some nine generations of slavery followed by three and a half generations of systematic discrimination means black households simply do not fare as well in the labour market as other households. What is more, the combination of de-industrialisation and welfare policies operate to further exclude black households from the labour market. Segregated housing, poor, inner-city schools and communities with weak attachment to the labour market combine to deliver complex social pathologies and a hysteresis of permanent economic exclusion. What is interesting is that in the South there has been an improvement in both wages and earnings relative to white wages despite the difficult backdrop of de-industrialisation and changes in the demand for labour.

There is one clear lesson, however, that should be recognised. Black men are more vulnerable to exclusion from the labour market through a combination of relatively lower levels of education and skill. This means they have a lower level of marginal revenue product. Any labour market institutional change that artificially increases employment costs through regulation is likely to disproportionately hinder black Americans' job prospects. This includes government regulation and the presence of an effective trade union mark-up in a competitive market, and such regulation and bargaining arrangements will in the long-run reduce employment and ultimately lower black household income. Such costs have a particular effect on manufacturing businesses that face much greater international challenge and domestic markets that are more contested.

Black wealth

Black household wealth is lower than white household wealth, and the gap is greater than the difference between black and white earnings.

Wealth is accumulated over generations, and given the historic endowment black households start with – going back to the end of slavery and Reconstruction – the difference in wealth will lag changes that narrow the gap in wages and earnings. The combination of low wages, lack of access to capital and obstacles to home ownership combine to hinder black wealth accumulation. Thomas Shapiro, in his book *Racial Wealth Gap* published in 2005, reports that in 2000 the average wealth of black households was $6,165 compared with $65,000 for white households, and there had been little change compared with the previous decade. In 2009, the census data difference was greater – black wealth was $5,325 and white wealth was $113,149.

Home ownership is a key factor in average wealth accumulation, and differences in housing tenure between black and white households are key drivers in wealth accumulation. During the Civil War, there was a suggestion that liberated slaves should be endowed with land. Apart from a few instances this did not happen in the Confederacy. In some of the new land developed in the West, however, there were examples of former slaves receiving land grants. Melinda Miller, in an article '*Land and racial inequality*' published in the *American Economic Review* in 2011, suggests land grants could and did have an identifiable effect on relative black household wealth. Miller found that black freedmen who had been Cherokee Nation slaves, who as citizens of the Cherokee Nation were able to acquire unused public land, had higher levels of income and wealth than other former slaves.

Historically, black people were explicitly barred from owning homes in certain districts. The migration to the north, combined with employment in manufacturing industries in large cities, boosted black earnings relative to white earnings, but reduced the probability of black households owning their own home.

Sharecroppers moving north often actually owned their own home in the south, but in northern cities they tended to rent. This meant black households did not accumulate wealth through equity in their homes. Mortgage lenders also discriminated against black borrowers, and so the relative accumulation of household wealth was further hindered. Katznelson catalogues how the federal government assistance given to GIs returning to civilian life in the 1940s in practice entrenched and extended differences in household wealth.

Black GIs were entitled to federal government loan guarantees. In the South, the attitude of lenders made such assistance next to useless. In circumstances where intimidation and lynching were present, property ownership does not have the same meaning as it does in a society where the rule of law and contract is enforced in its conventional meaning. In the North there were more opportunities, but there was also discrimination on the part of lenders and other constraints on black households acquiring land and property. In New York and northern New Jersey suburbs, fewer than 100 of the 67,000 mortgages insured through the GI legislation-financed homes were bought by non-whites, and this is why the GI Act in 1946 played an important part in extending differences in black and white household wealth.

Katznelson shows that the GI Act played a significant part in expanding and shaping the modern American middle class because the Veterans Administration helped to finance 5 million homes – interest rates were capped, down payments were waived and repayment periods were extended to 30 years. The GI bill massively extended the reach of home ownership and tilted the balance of housing tenure from renting to owning. In the immediate postwar years, the Veterans Administration financed 40 percent of new homes being added to the housing stock. Katznelson summarises the position by saying: 'Residential ownership became the key foundation of economic security for the burgeoning and overwhelmingly white middle class.'

The GI bill changed the location of middle-class housing and played a large role in creating the modern American suburb. The scale of the GI bill was such that by 1950, the federal government had spent more on it than it had on the Marshall Plan to rebuild Europe. Later, as white households moved to suburbs, there were more opportunities for black households to acquire often handsome Victorian and Edwardian homes at cheap prices. But these opportunities did not balance the obstacles that hindered relative black wealth accumulation. Differences in home ownership are important in explaining differences in black and white wealth, because housing wealth plays a critical part in modern American household balance sheets.

The dispersion in wealth between racial and ethnic groups widened as a result of the Great Recession and has been pronounced during the period when the economy recovered. This reflected the impact of the subprime crisis on black households and black homeownership. In 2013 differences in wealth were at their widest for 30 years. Rakesh Kochhar and Richard Fry in a study published by Pew Center in December 2014, *Wealth inequality has widened along racial, ethnic lines since end of the Great Recession*, uses data from the Federal Reserve Board's *Survey of Consumer Finances* to examine the impact of the contraction in output on black household wealth. They note that the crises in the housing and financial markets, was universally hard on the net worth of all American families, but it had a disproportionate impact on black household wealth. This became more pronounced as the economy returned to its trend rate of growth recovery and previously depressed asset prices rose. Households did no benefit in equal measure, and wealth inequality widened along racial and ethnic lines.

Figure 16.2: Racial, ethnic wealth gaps have grown since Great Recession, median net worth of households, (in 2013 dollars)

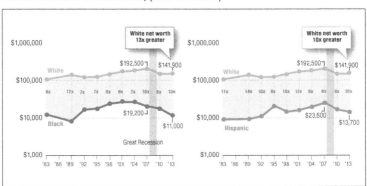

Source: Pew Research Center tabulations of Survey of Consumer Finances public-use data.

The wealth of white households was 13 times the median wealth of black households in 2013, compared with eight times the wealth in 2010, Pew Research Center reported. The difference between black and white household wealth widened to its greatest degree since 1989, when white households had 17 times the wealth of black households.

From 2007 to 2010, the median net worth of American households fell by 39.4 percent, from $135,700 to $82,300. Plunging house prices and a large fall in stock market equity prices, caused this fall in household wealth. From 2010 to 2013, the median wealth of non-Hispanic white households increased from $138,600 to $141,900, or by 2.4 percent, while the median wealth of non-Hispanic black households fell by 33.7 percent. The rate of homeownership of non-Hispanic white households fell from 75.3 percent in 2010 to 73.9 percent in 2013, a percentage drop of 2 percent. Rate of homeownership rate among minority households decreased from 50.6 percent in 2010 to 47.4 percent in 2013, a reduction of 6.5 percent, from $16,600 in 2010 to $11,000 in 2013. Researchers at the Federal Reserve Bank of St Louis's Center for Household Financial Stability used the same Federal Reserve Board data and their analysis broadly corroborated the Pew

Center study. *The Demographics of Wealth How Age, Education and Race Separate Thrivers from Strugglers in Today's Economy* published by Ray Boshara, William R. Emmons and Bryan J. Noeth in February 2015 also suggests that as well as differences in home ownership, differences in choices about the composition of household balance sheets also appear to influence the accumulation of wealth in black households relative to that of white and Asian households. Federal Reserve's Survey of Consumer Finances. More than the survey of 40,000 heads of households were interviewed between 1989 and 2013, showed that in terms of median family wealth, assets minus liabilities, the ranking of the four racial or ethnic groups did not change in order between 1989 and 2013. In inflation-adjusted dollars, the median wealth of a white family in 1989 was $130,102. In 2013, it was $134,008. For an Asian family, the two medians were $64,165 and $91,440. For a Hispanic family, they were $9,229 and $13,900. For a black family, they were $7,736 and $11,184. Across racial and ethnic groups, the St Louis study reported 'striking and persistent differences in wealth, income, the structure of these groups' balance sheets' and a measure of financial decision-making that the report describes as financial health. The report that 'with few exceptions, the financial patterns evident in 2013 echo those apparent throughout the period since 1989—at least among whites, Hispanics and blacks. Asian families have changed the most during the past 25 years, moving away from Hispanic and black families' wealth levels toward those of whites. Given the remarkable increase in educational attainment by younger Asians in recent decades, Asian families' median income, mean income and wealth levels already have or soon will surpass those of whites'. The St Louis study notes that the greater share of the assets invested in financial and business assets, which provide both asset diversification and higher average returns in the long run rather than a portfolio consisting mostly of tangible assets like a house, vehicles or other durable goods, contributes to the relative differences in rates of wealth accumulation between the ethnic communities.

Moynihan Commission revisited

Daniel Patrick Moynihan's 1965 report on black families pointed out that in a period of great prosperity, the conditions of black men in the labour market – particularly young black men – were not improving by as much as the general performance of the economy suggested it should. Moynihan also took a pessimistic view of the future prospects of young black men. The demand for labour was increasingly for the educated and higher skilled, and black people lacked access to those skills and education. He recognised the continuing role of discrimination and an increasing alienation among young black men. Moynihan argued that the lack of skill attainment, along with increased alienation, would rise the chances of young men turning to crime and that this would be aggravated by the structure of black families and the greater role of women as lone patents in the absence of fathers.

Harry Holzer, in a paper, *The Labour Market and Young Black Men: Updating Moynihan's perspective,* published in 2007, argues that Moynihan was prescient about the future labour market prospects of young black men and that he identified many of the causes of the problems – and some of the broad remedies. Young black men lag behind virtually all groups in terms of education, attachment to the labour market and earnings, and are also behind young black women in terms of education and employment. In the 1990s, the combination of the Clinton administration's welfare reform policy changes and the extension of the EITC increased the labour market participation of black women.

Incarceration and the labor market

The Bureau of Justice Statistics indicates that at any one time, over a third of all young black men are in prison, on parole or on probation. This level of imprisonment means that any conventionally reported labour market data on black participation rates, if anything, understates the degree to which black men are outside the labour force. This raises wider questions about the extent that the increasing use of incarceration is optimal, and has implications for public spending.

Imprisonment on this scale also does permanent damage to the employability of black men. Employers are reluctant to hire men with prison records. *The Economist*, in an article 'America's jobless men - decline of the working man*, published in April 2011, provides an example of an unemployed black man who cannot get a satisfactory job despite having a degree. The degree was in public administration, but he could only get a job as a telephone surveyor. His problem is that the degree was earned in prison. Most employers are reluctant to hire people with a criminal conviction, and the healthcare and education sectors will not consider ex-offenders. This is significant, because healthcare has been one of the fastest growing sectors of employment.

Holzer's view is that these factors result from changes in the demand and supply of labour in the way Moynihan's analysis implied. In terms of the demand for labour, employers' attitudes to hiring black men reduces the demand for their labour. Black men respond to an increasingly weak employment position by withdrawing from participation in the labour market altogether. Indeed, they may do so even before they enter it by withdrawing from mainstream institutions and potentially turning to unlawful activity.

Their withdrawal from the labour market is not simply because there are not enough job opportunities. Holzer argues it reflects labour supply being withdrawn, because wage rates have fallen below black 'reservation wages'. There also appears to be evidence that the black reservation wage may have risen in the 1960s and 1970s, which may have been caused by increased expectations in the 1960s and the growth of alternative illegal trading incomes from the market in unlawful drugs. The wages of legal work fell in the 1970s and 1980s relative to the incomes that could be extracted from unlawful activity. Holzer says that in those circumstances, a black withdrawal from the labour market would be consistent with the framework of economic analysis developed by Gary Becker to explain criminal behaviour.

Richard Freeman argued in '*Why do so many young American men commit crimes and what might we do about it?*', published in the *Journal of Economic Perspectives* in 1996, that young black men turned to crime in response to declining job opportunities in the 1980s and 1990s. In *Economic Inequality and the Rise in US Imprisonment* (2004) and *Did Falling Wages and Employment Increase US Imprisonment?* (2005) Bruce Western, Meredith Kleykamp and Jack Rosenfeld explored the way that for low-skilled young men, and young black men in particular, imprisonment became a common experience for those with a weak attachment to the labour market and one that was likely to entrench that labour market detachment.

Penal policy and the administration of justice in contemporary American shapes black economic welfare, employment participation, earnings and accumulation of wealth. The US has a punitive criminal justice system distinguished by condign punishments compared to other countries. The US accounts for about 5 percent of the world population, but holds a quarter of the number of people estimated to be subject to imprisonment. The per capita incarceration rate in the US is about one and a half times that of second-placed Rwanda and third-placed Russia, and more than six times the rate of Canada. A further 4.75 million Americans are subject to the state supervision imposed by probation or parole. *Jail Inmates at Midyear 2014* by Todd D. Minton and Zhen Zeng, published by the US Department of Justice in 2015 reported that the number of offenders confined in US county and city jails was estimated to be 744,600 at midyear 2014. From 2000, the jail inmate population increased about 1 percent a year. It peaked in 2008 at 785,500. The jail population remained stable in the 2012. The incarceration rate, the jail population per 100,000 U.S. residents—has fallen steadily from a peak of 259 inmates per 100,000 at mid-year 2007 to 234 per 100,000 at midyear 2014. The incarceration rate of adults has declined from a high of 340 inmates per 100,000 at midyear 2007 to 302 per 100,000 at midyear 2014.

The causes and consequences of the increased rate of incarceration and the increasingly condign character of punishment within the US criminal justice system are beyond the scope of a book that is focused on the US economy's long-term structural challenges. It appears to arise from measures to prohibit the use of drugs, greater use of minimum sentences and the exemplary punishment of repeat offending, such as the 'three strikes and you're out'. The use of the criminal justice system as an instrument for revenue collection also appears to play a role. In some local authorities the police are used as revenue collection agents when enforcing motoring offences and municipal codes relating to housing. In some localities local courts have become part of this revenue collection apparatus, delaying the presentation of evidence and trials, fining defendants for failing to appear at repeatedly delayed court procedures that take no account of the financial capacity of offenders to pay the fine. The Department of Justice's *Investigation of the Ferguson Police Department* published in May 2015 provides a cogent analysis of this revenue collection approach to the administration of justice. It is not limited to Ferguson, Missouri, examples of it can be found across the US.

It is a system that disproportionately punishes black residents of the US. White inmates accounted for 47 percent of the total jail population, blacks represented 35 percent, and Hispanics represented 15 percent. Black people make up some 13 percent of the US population. It is often asserted that there are more black men in prison than in college. Indeed President Obama told the NCCP in 2007 that 'We have more work to do when more young black men languish in prison than attend colleges and universities across America'. Professor Ivory Toldsom of Howard University in *Root.com* has challenged this as a myth, arguing that when the number of black men at college and university are properly counted that number exceeds the number in prison. In 2013 there were about 1.4 million black men at college compared to roughly half that number in jail. Professor Toldsom argues that the recorded number of black men enrolled in college by the National Center for Educational Statistics has risen as a result of better collection of statistics, more black men applying for college and greater opportunities arising from the expansion of community and private for profit colleges. While the comparison of college and prison numbers may be erroneous, Professor Toldsom points out that the rate of incarceration among black males is seven times that of white males. It has implications for life time black earnings, given that so many black men spend part of their early adult years outside of the labour market. It also damages the employability of black men, because it excludes them from employment in several of the principal sectors of the economy exhibiting growth in employment such as health and social care.

The increased use of imprisonment has had a disproportionate effect on black men, but it is a burden that has damaged all American communities. A 500 percent increase in incarceration over forty years is expensive. Jedd Rackoff in an article *The New York Review of Books*, published in the 15 May 2015 edition, *Mass Incarceration: the silence of the judges* points out that there is an increasing appreciation across the US political spectrum that something has gone seriously wrong in 'Congress, a bill to eliminate mandatory minimum sentences for nonviolent drug offenders was endorsed not only by the Department of Justice, but also by such prominent right-wing Republican senators as Ted Cruz and Rand Paul'. Although the bill to modify the applicability of mandatory minimum sentences never reached a vote.

Public intervention to improve black economic and social conditions

The social and economic position of many black people requires public intervention to improve their welfare. The fact that black people operate in the labour market with a series of handicaps arising out of continuing direct discrimination and previous discrimination that – in terms of education, employment and home ownership – result in significant difference in contemporary black and white endowment of human and physical capital, merits public intervention through regulation and expenditure to assist black individuals and communities.

The economic and social condition of black people in America is a continuing challenge for modern policymakers, one made greater given that many benign and well intentioned pieces of public policy may in practice operate to hinder rather than help black people with low levels of education, skill and training that result in low marginal product per capita.

Transfer payments can create complex changes in employment incentives that operate to detach the recipients from employment or reduce the intensity of their labour supply. The EITC, by concentrating on families with children, offers little help to young black men. Looking again at the original arguments surrounding a negative income tax proposed by Milton Friedman that Daniel Moynihan supported could offer opportunities to try to better attach young black men to the labour market. The New Hope project in Milwaukee, Wisconsin, demonstrated the positive effects on work effort of supplementing the earnings of young black men. It will not be easy to construct a benefit that does this without damaging work incentives at some stage, but at the very bottom part of the earnings distribution – where the relief of poverty is the key matter – there is almost certainly scope to intervene to raise take home pay from work.

Historically, blacks benefited from working in manufacturing industries that later became unionised. Where unions were able to extract an economic rent and there was clear evidence of trade union power and a union wage mark-up, black wages rose. It is not clear that such wage bargaining institutions would help now. First, markets are much more competitive, which limits the sustainable union wage mark-up. Second, while existing workers benefit as insiders, younger cohorts of black workers are excluded in what amounts to a segmented labour market. Additionally, new black labour market entrants are likely to be precisely the kind of person shut out by a labour market distinguished by insider power, people with little employment experience and low levels of education.

There are ways that public intervention may, however, improve black labour market outcomes. The first is improvements in black school and community college opportunities, and ensuring greater assistance in completing university programmes. The quality of black schools is a serious matter. In New York state, 21 percent of black school students were taught by teachers who had failed their general knowledge certification exam on the first attempt compared with 7 percent of white students. There is also a problem with high teacher turnover. Schools with students from minority and high-poverty households have much higher turnover of staff than in schools where the students come from more advantaged households.

Second, greater effort could be made with training and matching black people with viable local job opportunities, particularly in terms of careers advice for young people. Interventions of this sort fall very much within the OECD recommendations about active labour market policies. They appear to be particularly relevant in relation to high school graduates. There needs to be some way of presenting the knowledge and basic literacy and numeracy that young people leaving high school possess in a better and more systematic manner. There also need to be careers and employment services that connect young, inexperienced black people to the labour market. It is clear that this particularly applies to young black men leaving school and college.

Federal spending on active labour market policies has fallen by 60 percent in real terms since the 1970s. An obvious question is what role vocational training and employment experience programmes could have, as they have been effective in other OECD countries. The US spends much less on this area of public policy than almost any other advanced economy. Better labour market policies would improve the working of the US economy as a whole and should offer particular and necessary assistance to black people As well as better vocational training and links between secondary education and employment, there is significant scope to improve the advice that young black people receive when making choices about college and university. Professor

Ivory Toldson has noted that black male representation in higher education is proportional to black male representation in the adult population. However, 'lack of adequate guidance and academic rigour in high schools has resulted in black males being underrepresented at competitive universities like Rutgers and overrepresented at community colleges and online universities.'

Conclusion: the opportunity that the black community offers America

The good news for the US is that the black community presents it with an economic opportunity.

Black male earnings are almost 30 percentage points lower than average white male earnings. Given that around 13 percent of the population is made of black people, if the gap in black and white earnings were merely halved the higher GDP per capita would raise overall national income by about 1 percent. If the marginal revenue product of black women was also raised in a similar fashion, GDP could be raised by something close to 1.5 percent. This is a real and significant opportunity in the context of an ageing society where the ratio of people of working age to those who are retired is falling. Not only would it result in a higher national income, but it would also be accompanied by falls in public spending. Given the projections that the Congressional Budget Office and General Accountability Office are providing for the future course of public spending, anything that raises the level of national income and lowers the level of spending is extremely helpful in containing the ratio of public spending to GDP. Systematic policies directed at improving the labor market such as active labor market polices, improvements in secondary education and the connection between schools and community colleges and the labour market along with better focused in work benefits to help low income people to attach themselves to the labor market would help.

Chapter 17

America's Debate about Public Infrastructure Investment

Infrastructure is at the top of President Trump's domestic economic agenda. For more than 25 years there has been a debate about the amount and quality of the infrastructure in the US. As well as involving a discussion of the quantum of the capital stock this debate has widened into a consideration of the benefits and returns to infrastructure spending.

New growth theory and businessmen economics

The Economic Report of the President in 2016 elegantly summarised the established economic perception of the role of infrastructural capital. Reliable infrastructure facilitates the efficient exchange of goods, labor, and the diffusion of innovation and ideas. 'From the Erie Canal in the early 1800s to the Transcontinental Railroad in the 1860s, to the Interstate Highway System in the 1950s and 1960s, previous generations of Americans have made these investments, and they were instrumental in putting the country on a path for sustained economic growth'. In the 1990s it formed part of the debate surrounding new approaches to growth theory, the so called endogenous growth theories that identified unusually high returns to certain forms of investment and capital accumulation. This analysis fed into the President Clinton's election campaign platform in 1992. It was a central feature of the New Democrat policy agenda. Several of the principal protagonists in the technical economic debate, such as Brad De Long and Alicia Munnell came from academia and in Dr Munnell's case from the Federal Reserve Bank of Boston to serve in President Clinton's Treasury department. The Democrat Party platform in 1992 reflected the experience of a party excluded from executive office in the federal government in Washington DC for twelve years. Its mayors and state governors, of whom Bill Clinton was one, had developed a political network that emphasised public investment that mirrored their parochial political functions. Infrastructure investment is principally a state and local government responsibility in the US. Arguing the case for infrastructure investment enabled Democrat politicians to appear practical, moderate and business like. It also aligned them with business. Business interests themselves have a taste for politicians with an appetite for large scale and complex capital investment. The combination of construction contracts, complex off balance sheet financial vehicles, ultimately guaranteed by the taxpayer and the lobbying, media and stakeholder management consultancy opportunities represent a potent elixir. For the conference attending and commentating public sector and business executives it is an article of faith that public infrastructure is a good thing. Any challenge about cost or financing is to be brushed aside, apart from the understanding that the ultimate guarantor of such investment has to be the taxpayer.

The long standing consensus on the merits of infrastructure spending in November 1992 was reflected in the proudest boast of modern Democrat governors supporting Bill Clinton at that time. This was the readily repeated assertion that they had a list of bridges and infrastructure projects that were 'shovel ready' and waiting for federal finance. A good example was the late Bruce Sundlun of Rhode Island. What was interesting was not his list, but his much more guarded explanation of the economic and social returns that would arise from the list of projects and more particularly how the criterion used to assess them had been developed.

EU Trans-European networks and Japan's response to stagnation

This enthusiasm for infrastructure investment was not confined to the US. In the early 1990s as the EU completed its preparations the completion of the Single Market in 1993, the EU Commission emphasised infrastructure investment. The Commission in 1993 published the so-called Delors White Paper on *Growth, Competitiveness and Employment*. This argued for 'trans-European networks', principally new high speed railways lines to raise the rate of growth in the EU. This agenda drew on the perception that railway building was central to the economic history and development of the North American economy in the 19th century. While in Japan following the banking collapse in the 1990s and the years of stagnation, infrastructure has been an important part of the fiscal policy response to the years of economic to Japan's economic challenges.

The international economic consensus on benefits of public sector infrastructure investment

There are few things that the Trump administration and the American and the international policy making establishment agree on. If there is one thing where President Trump's agenda coincides with the establishment economic consensus it is on the benefits of infrastructure investment and modernising the US economy's capital stock. This was an important part of the Obama administration's economic analysis. Much of Mrs Clinton's domestic economic agenda rehearsed the previous investment agenda of her husband President Clinton.

The IMF identifies infrastructure investment as a route to raising rates of economic growth in the context of very low interest rates. The OECD shortly after President Trump was elected in November 2016 the *OECD Economic Outlook* argued that after a period of fiscal consolidation of debt to GDP levels the time had come to focus on expanding the denominator in that ratio – GDP growth. The OECD argued that very low interest rates had created a fiscal space that resulted from lower interest payments on debt arising from rolled over public debt being refinanced more cheaply. The OECD suggested that higher spending on investment and spending on active labor market polices would raise future growth rates and labor participation rates.

Yet a casual glance at the statistical annex of *OECD Economic Outlook* is not reassuring about the success of such policies in Japan. Since 1990 public debt has risen from 128 percent to 228 percent of GDP in 2016. Much of this debt was accumulated as a result of spending on infrastructure projects that yielded disappointing rates of return that have been caricatured as the roads and bridges to nowhere. Despite the infrastructure investment and borrowing GDP is roughly unchanged from the mid-1990s. The lost twenty years in Japan suggest that infrastructure spending and loose fiscal policies do not offer a guaranteed route out of secular stagnation. They may have contributed to the stabilisation of output and helped avoid a more intense debt-deflation, but they have not been a remedy for secular stagnation.

Infrastructure investment is a specific category of capital investment. Often there is a 'loose' use of the term public investment to include a wide range of spending on public services. The *OECD Economic Outlook* in November 2016 referred to 'soft investments' in things, such as education. Infrastructure proper is defined more narrowly as fixed capital assets that are used in various production processes that support economic activity. The heart of infrastructure investment is spending on roads, other transport facilities, such as rail and mass transit services, power generation plants and distribution networks and water treatment and sewage systems.

How much does the US spend on infrastructure investment?

Spending on water and transportation infrastructure by federal state and local authorities in the US accounted for 2.42 percent of GDP in 2014. This was 0.6 percentage points below its peak share of national income recorded in 1959. This is slightly higher than the slowest rate of spending on this form of capital accumulation when the annual ratio of GDP spent on infrastructure was 2.35 percent in 1998. Each year since 1956, state and local governments have accounted for about 72 percent of infrastructure spending. The *Economic Report of the President* in 2016 estimated that the stock of physical public capital relative to GDP was about 76 percent and that the marginal revenue product of this public capital was about 14 percent.

The *Economic Report of the President* drew attention to the fact that US infrastructure has aged rapidly. The average age of the public capital stock has risen in recent years. For example from 2010 to 2014, the average age of streets and highways increased 3.2 years. This was the greatest four-year change recorded and more than the 2.9 year increase in aging that took place over the previous two decades. Water supply facilities aged by an average of 1.2 years between 2010 and 2014. This rate of aging was significantly more rapid than the 0.7 year increase over the previous 20 years before that. Sewerage systems and power facilities aged slightly less between 2010 and 2014 than in the previous decade. The average age of public transport assets has increased by almost 20 percent in the ten years to 2014.

Economists working for the Obama administration estimated that to significantly improve the conditions of the road network and its performance, rather than allowing congestion to increase and road conditions to worsen, would require a capital investment in roads across all levels of US government of between $124 and $146 billion annually. The higher estimate reflected higher forecasts for the rate of growth and their potential impact on car and other motor vehicle use.

Composition of public spending on capital investment

The balance of spending on different forms of water and transportation infrastructure has changed significantly since the late-1950s. Spending on rail and mass transit public transport has increased relative to spending on roads. On average between

1956 and 1960, streets and roads accounted for over 62 percent of public spending on water and transportation infrastructure. In contrast while mass transit and rail accounted for only about 5 percent public capital spending. In the early 1980s spending on transport and roads had fallen to just under 43 percent. While spending on rail and mass transit had risen to over 15 percent of the total. Over the last thirty years the priority given to different forms of infrastructure investment has been roughly stable. Streets and roads get 42 percent of the total; water transportation, resources, and utilities account for 35 percent; mass transit and rail 14 percent; and aviation gets 9 percent.

Figure 17.1: Public Spending on Transportation and Water Infrastructure as a share of GDP, 1956 to 2014

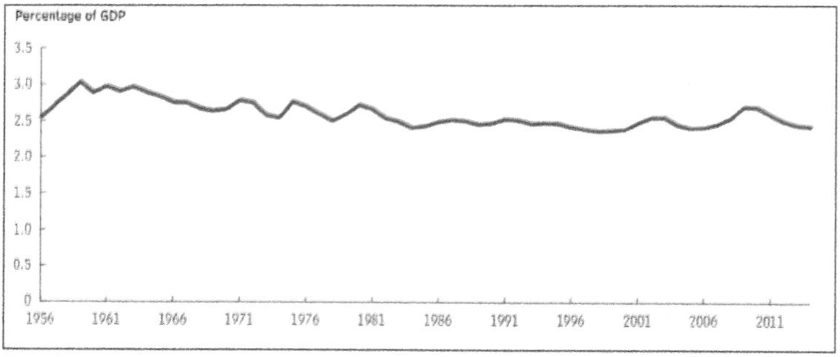

Source: Congressional Budget Office based on data from the Office of Management and Budget, the Census Bureau, and the Bureau of Economc Analysis

The fall in the priority given to infrastructure investment is not confined to the US economy. Spending in the G7 has fallen as a share of GDP. The perception that there has been a decline in the quality of infrastructure is not confined to the US. The World Economic Forum produces annual ratings that assess the quality of infrastructure throughout the world. These ratings are determined on a scale of 1-7, where a higher score indicates a higher level of quality. In 2015, the United States received a rating of 5.8 for its overall infrastructure. This was above the 5.5 average score of the G7 economies, the 3.8-average score across emerging and developing Asian nations, and the 4.1 global average score. Given the concern about the quality of the US infrastructure it is interesting that on these comparative figures the US does pretty well.

Table 17.1: Quality of Infrastructure in G-7 Member Countries

TYPE	CAN	FRA	DEU	ITA	JPN	GBR	USA	G-7 Average
2006								
Overall	6.0	6.5	6.6	3.7	6.1	5.6	6.2	5.8
2015								
Overall	5.4	5.9	5.9	4.1	6.2	5.3	5.8	5.5
Air	5.8	5.8	6.0	4.5	5.6	5.8	6.2	5.7
Ports	5.5	5.3	5.6	4.3	5.4	5.7	5.7	5.4
Roads	5.2	6.1	5.7	4.4	6.0	5.2	5.7	5.5
Railroads	4.7	5.8	5.6	4.0	6.7	4.8	5.0	5.2

Note: Scale of 1–7, with higher score indicating better infrastructure quality.

Source: World Economic Forum, Global Competitiveness Report Survey.

Maintenance and Repair of infrastructure is very important. The research evidence suggests that spending on maintaining existing infrastructure properly yields some of the highest rates of return. Spending on repair and maintenance is a cost-effective technique that avoids more expensive repairs in the future. One estimate referred to in the *Economic Report of the President* is that every $1 spent on preventive pavement maintenance reduces future repair costs by $4 to $10. The wear and tear on cars and other vehicles is higher and increases depreciations costs when the conditions of roads are allowed to deteriorate as a result of lack of repair. Cars and trucks driven on defective roads will inevitably need more frequent changes of tire and other wear and tear.

Ratio of public spending on operation and maintenance versus new investment

Between 1956 and 1970, the ratio of public spending on the operation and maintenance of existing infrastructure to public spending on new capital for water and transportation infrastructure averaged 0.61 percent. For every $1 spent toward new capital, $0.61 was spent on operation and maintenance. This relatively low public spending ratio largely reflected increased spending towards the end of the 1950s on construction of the Interstate Highway System. In the following 35 years, the ratio for operation and maintenance to new capital averaged 1.00, indicating a balanced approach between priority given to new capital investment and the need to operate and maintain the existing infrastructure. Public spending on water and transportation infrastructure has given greater priority to supporting the operation and maintenance of current infrastructure relative to the formation of new capital. The average public spending ratio of maintenance to capital accumulation is now 1.20. It is not clear what the optimal ratio is. Yet maximizing growth requires spending on both new infrastructure and importantly maintaining the existing stock of infrastructure assets.

Financing Infrastructure: the role states and localities and the federal government

The great bulk of public sector capital accumulation is undertaken by state and local government authorities. The federal government, however, plays a significant role in financing it through the tax expenditure arising from the exempting interest paid on municipal bonds from federal income tax. Between 2004 and 2013, the amount of tax-preferred debt issued to finance new infrastructure projects undertaken by the public and private sectors was $2.02 trillion. 73 percent, or around $1.5 trillion, was used by states and localities. While private capital investment funded projects with a public purpose, such as hospitals or social housing accounted for the remaining $542 billion.

Since the Great Recession the federal government has taken a number of measures to assist state and local government capital spending. Among these are the Build America Bonds (BABs) program introduced as part of the American Recovery and Reinvestment Act. This authorised state and local governments to issue special taxable bonds that received either a 35 percent direct federal subsidy to the borrower (Direct Payment BABs) or a Federal tax credit worth 35 percent of the interest owed to investors. Department of the Treasury was able to harness the efficiencies of the taxable debt market for states and localities, where it enjoys lower average borrowing costs than they do. This enabled state and local governments to obtain borrowing more cheaply. Some $181 billion was raised under the BABs program.

The Build America program and other federal capital programs have in recent years been introduced to ensure that states and localities could maintain their capital stocks during a period when their revenue base and balance sheets have been under pressure. In more normal economic circumstances the tax system in the US may create incentives that lead to something of a bias towards public sector capital accumulation, given that the municipal bond market enjoys a tax subsidy from the federal government.

Congressional Budget Office analysis *Approaches to make Federal Highway spending more productive* 2016 showed that he split between capital projects and operation and maintenance has not changed much since 1980. The federal share of capital spending has typically ranged between about 40 percent and 50 percent since 1959 shortly after construction began on the Interstate System. In 2014 spending by federal, state, and local governments on highways totalled $165 billion: $92 billion was allocated to capital projects and $73 billion was spent on operation and maintenance. Of the $46 billion in the Federal Government spent on roads almost all of it – some $44 billion, was used for capital projects. While almost all of the operation and maintenance spending for highway infrastructure came from state and local governments. The percentage varies significantly among states. In 2009, twelve states - mainly smaller states - relied on federal funds for two-thirds or more of their capital spending on roads. The CBO report drew attention to a combination of pressures that required policy makers to concentrate attention on the need to make road spending more effective. Revenue from gasoline and diesel fuel duties that are hypothecated to the Highway Trust Fund, the federal government's principal vehicle for funding funds roads, had been insufficient to pay for planned highway spending. Between 2008 and 2016, Congress therefore transferred about $143 billion, mainly from the Treasury's general fund, into the Highway Fund to ensure that the fund remained solvent. The second pressure has come from higher costs. The cost of goods and services that go into highway construction increased significantly in the ten years to 2016. The cost of building roads rose much more rapidly than prices in the economy as a whole. As a result, the CBO reported that the amount of federal spending for highways, as well as the amount of spending by all levels of government, declined from the early 2000s when adjusted for changes in the cost of those materials and other inputs. In total highway spending has bought less recently in real terms than at any time since 1993.

Figure 17.2: The Federal Government's and State and Local Goverments' Shares of Spending on Transportation and Water Infrastructure, by Category of Spending, 2014

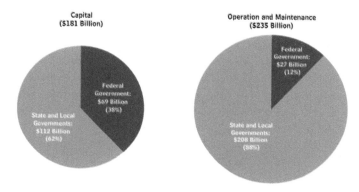

Source: Congressional Budget Office based on data from the Office of Management and Budget and the Census Bureau

The returns to investing in roads in the US

The allocation of federal highway funding is only loosely related to how much highways are used. Research suggests that the increases in economic activity from spending for new highways in the United States have generally declined over time. As the highway system has matured and changes to it have become more incremental and localized, spending to repair existing capacity may have become relatively more productive. Road use is not distributed evenly among the different kinds of roads. Although the Interstate system constituted only 3 percent of the lane-miles in 2013, it handled a quarter of vehicle-miles travelled. Similarly, other federal-aid roads—such as numbered U.S. and state highways and other connector highways between those roads—made up 26 percent of highway capacity and accounted for 60 percent of the traffic. Local roads provided most of the capacity but accounted for 16 percent of the traffic.

The CBO point out that investment in highways has made a significant positive contribution to economic growth. Studies of the economic returns from public investment in highways have found that the construction of the Interstate System was associated with significant increases in productivity, particularly in industries that use the road system relatively intensively. However, The CBO note that subsequent capital spending on roads has had a much smaller impact. As both the scope and age of the highway system in the United States have increased, greater attention has been given to the potential benefits from repairing and rehabilitating existing roads.

Attention has also turned to particular aspects of the contributions of highway investment. For example, projects focused on highways serving major airports and ports could increase the potential gains from international trade. Likewise, road construction that facilitates the growth of urban and metropolitan economies might promote greater economic activity arising from the clustering effects or agglomeration effects from increased interactions among individuals and businesses. Yet simply because highway infrastructure can have these previously recorded positive economic effects does not necessarily mean that it will. Roads, bridges, or other forms of transportation to sparsely populated places or little used infrastructure may provide few of the benefits, let alone enough to offset the costs.

Many of the returns to these sorts of investment have diminished over time. Since the early 1970s, when the Interstate System was largely completed, the CBO point out that investment in highways has displayed a much weaker link to productivity than before. This suggests a decline in the economic returns from this form of investment. An analysis of 68 studies conducted from 1983 to 2008—addressing not only highway spending but also investment in other kinds of infrastructure—also supports estimates of a decline in economic returns over time

There are a number of plausible explanations the CBO analysis explores. First, the availability of fast and reliable road transportation across the US, which was provided by the construction of the Interstate System and thousands of miles of other roads, enabled some businesses to become more productive to an extent that could not be replicated by subsequent, and more incremental, additions to the highway system. Second, the research literature has suggested that when new capacity is added to existing roads, the benefits—in terms of reduced congestion and, hence, travel times—diminish over time as the roads become more fully used again. More traffic uses the new lanes, travel speeds decline toward those that existed before the improvement. The addition of new lanes has little effect on congestion within ten years. The behavioural response of road users is: businesses use more trucking, residents drive more, new people move to an area, and traffic is diverted from other roads to the new lanes. Part of the higher "induced traffic" will be additional economic activity, and some it will represent the redistribution of economic activity from other areas.

Cost Benefit Analysis

Proper cost benefit analysis is imperative if investment spending of any kind is likely to yield and economic return. Yet proper cost benefit analysis appears to play a limited role in state and local governments' decisions about which projects to give priority to; and the type of formal project analysis and evaluation undertaken varies greatly. State governments have a degree of discretion in the way that they make decisions about how to spend the money they receive from federal highway grants. Accountability Office (GAO) in 2010 found that economic analysis of projects was of "great or very great importance" for only about 20 percent of states' departments of transportation. An earlier GAO survey, in 2004, of states' departments of transportation and transit agencies found that fewer than half used economic analysis on a regular basis and that when they did, they had considerable flexibility to use different models without being subject to minimum standards. Furthermore, that survey found that "although the costs and benefits of projects were almost always considered in some way, formal analyses such as benefit-cost analysis were not usually conducted when considering project alternatives, and they were completed less frequently for proposed highway projects than transit projects." GAO found that roughly 60 percent of states' departments of transportation indicated that political support and public opinion were factors of "great or very great importance" when decisions about highway projects were made. The research suggests that building more roads is sometimes an approach that is used to benefit areas with low population densities or poor and deteriorating economic circumstances, instead of an opportunity to maximize long-term economic growth in more dynamic economic communities.

Reviews of grant applications made under the Transportation Investment Generating Economic Recovery (TIGER) program established in 2009 under the American Recovery and Reinvestment Act, to provide competitive grants to fund infrastructure projects, found that funding requests exhibit common errors and that there is considerable variance in the quality of applicants' benefit-cost analyses. Although CBO found that the quality of submissions had improved, further assistance from the federal government could help to improve the quality of applications. This assistance could include offering staff expertise to states and localities wanting to carryout rigorous benefit-cost evaluations. The program includes benefit-cost analysis as a basis for evaluating grant applications, but some observers such as the GAO's report *Surface Transportation: Department of Transportation Should Measure the Overall Performance and Outcomes of the TIGER Discretionary Grant Program*, GAO-14-766 (September 2014), have raised concerns that many of the analyses submitted are of little use in the evaluation process and that in some instances the results of analyses undertaken do not appear to bear on the final project selection decisions

While concern about the amount and quality of infrastructure has been a concern for many economists and policy makers the emphasis on the infrastructure agenda has attracted a cogent note of dissent from several interesting economists. In the early 1990s John Tatom an economist at the Federal Reserve Bank of St Louis expressed doubts about much of the analysis that underpinned the Clinton administration's infrastructure program. In an article *Is an infrastructure crisis lowering the nation's productivity?* Tatom challenged much of the data that underpinned Alicia Munnell's work and expressed reservations about the asserted benefits arising from infrastructure investment and the purported link between public capital and private sector productivity. The issue that Tatom drew attention to was an identification problem in use of the data that inverted the causation between the two separate things. This resulted from spurious or unrelated movements in the quantity of public capital and business sector output and productivity being connected in a form of causation that was not present in his judgement. While both private sector productivity and the public capital stock per hour had risen over time, their movements have not been closely related. Indeed, in the 1980s the two measures generally moved inversely with one another.

   John Tatom also argued that there is a further tax issues favouring excessive investment in public physical capital facilities, which must considered in discussions of the public capital stock. This is 'a built-in bias in the United States favouring excessive investment in public physical capital facilities'. This bias occurs because the public sector is not taxed on the return or benefits from public capital formation. The private sector in contrast is taxed on the benefits from private sector capital formation. Tatom's argument is that capital formation is restricted in the taxed private sector. In contrast the cost of capital to the public sector is lowered, therefore boosting public capital formation. Tatom makes the further point that the federal income tax expenditure for public investment means that projects financed by the sale of tax-free bonds, gives many state investment projects a taxpayer-subsidy. These public sector bodies therefore have a lower cost of capital than the private sector. When government decision makers only take account of their own direct cost of finance rather than the full social opportunity cost (the before-tax return on private capital) Tatom argues that 'they will tend to invest in projects with benefits that are worth less than their cost to taxpayers. In this sense, the nation would "overinvest" in public capital'.

More recently Bent Flyvbjerg and Cass R. Sunstein in *The Principle of the Malevolent Hiding Hand; or, the Planning Fallacy Writ Large* examined over 2,000 large scale infrastructure projects in over 100 countries between 1927 and 2013. They look at the he claims made for them, their expected economic rates or return and their projected costs. Their conclusion is that social planners tend to be unrealistically optimistic, particularly when planners begin their projects. They greatly overestimate 'some factor or condition that is indispensable to success, and underestimate difficulties and costs'. They point out that people systematically underestimate the time that it takes to complete projects. Flyvbjerg and Sunstein identify what they call a "pseudo-imitation" technique, where planners pretend, or think, "that a project is nothing but a straightforward application of a well-known technique that has been successfully used elsewhere." Such "pseudo-comprehensive-program" techniques, enable planners to dismiss previous efforts as piecemeal, and portray their own work as novel and comprehensive. This technique gives policymakers the illusion "that the 'experts' have already found all the answers," and all that is needed is faithful implementation.

They found that a typical project experiences a double whammy of higher-than-estimated costs and lower than estimated benefits. Their data suggest that the cost-benefit ratio is typically overestimated by between 50 and 200 percent. This results in decision makers agreeing to projects that should never have been embarked upon. Moreover, Bent Flyvbjerg in a separate article in the Oxford Review of Economic Policy in 2009 *Survival of the unfittest: why the worst infrastructure gets built – and what we can do about it* argued that rapid increases in stimulus expenditure and more spending on information technology 'is catapulting infrastructure investment from the frying pan into the fire.'

Did the building of railways play the role in 19th century American economic history that policy makers so readily assert?

An earlier debate over the role of infrastructure focused on many of the same issues as the recent discussion of public capital formation. This earlier literature concerned the mainstream view of the indispensable role of the railways in stimulating economic growth in the 19th-century America. The standard analysis emphasised the role of substitutability of competing transportation modes. Robert Fogel received the Noble Prize for his work on this set out in his book *Railroads and American Economic Growth: Essays in Econometric History* published 1964. This seminal work looked at the hypothesis about the substitutability of different forms of transportation. Fogel compared the actual American economy 1890 economy to a hypothetical 1890 economy where transport was limited to wagons, canals, and natural waterways. Without that railways transport costs would have been higher. Taking agricultural products from farms to markets, particularly in the Midwest would have been more expensive and the geographic location of agricultural production would have been different. Yet despite this, the overall effects of higher transport costs and the "social savings" that could be attributed to the development of railways, were modest. Fogel estimated that they were something around some 2.7 percent GNP in relation to the American economy in 1890. His main point to explain this was that alternative technologies, such as a more extensive canal system or improved roads, would have further lowered the importance of railways.

Conclusion

While there is much anxious debate about the amount and the quality of American infrastructure and careful examination of this part of the US capital stock probably offers a more nuanced picture than the election platforms of either President Clinton in 1992 or the presidential candidates in 2016. US spending on infrastructure has fallen as share of national income since the end of the 1950s. This peak in infrastructure investment in the 20th century reflected the Eisenhower administration's investment in the interstate network of highways and its completion by the 1970s.

There was a similar pattern in investment in educational buildings. The share of the school age population (ages 5 to 24) rose from about 31 percent of the total population in 1949 to around 37.5 percent in 1970. It then fell top 29 percent in 1990. Education spending capita in that period peaked in 1974. The fall in the rate of public investment in education that followed reflected the change in demography.

Some economic commentators and policy makers regard spending on infrastructure investment as a potential silver bullet that could remedy many of the wider challenges in the modern American economy. The debate on infrastructure spending forms part of a much broader contemporary debate over secular stagnation that has been led by the Professor Lawrence Summers of Harvard, the former US Treasury Secretary. Professor Summers argues that slow rates of growth in productivity result from weaker capital accumulation and the reluctance of the private sector to take risks. This provides an opportunity for the public sector to remedy this slower rate of private accumulation of capital with investment in infrastructure. An opportunity made more compelling by the low level of interest rates and debt service costs that the OECD has identified. It is not clear that two forms of capital are neat substitutes. Infrastructure investment projects that yield low rates of return are unlikely to bring about the remedy that will increase productivity. Moreover, Professor Robert Gordon in his book *The Rise and Fall of American Growth* published in 2016 points out that there may be good reasons why investment has been weak given the opportunities afforded by the marginal returns on investment in modern technology compared to the returns from investment in refrigeration and sanitation and water processes in the hundred years before 1970. Professor Gordon makes the point that low interest rates and strong equity markets have provided plenty of capital potentially worthwhile projects and that public policy may not provide a ready remedy to the US productivity challenge.

Bibliography

A

Daniel Aaronson and Jonathan Davis *How much has house lock affected labor mobility and the unemployment rate?* Chicago Fed Letter (September 2011)

Ronen Abraham, Leemore Dafny and Max Schanzenbach in *The Impact of Tort Reform on Employer-Sponsored Health Insurance Premiums*

Benjamin A Anderson *Economics and Public Welfare A Financial and Economic History of the United States 1914-1946* D Van Nostrand Company 1949 Liberty Press 1979

Kenneth Arrow *Uncertainty and the Welfare Economics of Medical Care* American Economic Review in December 1963

David H Autor Lawrence F Katz and Melissa S Kearney *Measuring and Interpreting Trends in Economic Inequality: The Polarization of the US Labor Market* American Economic Review May 2006

Alan J Auerbach, William G Gale and Benjamin H Harris *Activist Fiscal* Policy Journal of Economic Perspectives Fall 2010

B

Josh Barro *Two Americas: Public Sector Gains In Recession* Manhattan Institute February 2010

Robert J Barro *Are Government Bonds Net Wealth?* Journal of Political Economy 1974

Gary S Becker *Crime and Punishment: An Economic Approach* The Journal of Political Economy 1968

Gerwin Bell and Norikazu Tawara *The Size of Government and US-European Differences in Economic Performance* IMF Paper 2009

Andrew Biggs *Pampered Public Sector Employees Why Government sees higher Wages and Benefits* The Atlantic August 22 2010

Andrew Biggs and Jason Richwine *Federal Employees Are Not Underpaid 22 Percent* Washington Examiner 1 September 2010.

Keith Bender and John Heywood *Out of Balance? Comparing Public and Private Sector Compensation over 20 Years,* Center for State and Local Government Excellence April 2010

Alan Auerbach, William Gale and Benjamin Harris *Active Fiscal Policy*

Robert Bacon and Walter Eltis *Britain's Economic Problem: Too Few Producers* 1976

Barclays Capital *Taxable Municipal Market Commentary 2011*

Nicoletta Batini et al *United States Selective Issues* IMF Country Report 2010

George Borjas *Immigration Policy and Human Capital, in Reshaping the American Workforce in a Changing Economy,* eds. Harry J. Holzer and Demetra Nightingale Washington, DC: Urban Institute Press, 2007

Christian Broda and David Weinstein *Prices and Inequality Why Americans Are better Off Than You Think American* Enterprise Institute 2008

Cary Brown looked at this in *Fiscal Policy in the Thirties: A Reappraisal,* in the American Economic Review 46 December 1956

Thomas Buchmueller and Alan Monheit *Employer-Sponsored Health Insurance and Health Reform* NBER Working Paper 14839

Kate Bundorf and Mark Pauly *Is Health Insurance Affordable to the Uninsured?*

Walter J Blum *The Effects of Special Provisions in the Income Tax on Taxpayer*

Leonard Burman *Tax Expenditures, the Size and Efficiency of Government, and Implications for Budget Reform* Spring 2011

Budget of United States Government Year Fiscal 201x

Budget of US Government Analytical Perspectives Fiscal Year 2012

Budget of US Government Historical Tables Fiscal Year 2012

C

David Card *Is the New Immigration Really So Bad?* Economic Journal 115 no. 506 (2005)

David Card *Immigration and Inequality* American Economic Review 99 no. 2 (2009) Centre on Budget and Policy Priorities in July 2010

Cristina Checherita, Christiane Nickel and Phillipp Rother *The Role of Fiscal Transfers for Regional Economic Convergence in Europe* ECB Working Paper No 1029/March 2009

Robert Clark and Melinda Sandler Morrill Retiree *Health Plans in the Public Sector: Is there a Funding Crisis?* Edward Elgar 2010

College Board Advisory and Policy *Center Trends in College Pricing* 2010

Timothy Conley and Bill Dupor *The American Recovery and Re-investment Act Public Sector Jobs Saved, Private Sector Jobs Forestalled* 17 May 2011

Congressional Budget Office CBO's *Analysis of the Major Health Care Legislation Enacted in March 2010* 30 March 2011

Congressional Budget Office *Estimated Impact of the American Recovery and Reinvestment Act on Employment and Economic Output as of September 2009* November 2009

Congressional Budget Office *Estimated Impact of the American Recovery and Reinvestment Act on Employment and Economic Output from January 2010 Through March 2010* May 2010

Congressional Budget Office *Fiscal Stress Faced by Local Governments* published in December 2010

Congressional Budget Office *CBO's 2011 Long-Term Budget Outlook* June 2011

Congressional Budget Office *New York City's Fiscal Problem: Its Origins, Potential Repercussions, and Some Alternative Policy Responses* October 1975

Congressional Budget Office *The Economics of US Tort Liability: A Primer* 2003

Congressional Budget Office *Changes in the Distribution of Workers' Hourly wages Between 1970 and 2000* February 2011

Congressional Budget Office *Trends in the Distribution of Household Income Between 1979 and 2007* October 2011

Congressional Research Service *The Debt Limit: History and Recent Increases* July 2011

Congressional Research Service *Tax Expenditures and the Federal Budget* June 2011

Michael Cooper and Mary Williams *Mounting Debts by States, Stoke Fears of Crisis* New York Times 4 December 2010

Carlo Cottarelli and Andrea Schaechter *Long-Term Trends in Public Finances in the G-7 Economies* 1 September 2011

Bill Costello *The Erosion of American Higher education (cost of College rising faster than inflation)* American Thinker 5 October 2010.

David Cutler in *Where are the Health Care Entrepreneurs? The Failure of Organisational Innovation in Health Care* NBER Working Paper

No 16030

Lawrence Christiano, Roberto Motto and Massimo Rostagno in an ECB working paper *The Great Depression and the Friedman-Schwartz Hypothesis* 2004

Lauren Cohen, Joshua Coval and Christopher Mallory *Do Powerful Politicians Cause Corporate Downsizing?* March 2011

Sarah Cunnane *A weather eye on the US storm* Times Higher Education Supplement 28 February 2011

Thomas C Leonard *American Economic Reform in the Progressive Era: Its Fundamental Beliefs and Their Relation to Eugenics History of Political Economy* 2009

D

Mary Daly, Bart Hoijn and Rob Valletta *The Recent Rise of the Natural Rate of Unemployment Federal Reserve Bank of San Francisco* January 2011

E

Economic Report of the President 2003

Economic Report of the President 2004

Economic Report of the President 2005

Economic Report of the President 2006

Economic Report of the President 2009

Economic Report of the President 2010

Economic Report of President 2016

The Economist *America's Jobless men Decline of the working man* 28 April 2011

The Economist *Secrets of Success America's System of higher education is the world that is because there is no system* 8 September 2005

Christine Eibner and Susan Marquis *Employer's health insurance cost burden, 1996-2005* US Monthly Labour Review June 2008

Nada Eissa and Hilary Hoynes *The Earned Income Tax credit and the Labour Supply of Married Couples* NBER Working Paper No 6856

F

Brett Fawley and Lucinda Juvenal *Unemployment and the Role of Monetary Policy Economic Synopses* Federal Reserve Bank of St Louis December 2010

Martin Feldstein *Why Has America's Economic Recovery Stalled?* Project Syndicate 25 October 2010

Price Fishback in an article *US monetary and fiscal policy in the 1930s* in the Oxford Review of Economic Policy (Vol 26 No 3 2010)

Price V. Fishback shows in his paper *Social Welfare Expenditures in the United States and Nordic Countries 1900-2003* NBER Working Paper No 15982 May 2010

Richard Freeman *Why Do So Many Young American Men Commit Crimes and What Might We Do About It?* Journal of Economic Perspectives Winter 1996

Milton Freidman *Capitalism and Freedom* 1962

Milton Freidman and Anna Schwartz in their *A Monetary History of the United States, 1867-1960* (1963)

Rober W Fogel *Remarks to Association of American Universities on The influence of economists in shaping and developing the welfare state 17* April 2000

G

William G Gale and Benjamin H Harris *A Value-Added Tax for the United States: Part of the Solution* Brookings Institution and Tax policy Center July 2010.

Alan Garber and Jonathon Skinner in *Is American Health Care Uniquely Inefficient* NBER Working Paper 14257

General Accountability Office *Debt Limit Delays Debt Management Challenges and Increases* February 2011

General Accountability Office *State and Local Government's Fiscal Outlook* April 2011 Update

General Accounting *Office State and Local Government Retirement Benefits: Current Funded Status of Pensions and Health Benefits* January 2008

General Accountability Office *State and Local Government Retiree Health Benefits: Liabilities Are Largely Unfunded, but Some Governments Are Taking Action*, November 2009

General Accountability Office *Value-Added Taxes Potential Lessons for United States from Other Countries' Experiences* July 2011

Jagadeesh Gokhale, Laurence Kotllikoff and Alexi Sluchynsky *Does Work Pay?* NBER (November 2002)

John Gunther *Inside America* Hamish Hamilton 1947

Laurence Kotlikoff and David Rapson *Does It Pay, at the Margin to Work and Save? – Measuring Effective Marginal Taxes on Americans' Labour Supply and Saving* NBER (October 2006)

Christian Grisse, Thomas Klitgaard and Aysegul Sahin *The Vanishing US-EU Employment Gap* Federal Reserve Bank of New York Liberty Street Economics July2011

Jonathan Gruber *End a Health Insurance Subsidy* New York Times (14 November 2010

Jeremy Guest and Daniel Wilson *Fiscal Crises of the States: Causes and Consequences* Federal Reserve Bank of San Francisco 28 June 2010

H

Jacob S Hacker *Health Care Reform 2015* in Democracy a Journal of Ideas (Fall 2010)

Alexander Hamilton First *Report on Public Credit*

Arnold C Harberger *Taxation, Resource Allocation and Welfare* (1964) in Herberger *Taxation and Welfare* Chicago University Press 1974

Michael Harrington *The Other America Poverty in the United States* Penguin 1962

Kevin A Hassett Director of American Enterprise Institute *Testimony before House Ways and Means Committee Regarding the Importance of Tax Reform* January 2011

John Heywood *Out of Balance? Comparing Public and Private Sector Compensation over 20 Years*, Center for State and Local Government Excellence April 2010

Elsby, Hobijn and Sahin in *The Labour Market in the Great Recession* Brooking Papers on Economic Activity Spring 2010

Jonathan Heathcote, Fabrizio Perri and Giovanni Violante *Unequal We Stand: An Empirical Analysis of Economic Inequality in the United States, 1967 to-2006* Federal Reserve Bank of Minneapolis October 2009

Douglas Holtz-Eakin *Higher Costs and the Affordable Care Act* American Action Forum 9 March 2009

Harry Holzer *The Labour Market and Young Black Men: Updating Moynihan's perspective* Urban Institute 2007

Harry Holzer *Immigration and Less-Skilled Workers in the United States* (Urban Institute January 2011)

Christopher Howard Hidden *Welfare State: Tax Expenditures and Social Policy in the United States* (Princeton1997)

Peter W Huber Liability *The Legal Revolution and Its Consequences* Basic Books 1988

I

IMF *World Economic Outlook 2008*

J

Joint Economic Committee of Congress *Improving the American Legal System: Economic Benefits of Tort Reform* 1996

Joint Economic Committee of Congress *2001 Economic Report of the President* 2002

Joint Economic Committee of Congress *Hidden Costs of Government Spending* 2002

Joint Committee on Taxation of Congress *A Reconsideration of Tax Expenditure Analysis* May 2008

K

Ira Katznelson's W*hen Affirmative Action was White An Untold History of Racial Inequality in Twentieth-Century America* Norton 2005

Natalia Kolesnikova and Yang Liu in *A Bleak 30 Years for Black Men* The Regional Economist Federal Reserve Bank of St Louis July 2010

J M Keynes *General Theory of Employment, Interest and Money* 1936

Kevin L. Kliesen, Daniel L. Thornton T*he Federal Debt: Too Little Revenue or Too Much Spending?* Federal Reserve Bank of St Louis July 2011

Alan Krueger *Are Public Sector Workers Paid More than their Alternative Wage? Evidence from Longitudinal Data and Job Queues'* in *When Public Sector Workers Unionize* Edited by Richard B Freeman and Casey Ichniowski (Cambridge MA 1984).

L

Iris Lav and Elizabeth McNichol *Misunderstandings Regarding State Debt, Pensions, And Retiree Health Costs Create Unnecessary Alarm* Center on Budget Policy January 2011

David Leonhardt America's *Sea of Red Ink Was Years in the Making* The New York Times (10 July 2009)

Darren Lubotsky Bhashkar Mazumder Zach Seeskin *New perspectives on health and health care policy* Chicago Fed Letter (July 210

M

Angus Maddison *Contours Of The World Economy, 1-2030 Essays in Macro-Economic History* Oxford 2007

Donald B Marron *How Large are Tax Expenditures* Tax Notes March 28 2011

Richhard Mattoon *Charting Illinois's fiscal future* Chicago Fed Letter August 2010

Charles Ian Mead, Karin Moses and Brent Moulton *The NIPAs and the System of National Accounts* Bureau of Economic Analysis Survey of Current Business, December 2004.

Medicare Trustees *Annual Report of the Medical Insurance Trust Fund* May 2010

Melinda Miller *Land and Racial Inequality* American Economic Review May 2011

C Wright Mills *The Power Elite* OUP 1956

Daniel Patrick Moynihan *Moynihan Report The Negro Family: The Case for National Action* 1965

Alicia Munnell, Jean-Pierre Aubry and Laura Quinby *The Funding of State and Local Government Pensions 2009-2013* Center for Retirement Research, Boston College (April 2010)

N

National Association of State Budget Officers *2009 State Expenditure Report* December 2010

National Governors Association and Association of State Budget Officers *The Fiscal Survey of States* June 2010

National Congress of American Indians *Investing in Tribal Governments Case studies From The American Recovery Act* March 2010

Nelson Rockefeller Center and Pew Centre for the Study of States *States' Revenue Estimating: Cracks in the Crystal Ball* March 2011

O

OECD Economic Outlook Volume 2011/1, June 2011

OECD Economic Surveys: United States, September 2010

P

A C Pigou *The Economics of Welfare* 1920

Waltraut Peter *The Earned Income Tax Credit : A Model for Germany?* American Institute for Contemporary German Studies September 2004

Samuel Preston and Jessica Ho *Low Life Expectancy in the United States: Is the Health Care system at Fault?* NEBR Working paper 15213

Pew Centre for the Study of States *The Widening Gap: The Great Recession's Impact on State Pension and Retiree Health Care Costs* April 2011

R

Carmen M Reinhart Kenneth S Rogoff *This Time Is Different Eight Centuries of Financial Folly* Princeton 2009

Arnold Relman in *Second Opinion Rescuing America's Health Care* Public Affairs 2007

Arnold Relman *The Health Reform We Need and Are not Getting* New York Review of Books July 2009

Alice M Rivlin *Reviving the American Dream The Economy, the States, and the Federal Government* Brookings Institution 1992

Marshall Robinson in *The National Debt Ceiling : An Experiment in Fiscal policy* Brookings Institution 1959

Christina Romer Lessons from the Great Depression for *Economic Recovery in 2009* Brookings Institution Presentation 9 March 2009

Joshua Rauh and Robert Novy-Marx *Public Pension Promises: How Big Are They and What are They Worth?* October 2010

S

Emmanuel Saez *Striking it Richer: The Evolution of Top Incomes in the United States* August 2009

Emmanuel Saez Joel Slemrod and Seth Giertz *Striking it Richer: The Evolution of Top Incomes in the United States*, revised August 2010

Jason Saving *Can the Nation Stimulate Its Way to Prosperity?* Economic Letter Federal Reserve Bank of Dallas August 2010

John Schmidt *The Wage Penalty for State and Local Government Employee* Centre for Economic and Policy Research in March 2010

Mark Schneider *The Costs of Failure Factories in American Higher Education* American Enterprise Institute October 2008

Amity Shlaes *The Forgotten Man New History of the Great Depression* Jonathan Cape 2007

Thomas Shapiro in *Racial Wealth Gap* 2005

James Sherk and Jason Richwine *Federal Pay Still Inflated After Accounting for Skills* Heritage Foundation 14 September 2010.

Theda Skocpol. Lawrence R. Jacobs *Reaching a New Deal Ambitious Governance, Economic Meltdown and Polarised Politics in Obama's First Two Years* Russell Sage Foundation 2011

Werner Sombart *Why is there no Socialism in the United States?* 1906

Richard Sterner's *The Negro's Share A Study of Income Consumption Housing and Public Assistance* Harper & Brothers 1943

T

Vito Tanzi and Ludger Schuknecht *Public Spending in The 20th Century a Global Perspective* CUP 2000

Vito Tanzi *Governments versus Markets The Changing Role of the State* CUP 2011

Eric J Toder Co-Director Urban-Brooking *Institute Evidence to US Senate Committee on Responses to Tax Incentives in a Complex and Uncertain Tax Law* 30 March 2011

Towers Watson *US Tort Cost Trends 2010* Updated

Teresa Tritch *How the Deficit Got This Big* New York Times 23 July 2011

U

US Census Bureau *Current Population Survey 2008*

US Census Bureau *State Government Finances Summary: 2009* January 2011

US Census Bureau *Income Poverty and Health Insurance Coverage in the United States 2009*

US Census Bureau *Income Poverty, and Health Insurance Coverage in the United States 2010*

US Census Bureau *Statistical Abstract of the United States 2011*

US Department of Labor US Bureau of Labor Statistics *Occupational Employment Survey and the National Compensation Survey 2007*

US Department of Labor US Bureau of Labour Statistics *Labor Force Characteristics by Race and Ethnicity, 2009*

US Department of Labor US Bureau of Labor *Statistics Union Members 2010 January 2011*

US Historic Budget Tables Office for Management and Budget 2012 2011

US Treasury Department Office of Economic Policy *Treasury Methodology For Estimating Total Taxable Resources* November 2002

US Treasury Department Office of Economic Policy *Total Taxable Resources (by State)* December 2010

V

Lise Valentine and Richard Mattoon *Public and Private Sector Compensation: What is Affordable in This Recession and Beyond* Chicago Fed Letter May 2009

Richard Vedder *Going Broke By Degree Why College Costs Too Much* AEI Press 2005

W

Finis Welsch *Catching Up: Wages of Black Men* American Economic Review May 2003

Bruce Western, Meredith Kleykamp and Rosenfeld Economic *Inequality and the Rise in US Imprisonment* (2004)

Bruce Western, Meredith Kleykamp and Rosenfeld *Did Falling Wages and Employment Increase US Imprisonment?* Russell Sage Foundation 2004

Index

Lightning Source UK Ltd.
Milton Keynes UK
UKOW06f0235241117

9 781907 720659